WILLIAM K. KILPATRICK

SIMON & SCHUSTER

New York   London   Toronto   Sydney   Tokyo   Singapore

WHY JOHNNY CAN'T TELL RIGHT FROM WRONG

SIMON & SCHUSTER
Simon & Schuster Building
Rockefeller Center
1230 Avenue of the Americas
New York, New York 10020

Designed by Liney Li
Manufactured in the United States of America

10 9 8 7 6 5 4 3 2 1

Library of Congress Cataloging-in-Publication Data
Kilpatrick, William. date.
    Why Johnny can't tell right from wrong : moral illiteracy and the
case for character education / William K. Kilpatrick.
        p.   cm.
    Includes bibliographical references (p.) and index.
    1. Moral education—United States.   2. Education—United States—
Aims and objectives.   3. Public schools—United States.   I. Title.
    LC311.K55   1992
    370.11'4'0973—dc20   92-25864   CIP
    ISBN 0-671-75801-2

ACKNOWLEDGMENTS

I would like to acknowledge my thanks to the following people for their contribution to this book: Clyde Feil, Geoffrey Kilpatrick, Kathleen Rice, Allan Converse, and Michael Mayer for their invaluable assistance in helping to prepare the children's book list; Michael Raiger, Susannah Robbins, and again, Clyde Feil for reading and criticizing the manuscript and offering sound advice; Christina Hoff Sommers, Kevin Ryan, Ed Wynne, and Tom Masty for generously sharing their time and knowledge; Elizabeth Rudow for her help in gathering materials; Marguerite Tierney for typing multiple versions of the manuscript without losing her patience or good humor; Ann Donaruma, Kay Feeley, and Beth Kennedy for additional typing help; the National Endowment for the Humanities and the Wilbur Foundation for support of the studies on which this book is based; Boston College for supporting my work with a faculty fellowship; and the Earhart Foundation for providing research support.

I am particularly indebted to Bob Bender, my editor, for his expert guidance at every stage of the process; to his assistant editor, Johanna Li; and to Jean Touroff and Gypsy da Silva for their thorough copy editing. Special thanks are also due to my agent, Carol Mann, for her good advice and her hard work on my behalf. I owe more than I can express to several good friends for their support and encouragement over the years, especially Tony Chemasi, Tom Howard, Paul Vitz, Regis Martin, Michael Waldstein, Fr. Ron Tacelli, S.J., and Harold Fickett. Finally, I wish to thank Kathleen and Carl Rice for their moral support during the writing process.

FOR CRYSTAL AND HEATHER

CONTENTS

THE CRISIS IN
MORAL
EDUCATION

Educational fads come and go, but some stay long enough to do substantial harm. In 1955 Rudolf Flesch wrote *Why Johnny Can't Read*, a stinging indictment of one such fad. Children couldn't read because they were being taught by the wrong method, said Flesch. The method was called "look-say." It was meant to make reading easier but actually served to confuse children, with the result that many were developing reading problems—if they were learning to read at all. Flesch accurately predicted that if the method was not abandoned, SAT scores would plummet and functional illiteracy would soar.

But the educational establishment clung to the look-say method, all the while studiously ignoring a proven method of teaching reading—the "phonics" approach. Phonics was used in every other country with an alphabet system. And study after study had demonstrated its superiority. For most children it provides the best road to reading success. Belatedly, in 1986, the U.S.

Department of Education endorsed the method suggested by Flesch. But school systems, teachers colleges, and textbook publishers have been reluctant to give up the inferior method. As of this date look-say—or some variation of it—is the method used to teach reading in the vast majority of American schools, and large numbers of children and adults continue to be held back in life by their lack of reading skills.

A similar situation exists with regard to moral education. In addition to the fact that Johnny still can't read, we are now faced with the more serious problem that he can't tell right from wrong.

Not every Johnny, of course, but enough to cause alarm. An estimated 525,000 attacks, shakedowns, and robberies occur in public high schools each month. Each year nearly three million crimes are committed on or near school property—16,000 per school day. About 135,000 students carry guns to school daily; one fifth of all students report carrying a weapon of some type. Twenty-one percent of all secondary school students avoid using the rest rooms out of fear of being harmed or intimidated. Surveys of schoolchildren reveal that their chief school-related concern is the disruptive behavior of their classmates. Teachers have similar concerns. Almost one third of public school teachers indicate that they have seriously considered leaving teaching because of student misbehavior.

The situation is no better outside of school. Suicides among young people have risen by 300 percent over the last thirty years, and one in seven teens say they have tried to commit suicide. Drug and alcohol use is widespread. Teenage sexual activity seems to be at an all-time high. Despite a much smaller teen population and despite more frequent contraceptive use, about 1.1 million teenagers became pregnant in 1991—roughly the same figure as for the last ten years. Forty percent of today's fourteen-year-old girls will become pregnant by the time they are nineteen.

These behaviors are troubling enough, but just as worrisome are the attitudes that accompany them. Many youngsters have a difficult time seeing any moral dimension to their actions: getting drunk and having sex are just things to do. An increasing number of brutal crimes—such as the "wilding" incident in New York's

Central Park—are committed "just for kicks." Hundreds of equally disturbing cases exist. Police say that juveniles are often found laughing and playing at homicide scenes.

One natural response to these grim statistics might be to ask, "Why aren't they teaching values in the schools?" To someone with that idea it might come as a surprise to learn that moral values courses have been in the schools for over twenty-five years. In fact, more attention and research have been devoted to moral education in recent years than at any time in our history. Unfortunately, these attempts at moral education have been a resounding failure.

Why?

Flesch's analysis of the reasons why Johnny can't read is helpful here because the failure of moral education in the schools parallels the failure of the schools to teach reading. In brief, students are being taught by the wrong method—a method that looks more and more like a fad that won't go away. Ironically, this method, which made its appearance in the 1960s, not only fails to encourage virtuous behavior, it seems to actively undermine it, leaving children morally confused and adrift. On the other hand, there is an approach to developing character that does work. It is not a radically new method but, like phonics, an approach that has been tried and proven. It does not work perfectly, but it does seem to be considerably more effective than the current fads when it comes to encouraging responsible character traits in youngsters.

But, like phonics, this tried-and-true method doesn't fit in with the prevailing ideologies in education. The same educators and experts who still cling to the look-say method seem to want desperately to hold on to this failed philosophy of moral education. The resulting impact on our society may turn out to be far more serious than the decline in the SAT scores.

What are the two approaches?

One is called "character education." It is based on the idea that there are traits of character children ought to know, that they learn these by example, and that once they know them, they need to practice them until they become second nature. The other approach is called "decision making" or "moral reasoning" or "the dilemma method" or "Values Clarification." I'll generally use "decision making" as the designation for this approach.

Character education was what took place in school and society in the past. It was sometimes heavy-handed and always liable to abuse, but it seemed to serve our culture well over a long period of time. It has been criticized as being indoctrinative, but in some crucial respects it may have made possible more real freedom of choice than we now possess. It has been dismissed as naive, but new evidence suggests that it is more psychologically sophisticated than the methods that replaced it. There are signs it is now making a comeback. But what we have now, for the most part, is the decision-making approach. In one form or another—sometimes as a course in itself, sometimes as a strategy in sex education classes, sometimes as a unit in civics or social science—it has set the tone for moral education in public and even private schools.

The shift from character education to the decision-making model was begun with the best of intentions. The new approach was meant to help students to think more independently and critically about values. Proponents claimed that a young person would be more committed to self-discovered values than to ones that were simply handed down by adults.

That was the hope. But the actual consequences of the shift have been quite different:

- It has turned classroom discussions into "bull sessions" where opinions go back and forth but conclusions are never reached.
- It has resulted in classrooms where teachers act like talk show hosts, and where the merits of wife swapping, cannibalism, and teaching children to masturbate are recommended topics for debate. It has resulted in nonjudgmental drug education programs in which drugs are scarcely mentioned except to say that taking them is a personal choice.
- For students, it has meant wholesale confusion about moral values: learning to question values they have scarcely acquired, unlearning values taught at home, and concluding that questions of right and wrong are always merely subjective.

- For adults it has provided a theoretical basis for questioning the importance or necessity of setting a good example to the young.
- For church schools it has meant adopting curriculums completely at odds with traditional beliefs, and a seeming inability to discern their own best interests—illustrated in one instance by the collapse of a large Catholic school system after it invited one of the movement theorists into its midst.
- It has meant that the development of moral education curriculums has been turned over to theorists who have repeatedly expressed disdain for concepts such as virtue, character, and good example; the same theorists have dismissed past culture and history as being irrelevant to the search for values.
- It has involved the creation of curriculums that, while claiming to be nonindoctrinative, are anything but.
- It has created a generation of moral illiterates: students who know their own feelings but don't know their culture. On the college and graduate level it has helped to produce students who are unable to identify the Book of Job or to name the Ten Commandments.
- It has led to the creation of sex education classes where, on the one hand, students are encouraged to explore every conceivable option, and on the other, "safe sex" is an ironclad doctrine which cannot be questioned.
- It has involved teachers and administrators in deceptive attempts to keep parents in the dark about the content of the new curriculums.
- It has helped produce a citizenry unable to distinguish reasonable moral arguments from mere rationalizations.
- Finally, it has helped create an educational system with a de facto policy of withholding from children the greatest incentive to moral behavior—namely, the conviction that life makes sense—a policy of doing everything possible to prevent them from learning the larger purposes or stories that give meaning to existence. In failing to impart these stories, schools have deprived children of both moral context and moral energy.

How and why the shift from character education to decision making took place is the subject of this book. It is a fascinating story with roots going back to the time of Socrates. For those not acquainted with the hothouse world of education it may contain surprises: how, for example, in the name of Plato and Socrates, contemporary moral educators introduced a teaching technique that Plato himself considered inappropriate for children; how some of the most popular current ideas about educating children have their source in the writings of a man who locked away his own children in an orphanage; and how Watergate, Vietnam, and social turmoil provided the opportunity that educators needed to introduce their experimental curriculums.

What are these curriculums like? The common feature they all share is the assumption that children can learn to make good moral decisions without bothering to acquire moral habits or strength of character. The underlying strategy is to elicit the youngster's opinion on a wide variety of topics.

- For example, from a questionnaire used in several Massachusetts schools, "On a scale of 1 to 7 how do you rate the importance of being honest when dealing with parents? with peers? with strangers?"
- From the *Values Clarification* handbook (a half-million-copy best-seller): "Tell where you stand on the topic of masturbation"; "How important are engagement rings to you?" "Tell how you feel and what you actually do about alcohol or pot"; "Talk about your allowance—how much you get, when and how, and whether you think it's fair."
- From the same book: "To whom would you tell you have had premarital sexual relations?" "—you have considered suicide?" "—you use illegal drugs?" "—you have had an abortion?" "—your method of birth control?" "—you had once taken money from your dad's dresser?"

As these examples suggest, this is not education in the traditional sense. It has overtones of sensitivity training, and it borders on invasion of privacy. Some experts worry that it amounts to unlicensed therapy (the chief architect of this kind of education was, in fact, not an educator but a psychotherapist). Many parents are concerned as well. They are not convinced that such exercises make for more honest or responsible children.

Some exercises, such as these recommended in popular drug education and "life skills" programs, don't seem to have any connection with morality:

- "Each group takes a minute or so to form a 'pretzel.' This is done by continuing to hold hands and entwining themselves with each other (people passing under arms, stepping over, etc.) until they are a mass of bodies still linked."
- "Ask the children to lie down on the floor . . . present the fantasy, speaking slowly and calmly. 'Close your eyes and pretend that you're floating on your back. The water is gently splashing around you. The sun feels warm on your body, and you can feel the waves passing under you. Just quietly drift along on the water and feel the warm sun. Let all thoughts leave your mind.' "

Parents invest a considerable amount of time and taxes in their children's education. While some would be very pleased with these exercises, others would not. Depending on your point of view, the second activity could be construed as a harmless relaxation technique or else as an introduction to New Age sensibilities. In either case parents might be surprised to learn that activities like these, in combination with exercises for exploring feelings, make up the *bulk* of some drug education programs and extend over many years of the curriculum.

Exercises in guided fantasy are designed to give free play to the imagination. When it comes to sex education programs, however, the tendency in recent years has been to leave very little to the imagination.

- For example, in an elementary school in St. Louis, children are encouraged to use the four-letter words for intercourse, the genital organs, and cunnilingus. A workbook used in another state invites children to "draw mother and father making love."

· On Valentine's Day in Missoula, Montana, the administration of a junior high school gives out valentines with condoms inside to every student.

· In a southern high school classroom, students are shown a steamy film of a couple making love. After the film is over, the boys and girls are asked to pair off and each girl is required to unroll a condom over her partner's finger.

· *Changing Bodies, Changing Lives,* a text widely used in schools and recommended by the *School Library Journal,* is liberally sprinkled with quotes from teens describing their sexual experiences in minute detail. Fred, a gay student, relates, "I was so excited the first time I had sex with a guy that I came just taking my pants off . . ." Donna, a seventeen-year-old, describes her experience: "I was with this guy who said, 'Let me do something to you that I think you'll really like.' And that was when he went down on me and started licking me. I was really kind of embarrassed . . . But it felt really, really good, and I relaxed and just got into it." At regular intervals the authors remind their young readers, "There's no 'right' way or 'right' age to have life experiences," and "only you can decide" what is right.

Another key teaching tool in the decision-making approach is the open-ended discussion of an ethical dilemma.

Here are three commonly used examples of these dilemmas:

· A man's wife is dying of a rare kind of cancer. A local druggist has developed a cure for this type of cancer but demands far more than the man can afford to pay. Later the husband breaks into the store and steals the drug. Should he have done that?

· A girl and boy are in love but they live on two separate islands and the bridge joining the islands has been destroyed by a storm. It may be months before they can see each other again. The owner of a sailboat offers to take the girl across but only on the condition that she sleep with him. What should she do?

- A band of settlers is hiding from marauding Indians. A mother is faced with the choice of suffocating her infant son to prevent him from crying out, or allowing him to live and risking the lives of all the settlers. What should she do?

If you are a young teacher fresh out of education school, this last set of exercises might seem like a good way to sharpen a youngster's critical thinking skills or help him clarify his values. You will probably also note that they will make for a lively class period. On the other hand, if you are a parent with one or more children in school, these exercises might make you feel a little uneasy—although it might be difficult to say why; we have become rather used to this way of framing moral issues. One way to get at the source of the unease is to ask yourself how these exotic dilemmas would translate into matters of everyday conduct. For example, would the dilemma about the man stealing the drug help your youngster resist a temptation to steal change from your dresser? Would the story of the island boy and girl help your son or daughter learn anything about chastity or self-restraint? As for the pioneer woman's dilemma, is it a good idea to introduce youngsters to extreme situations where one life is weighed against another? (Teachers report that boys have a tendency to attack such dilemmas as though they were interesting math problems.)

A parent's intuitive answer is likely to be no. And it so happens there is a good deal of research demonstrating that the intuitive answer is the right one. For example, when drug education programs are patterned on the decision-making model, the result is increased drug use. Sex education programs of this type result in increased sexual activity.

Why?

The underlying problem became apparent to me one day when a graduate student from Japan asked, "Where's the 'moral' in 'moral education'?" In these curriculums a lot of time and energy are spent exchanging opinions and exploring feelings, but practically no time is spent providing moral guidance or forming character. The virtues are not explained or discussed, no models of good behavior are provided, no reason is given why a boy or girl should want to be good in the first place. In short, students are given nothing to live by or look up to. They come away with the impression that even the most basic values are matters of dispute. Morality, they are likely to infer, is something you talk about in class but not something you need to do anything about.

In one sense the decision-making curriculums have been a roaring success. They were set up to create a nonjudgmental attitude about values, and it worked. When members of a high school class in a Toronto suburb were asked to express their views on morality, all but a few came up with a variation on the theme that morality is purely personal. One boy, whose view is representative, wrote:

> Moral values cannot be taught and people must learn to use what works for them. In other words, "whatever gets you through the night, it's alright." The essence of civilization is not moral codes but individualism . . . The only way to know when your values are getting sounder is when they please you more.

When teachers carefully preface each discussion with the caution that there are no right or wrong answers, that is the distinct impression students come away with. Who says they don't listen? The irony is that instead of developing their own values, young people seem increasingly at the mercy of peer and media values.

How do these programs manage to survive and prosper? Part of the answer is that parents don't know they exist or, if they do know, have only a vague notion of what they entail. Quite often this is a matter of deliberate policy. In one community, when a teacher asked what she should do if parents objected to the new Values Clarification program, she was told by a seminar leader, "You call it 'life skills' and you do it anyway." In other communities, parents have been forced to sue under the Freedom of Information Act in order to find out what materials were being used in their children's classes. Professor Sidney Simon, who created the Values Clarification method, boasted that as a young teacher at Temple University he "always bootlegged the values stuff under other titles": "I was assigned to teach Social Studies in the Elementary School, and I taught values clarification. I was assigned Current Trends in American Education, and I taught *my* trend."

Teachers themselves are often in the dark about these curriculums. They may be unaware that the "innovative" program they are using has a long and sad history, and has simply undergone a name change and some cosmetic face-lifting. Unfortunately, many educators have little sense of history. In my own experience the two courses most avoided by education majors, whether graduate or undergraduate, are history of education and philosophy of education. Students will do anything to wriggle out of these "irrelevant" courses, and faculty advisers often aid and abet them in these attempts. Once these students become teachers, they are in a poor position to evaluate new developments in education, or to distinguish fads from genuine educational advances. As a result, education keeps circulating its errors. Failed ideas and theories keep popping up under new names, and no one seems to notice.

Until recently, that is.

Recently the new values curriculums have come under fire from critics both inside and outside the educational establishment. The result has been a clash of both ideas and institutions involving, among other things, a running battle between a secretary of education and the nation's most prestigious colleges, showdowns between parents and public schools, and a lawsuit against the Department of Health and Human Services intended to halt the development of abstinence-based sex education programs.

These skirmishes have, in turn, been part of a larger cultural war. One of the most publicized events of that war—the battle over public funding of exhibitions of the Mapplethorpe and Serrano photos—raises a fundamental question that has been ignored by our culture for a long time: not the question of censorship, and not the question of what is obscene, but the question of what is, or should be, the role of the arts in our culture.

Enclosed in that question is the more specific question of their role in education, and still more specifically, their role in moral education. Traditional cultures made generous use of epics, stories, songs, painting, and sculpture in educating and socializing the young. In many ways it was a surprisingly up-to-date approach—what we would now call "teaching to the right brain."

But much of this has been lost. In recent decades educators have turned a deaf ear and a blind eye to the crucial role of music, art, and story in moral formation. The result has been that these powerful influences have been left almost entirely in the hands of the entertainment industry, which has, in effect, become the real moral educator of the young.

The argument against employing these influences seemed to make sense in the postwar years. Songs, film, marches, and myths played a large part in the indoctrination that young Nazis and young Communists received. To avoid the possibility of indoctrination, educators wanted a stripped-down form of moral education, one that would be free of emotional appeals. Curriculums that claimed to teach "critical thinking" and "rational strategies" found a ready audience. All of this is understandable, but it is also mistaken. History strongly suggests that the dream of a rational morality or a rational society is always just that—a dream; a dream, moreover, that can easily turn into a nightmare, creating systems and societies just as inhuman as the ones they are meant to avoid.

It is realistic to worry about the possibility that art and myth will be misused. It is realistic to insist that their educational use be guided and balanced by reason and experience. It is not realistic to imagine there is a substitute for them. The arts are a two-edged sword, but sometimes a sword is what is needed. The argument about Nazi indoctrination is essentially correct. It was an evil use of powerful tools—song, story, sports, heroes, a grand vision— that allowed Hitler to appeal to so many. What is forgotten is that it was similar methods—along with a very different vision—that produced soldiers and civilians brave and determined enough to resist him.

I hope this will not be construed as an argument for war. It is not. But I do want to make an analogy between nations and individuals in one particular. One of the metaphors that can be used to describe an individual's moral life is that of warfare or battle. It was a metaphor much used in the past, but it has fallen out of use. It is, of course, not the only metaphor that can be employed, but it may be one worth reconsidering. Because, if it is an accurate metaphor—if, for example, the struggle to overcome a drug addiction is in part a spiritual battle with evil (as many recovered addicts describe it)—then it might be important to look at forms of moral education that would equip our young accordingly. If one has to do battle in life, one needs to be trained to do battle.

None of us want to go to untrained doctors, or fly with untrained pilots, or have untrained soldiers protect our country, but for some reason we have come to believe that one can be a good person without any training in goodness. We have succumbed to a myth that claims that morality comes naturally, or at most, with the help of a little reasoning. But it seems increasingly clear that these metaphors and the models that flow from them aren't working. The "natural" thing to do in most situations is to take the easy way out. The most perfectly rational plan of action is to always put yourself first.

Americans have been led to believe that their children will be able to fight their personal moral struggles with weapons that, upon examination, turn out to be very flimsy: there is not much evidence that values curriculums or the "self-esteem" they claim to foster have much effect on behavior. It is perhaps for this reason that values educators have shifted the focus of moral education away from personal behavior and toward public policy issues. What seems to matter for them is not whether one is a good son or daughter, brother or sister, but whether one has formulated a position on nuclear weapons, the environment, or surrogate motherhood.

That sort of approach—if it were done in a thorough and objective way—might help produce individuals with greater political and social awareness, but that is not the same thing as producing individuals of character and integrity. Having the "right" attitude about the environment or civil rights does not translate into keeping commitments to one's family. And it is in these latter respects that today's "moral education" fails.

Can anything be done to correct this failure? Can Johnny learn to tell right from wrong and act accordingly? The following chapters offer criticism of present approaches, but in addition, they offer an alternative. It's an old alternative, to be sure, but a large part of our education consists in rediscovering things we once knew to be true but forgot. In looking at them again, we often see that, however demanding they may be, there is really no workable alternative to them. The traditional character education model seems to be one of those basic forms to which we must always eventually return.

In the past ten years a number of exciting new developments in theory and research have done much to substantiate the case for character education. Philosophers, psychologists, and educators, working separately and pursuing different lines of inquiry, have been arriving at similar conclusions about the need for stories and models in moral formation. In addition, new curriculums are already under development: sex education and drug education programs that encourage abstinence and self-control rather than multiple-choice lifestyles; character education programs that use stories to teach virtues.

But it would be a mistake to think that this kind of education is, or should be, the sole property of schools, or that schools are even the best place for it. Most of all, it would be a mistake to think that character formation is something that can be capsulized in a specific course taught each year for that purpose. To the extent that character formation takes place in school, much of it is accomplished through the spirit and atmosphere of a school, its sports and symbols, its activities and assemblies, its purposes and priorities, its codes of conduct and responsibility—most of all, through its teachers and the quality of their example. Ultimately, character education is the responsibility of the whole culture. That makes it a very big undertaking, but that is not to say it is impossible. Schools are not the only arena for it, but schools are a very important arena and are one place to start.

How about parents? What can they do to encourage character development? They can, of course, do a great many things—from setting good examples to involving children in helping the hungry. But one of the most important things is also one of the simplest. Parents can spend time reading to their children. It may come as a surprise that a book on moral education places so much emphasis on stories. We have grown accustomed to thinking of stories as no more than entertainment. But they are, or can be, a lot more than that.

Let me add to the earlier discussion on reading that no reading method, however good, will bring the child very far unless he is given something meaningful to read. A student may master the rudimentary mechanics of reading, but if his only contact is with bland school readers, he will conclude that reading is not a very interesting pursuit. To rise above the level of minimal literacy, he needs to read exciting and vital stories. Much of that excitement comes from stories that we read with the sense that we are "onto something," with the expectancy that something of importance is about to be revealed.

Those who become accomplished readers are those who have learned to love reading. And they learn to love it because it helps to make sense out of their lives. The same principle applies to moral education. In recent years educators have become preoccupied with developing critical-thinking strategies. That is not a bad thing in the right context. But it is useless to learn the "mechanics" of moral decision making if the child's world is void of meaning, if life itself seems random and incomprehensible. Without the sense that life makes sense, all other motives for virtuous behavior lose their force. If life is "a tale told by an idiot . . . signifying nothing," then it doesn't really matter how one behaves. Moral decisions are not something divorced from our personal history. And our personal stories, in turn, need to be connected to some larger story or stories that give meaning to our lives and actions.

Stories help to make sense of our lives. They also create a desire to be good. Plato, who thought long and hard about the subject of moral education, believed that children should be brought up in such a way that they would fall in love with virtue. And he thought that stories and histories were the key to sparking this desire. No amount of discussion or dialogue could compensate if that spark was missing.

Yet today very little attention is paid to this aspect of a child's development. Contemporary educators have for too long assumed that the desire to be good will just be there. But we have learned in recent years that this is not the case. The desire has to be instilled by caring parents and thoughtful teachers. As Plato understood, one of the best ways to do it is with stories. They allow us to identify with models of courage and virtue in a way that "problem solving" or classroom discussion does not.

This is the normal way children achieve in other areas of life. Success in sports or music, for example, can usually be traced to a desire to emulate a "hero" of the sports world or music world. Stories supply examples of virtue in action; they can supply strength and wisdom as well. An important dimension of character is the ability to understand and persevere in difficult situations that can't for the moment be changed. Stories and fairy tales, as Bruno Bettelheim points out, have a way of helping children work through such times of adversity. A college student who had just read Katherine Paterson's *Jacob Have I Loved* once confided to me, "I wish I had read that as a teenager. I think it would have helped me to handle a lot of my anger toward my mother." In a similar vein a mother of a ten-year-old boy told me that the most important factor in keeping his spirits up during a series of painful operations was reading and rereading the story of the labors of Hercules in a book of myths.

Stories have always been an important way of transmitting values and wisdom. They become all the more important in a society that, like ours, has experienced so much disruption in the family and in the community. The lessons contained in good stories are lessons the child might not otherwise get in a world of harried adults and fractured social institutions.

The last chapter of this book provides an annotated list of stories that can help awaken the moral imagination of children and teens. They are not didactic or preachy stories. On the contrary, they are exciting and compelling. They are the kind of stories that throw off sparks.

Becoming acquainted or reacquainted with these stories carries some benefits for adults also. You may find that these stories touch chords for you as well as for your child. My daughter, now grown, tells me that the times I read to her were some of the best parts of her childhood. They were important times for me as well.

Those nights when I was reading from *The Hobbit, The Chronicles of Narnia,* from Bible stories and the *Little House* series not only brought us closer but also, I am convinced, accounted for a good deal of my own moral and spiritual growth. They helped me remember any number of things I had conveniently stowed in the cold storage part of my soul.

Finding good books for a child is a step that parents can take right away. Finding out what transpires in their child's school might well be the next important step. The following three chapters take a look inside Johnny's classroom.

DRUG EDUCATION

Dr. William Coulson is a distinguished-looking man in his late fifties, whose mild-mannered affability is complemented by a sophisticated sense of humor. Coulson was the founding director of the once prestigious Center for Studies of the Person and coeditor of an important series of texts on humanistic education. He now directs a much smaller organization known as the Research Council on Ethnopsychology. In addition to his research and writing activities, Dr. Coulson occasionally plays the trombone in the family jazz band he and his wife, Jeannie, formed years ago. The other members of the band are their seven children, although now that the children are grown, the performances are less frequent. Coulson is also a talented speaker who is much in demand. He has been known to enliven his already lively talks with a horn solo.

Lately Dr. Coulson's talks to various college and parent groups have centered on the theme of apology. He wants to apologize for himself and for several of his former colleagues who, having passed away, are unable to apologize for themselves. Dr. Coulson may be described as the affective educator who came in from the cold. The reasons for his defection make for an interesting story, and they also reveal why drug education in America got off to a bad start.

In the 1960s and 1970s Coulson was one of the leading figures in what came to be known as the human potential movement—a loose alliance of psychologists and educators interested in expanding human possibilities by encouraging greater self-awareness. One of the chief goals of human potential psychology was to help individuals "get in touch" with their feelings, or to use the psychological term, with their "affective" side—thus the term "affective education." Dr. Coulson was a colleague of both Abraham Maslow and Carl Rogers, the two men who are generally credited with starting the movement. Coulson, in fact, was considered to be the most likely successor to Rogers. In collaboration with Rogers he edited books on different facets of affective education, ran workshops and seminars, and helped to direct some of the movement's key organizations.

But Coulson began to have second thoughts about the movement, and by the middle of the seventies he had parted company with it. He was disturbed by the large number of casualties the movement seemed to produce in its wake: irresponsible experimentation with drugs and sex, broken relationships, and emotional disorders. In particular he became alarmed at the results that occurred when "humanistic" ideas were translated into school curriculums.

The drug education curriculums were especially distressing. Many, if not most of them, were modeled on the nondirective pattern that had been developed at the Western Behavioral Sciences Institute in La Jolla, California, under the leadership of Carl Rogers. Like other human potential offshoots such as the encounter group, these programs relied heavily on group discussion of feelings—a process that had come to be known simply as "the group experience." But when, beginning in the mid-seventies, research on the effectiveness of such programs was conducted, the news was not good.

In 1976 at Stanford University, Dr. Richard Blum and his research associates published the results of a four-year study of an
"affective" drug program called Decide. The students in the program were compared with a control group that received no drug
education. Blum had expected the study would favor the affective
program, but to his surprise it was the control group that showed
the most resistance to drugs. Those receiving affective education
used alcohol, tobacco, and marijuana sooner than the controls
and they used drugs more extensively.

Dr. Blum found much the same results in a similar study of
Decide in 1978. In the 1980s, when other affective drug prevention
programs such as Smart, Here's Looking at You, and Quest were
evaluated by other researchers, the results were almost identical:
these drug education programs increased drug use.

The studies came as no surprise to Coulson. He already knew
from personal experience that the approach pioneered at La Jolla
and at the celebrated Esalen Institute was designed to encourage
experimentation, not to prevent it. In fact, the group experience
was an almost sure-fire formula for disrupting previously stable
lives. The group encounters had led to a string of divorces and sex
scandals and not infrequently to episodes of psychological distur-
bance for the participants. The leaders encountered problems of
their own. One of Coulson's colleagues even managed to actual-
ize himself into prison.

One story Coulson tells is representative. When Rasa Gustaitis,
a free-lance journalist, visited Esalen in the late sixties, she had a
contract with Macmillan publishers for a book to be titled *Turning
On Without Drugs*. But the group experience changed all that:

> Once she arrived at Esalen Institute, the first thing that hap-
> pened was to be drawn into a "milling-around" exercise.
> Next she was placed in a circle to talk about feelings. Resist-
> ant at first, she finally yielded. The next day she took LSD. So
> when Macmillan published her book in 1969, it needed a
> different title. *Turning On Without Drugs* became, simply,
> *Turning On*.

Coulson was not the only one to have reservations about the
human potential movement. Years before Coulson's defection,

Abraham Maslow had expressed grave misgivings about the whole enterprise. Maslow's name is one of the most revered in psychology. Unlike other psychologists, he concentrated his studies not on pathology but on health. His interest was in human potential and the capacity for growth. Along with Rogers he had opened up a new path in psychology—what came to be known as "the Third Force" (the two other "forces" are Freudian psychology and behavioral psychology).

Yet, unknown to most of his followers, Maslow had, in the years before his death, repudiated much of the agenda connected with his name. In a journal entry dated May 5, 1968, he asks:

Who should teach whom? Youngsters teach the elders or vice versa? It got me in a conflict about my education theory. I've been in *continuous* conflict for a long time over this, over Esalen-type, orgiastic, Dionysian-type education.

Maslow was concerned that "my Jewish heritage of books and libraries" was in jeopardy from the anti-intellectualism of human potential psychology. He was afraid that his own daughters were being harmed by humanistic education. To have had daughters "made the psychology of the time look trivial and totally inadequate," he wrote in his journal.

In the preface to the second edition of *Motivation and Personality,* he was more pointed. Self-actualization, he wrote, was not a concept to be applied to children:

In Chapter 11 on self-actualization I have removed one source of confusion by confining the concept very definitely to older people. By the criteria I used, self-actualization does not occur in young people . . . [they have not] learned how to be patient; nor have they learned enough about evil in themselves and others . . . nor have they generally become knowledgeable and educated enough to open the possibility of becoming wise; nor have they generally acquired enough courage to be unpopular, to be unashamed about being openly virtuous, etc.

Dr. Coulson's own disaffection began after the failure of the Educational Innovation Project, an experiment in sensitizing an entire school system. Operated by the Sisters of the Immaculate Heart of Mary, the system included fifty-nine schools in the Los Angeles area. The nuns had responded to an article in which Carl Rogers had, in effect, advertised for a school system that would let him put his educational theories into action.

At first the experiment seemed promising. An elementary school teacher wrote:

> When I got back from the first weekend, I simply could not teach. There were too many things going on in me. So I told my children about my experience and tried to convey something of the spirit of the thing. They were fascinated and some of them even wept as I told them about it. Since then the class relationships have been *so much* better. They see me as a person and I see them as persons. They come to me much more often individually. They come to me for hugs and love. It is just fabulous what has happened in our class.

One of the teachers at Immaculate Heart College prepared a written announcement for her students which contained the following:

> Some of you might be frightened by this type of course. Please feel free to express this or any other reaction you may have enroute. I myself am apprehensive on many scores but I feel the risk is worth taking. How about you?

But the final result of month after month of in-depth sharing was quite different. Deep divisions emerged between parents and teachers. The sisters, who had initially been enthusiastic about revitalizing their schools, became absorbed with questions of self-actualization. Teaching took a back seat. Many lost their faith as well. The order secularized itself and broke its ties with the Catholic Church. The schools were shut down. Coulson, who was project coordinator, later wrote, "When we started . . . there were six hundred nuns and fifty-nine schools . . . Now, four years later, as I write, a year following the formal completion of the project there are two schools left and no nuns."

One would have to go back to seventeenth-century France and the appearance of the devils in the convent at Loudun to find a more radical transformation of a group of sisters. Even Rogers, who considered turmoil a necessary accompaniment of growth, was dismayed. "Why did I ever write that crazy plan?" he later asked colleagues. It was the beginning of what he was eventually to call "a pattern of failure."

At the heart of the plan was the concept of the therapeutic classroom. In the forties and fifties Rogers had pioneered the client-centered method of therapy, a technique that was highly regarded and widely used. As early as 1955 he began to think that it could be successfully transplanted into schools.

Rogers's therapeutic approach was based on the assumption that each person has two selves, a real self and a false self, which is constructed in response to social expectations. The real self, which is basically good and trustworthy, tends to be repressed but can be released under certain conditions. What conditions? In therapy, "unconditional positive regard"—a sort of complete acceptance—is the main ingredient. Given that climate, clients will be able to take the risks necessary to growth. But complete acceptance necessitated a second principle: Therapists must be nonjudgmental about their clients' values and behaviors. (It was an idea that struck a chord outside of therapeutic circles. Much of our current talk about "not imposing values" is simply a borrowing of Rogers's therapeutic vocabulary.) What then is the therapist's role? In brief, to let the client find his own directions. Rogers, like Maslow, believed in the existence of natural healthy instincts which would point each individual in the right direction. What that direction was to be was not for the therapist to say. Hence, client-centered therapy's other name—"nondirective counseling."

Could these ideas be applied to teaching? Rogers and Coulson thought so. Between 1968 and 1974 they edited a series of seventeen books for C. E. Merrill Publishing Company, most of them about nondirective teaching. The most important of these was Rogers's own *Freedom to Learn*, a book that was soon selling on the order of 150,000 copies per year.

In a sense, the book was not really about teaching at all. Not in any traditional sense. For Rogers the idea of instructing or teaching held little appeal. Instead, *Freedom to Learn* was a guidebook for turning teachers into facilitators. The model for the classroom was the sensitivity group:

> The intensive group or "workshop" group usually consists of ten to fifteen persons and a facilitator or leader. It is relatively unstructured, providing a climate of maximum freedom for personal expression, exploration of feelings, and interpersonal communication . . . Individuals come to know themselves and each other more fully . . . the climate of openness, risk-taking, and honesty generates trust, which enables the person to recognize and change self-defeating attitudes, test out and adopt more innovative and constructive behaviors.

Rogers was largely successful in getting his ideas across—at least, that is my impression after twenty years of teaching future teachers. They view their job as a therapeutic one: to facilitate self-expression, to enhance self-esteem, to be more open and nonjudgmental. In short, to be more like therapists. They may change their minds about it later on, but this seems to be the initial motivation. I think I understand how they feel. Those were exactly my sentiments at the time I started teaching, and in those days Rogers's theories were like scripture to me.

But Rogers himself was taken aback by the reverence with which his ideas were treated: "When I write up my theories, at least I try to make it clear that they're tentative . . . But when they get into textbooks, they sound like they came down on tablets from Mount Sinai . . ." He had two other misgivings. First, he didn't think the group experience should be forced on anyone. Second, in 1973, perhaps recalling the Immaculate Heart debacle, he concluded that it was never appropriate for children to participate in classroom encounter groups. Dr. Coulson, who knew the family well, observes that Rogers did not practice nondirectiveness with his own children and grandchildren.

As with Maslow, Rogers's misgivings were either unknown to his followers or ignored by them. His theories had already stimulated what Coulson calls a "wild psychologizing" among curriculum writers. The "affective approach," as Rogers's brand of education came to be called, seemed the answer to every educational problem.

Including drug education.

The largest independent drug education program in the United States is called Quest. Quest is described in a promotional brochure as a "non-profit educational organization founded in 1975 whose mission is to 'create a world that cares deeply about its young people.'" According to the organization's literature, its Skills for Living program has been installed in "more than 2000 school systems in 47 states and seven countries," while its Skills for Adolescence program is in use in "more than 12,000 communities and schools throughout the world." Quest, like many of the other drug prevention programs developed in the seventies and early eighties—Positive Action, Project Charlie, Here's Looking at You, Me-ology, Values & Choices—is modeled on Rogers's thera peutic education scheme. In fact, Howard Kirschenbaum, the author of the first Quest program, Skills for Living, is also the author of an adulatory biography of Carl Rogers.

Group leaders or "facilitators" of the Quest program are required to attend a three-day workshop which is basically a crash course in the techniques of client-centered therapy. The advice they receive is similar to the advice a fledgling therapist might receive before meeting his first client:

- Paraphrase. ("So, you've had a similar experience.")
- Reflect feelings. ("I can see that really annoys you.")
- Watch advising, evaluating, or moralizing.
- Remind yourself you're asking for opinions; everyone has a right to his or her own.
- Ask nonjudgmental questions to promote further thinking.
- Express your own feelings.
- Push their risk levels gently.
- Trust the process.

The language is so sensitive and democratic that a casual observer might wonder why there is any fuss over this kind of approach. But there is—enough of a fuss to divide school districts all over the country into warring factions.

Critics of the therapeutic approach claim that while it may be useful in therapy, it has no place in drug education. Coulson points out that the cardinal rule of the clinic, "I will never censor you—nor must you censor yourself," should not apply in schools, especially when the topic is drug taking. On the subject of drugs and other life-and-death issues, children need "authoritative guidance," says Coulson, not techniques designed to explore options and feelings. As Coulson points out, the teachers' guides for these various programs invariably urge the instructor to conduct discussions "free of right and wrong answers." Students, says Coulson, will gain the impression that the rightness or wrongness of drug use is a subjective matter. This, he claims, is a highly irresponsible message—especially in view of the fact that the law does not consider drug use to lie in the subjective realm.

Coulson, in turn, has been accused of being a right-wing fundamentalist, of lying about his credentials, and of misrepresenting his ties with Rogers and Maslow. Apparently, when it comes to defending their own programs, not even affective educators can hope to be consistently nonjudgmental. And besides, they like what they do. Teachers in these programs become what Rogers had hoped they would become—neutral facilitators. "Try not to lecture," cautions one teachers' guide; "Practice using the skills of facilitation . . . listening and processing," prompts another.

In exchange for this abdication of authority, teachers get to teach classes that are fairly popular. Quest, Project Charlie, Here's Looking at You, and Me-ology all utilize games and activities that are "fun" and "exciting"—"a really good time," as one Project Charlie coordinator put it. In addition, the therapeutic enterprise has attractions of its own. To be an encourager of self-discovery, growth, and personal liberation is no small thing.

What is the role of parents in this scheme? Parents have been the most vociferous opponents of affective education, and little wonder. If teachers are instructed to be nondirective, parents are expected to recede even farther into the background. After all, from the viewpoint of human potential psychology, they are the largest part of the problem. Consequently, it wasn't long before the idea of the teacher as therapist was followed by the idea of the parent as therapist. The chief exponent of the idea was Thomas Gordon, a student of Rogers, who, in a book titled *Parent Effectiveness Training,* urged the techniques of therapeutic listening and nonjudgmentalism on parents. The idea spread rapidly among therapists, educators, and parents as Parent Effectiveness workshops sprang up across the country. Coulson sums up the mood of the time this way: "We were to be the first generation of parents not to oppress our kids."

Drug educators were eager to press the point. Helping Youth Decide, a program targeted at parents, reminds them, "Remember that these techniques may backfire if you preach. This approach is designed to help youth explore and develop their *own* values and morals . . ." Curriculum developers seem eager that children also realize the limited nature of the role their parents ideally should play. "The Family," says one Quest worksheet in headline letters, "Should Be Like an Elephant—All Ears." Unfortunately, of course, most parents haven't been working on their therapeutic skills, and Quest takes note of this, too. The workbooks contain many scenarios of family conflict for students to discuss and role-play. But, as a mother of a Quest student observes, "It seemed as if the parents were always put in a bad light. The story would be about a father and his son, say; and the father was *always* overbearing, *always* too strict, *always* unfair."

This is rather standard fare in the health education curriculum. "You must decide for yourself which role to adopt," says one typical high school text. Another advises: "A major influence on you has been the attitudes and behaviors of each of your parents. . . . You have probably learned some fairly traditional ideas . . . Many believe that these traditional attitudes hinder growth and development of a person because they limit possibilities . . ." "Only you can judge," counsels another text.

Any parent who has traditional ideas about right and wrong and the conduct of family life is likely to suffer by comparison with facilitative teachers. "Your parents don't understand you, but we do" seems to be an implicit message in the affective classroom. And of course, it's a message that sits well with the average youngster. Parents of an eight-year-old boy in Washington State asked the child what Quest meant to him. They learned it meant "choosing for himself no matter what his parents might say."

But if you don't have to listen to your parents and teachers, whom should you listen to? The answer given by affective educators is fairly consistent on this point—"yourself." What part of yourself? The emotional part. "This evocation of feeling is the most prominent feature in every program I reviewed," writes Coulson of his work as a technical adviser to the U.S. Department of Education. The Quest student workbooks contain several examples. In one exercise titled "Emotion Clock," students keep track of their feelings over a twenty-four-hour period. Another is called "My Emotions" and asks students to keep a record of "everything that makes you feel good or uncomfortable for one day." "I'm Comfortable" asks students to complete sentences such as "It's easy to share my feelings with others when they _____." Other activities involve drawing a "Rainbow of Feelings" and a "Mood Continuum." This emphasis on self-affirmation even extends to the teachers. In a training session for one program, Coulson observed teachers drawing rainbows and writing the following caption: "The most wonderful thing in the world." He asked, "What do you say it is, this most wonderful thing in the world?" "The answer," Coulson reports, "was unanimous. 'Me!' " Were they putting him on? I doubt it. Not too long ago, when seniors at Boston College's School of Education had to choose a class song for graduation, they came up with Whitney Houston's hit "The Greatest Love of All"—a song about learning to love yourself.

One interesting consequence of all the "self talk" in drug education is that there is relatively little said about drugs themselves. Of his visit to a San Diego program, Coulson remarks, "There was no talk of drugs in the session I observed and I was told that, by design, there would be none till the last three weeks of the course." Out of a total of seven units, Quest has only one that deals with any factual information on drugs. Coulson concludes, "The subject is not drugs but selves."

On the other hand, defenders of Quest and similar curriculums say this is exactly the point. Quest is part of a larger educational effort which may be called "the self-esteem movement." In 1987

California created a "Task Force to Promote Self-Esteem," which concluded that "the lack of self-esteem is central to most personal and social ills plaguing our state and nation as we approach the end of the 20th century." Other states followed suit and created their own task forces. Soon there was a National Council for Self-Esteem and a Foundation for Self-Esteem. The National Education Association tells its 2 million member teachers that schools "must structure self-esteem building into the curriculum." After an extensive examination of teacher education programs, writer and researcher Rita Kramer concluded that elementary teachers "are being taught to concern themselves with children's feelings of self worth and not with the worth of hard work . . ."

Chester Finn, who served as assistant secretary of education, observes that "near-magical powers" are ascribed to self-esteem. For example, the California Task Force says self-esteem "inoculates us against the lures of crime, violence, substance abuse, teen pregnancy, child abuse, chronic welfare dependency, and educational failure." From this viewpoint, bad choices and destructive behaviors—such as drug taking—are a result of low self-esteem. If schools would go to work on raising self-esteem, the other problems would take care of themselves. By this reasoning, it makes sense to devote the greater part of a drug education curriculum to cultivating feelings and self-awareness. This, of course, is really just a reworking of Rogers's idea that the true self is inherently good and trustworthy and needs only to be liberated. Students thus liberated will, in the words of the Quest brochure, be able to make "wise and healthy decisions."

But there are some problems with this approach. Real self-esteem is a by-product of real learning and achievement. We feel good about ourselves because we've done something good or worthy. Most self-esteem-based curriculums, however, don't make any connection between self-esteem and achievement or between self-esteem and behavior. People are just simply good as they are. A central message of Quest and similar programs is "You're fine as you are." But, if that's so, there is no need for moral improvement or self-betterment. Being completely self-accepting is not exactly a formula for responsible behavior. Some of recent history's worst scoundrels—Joseph Stalin, Idi Amin, Saddam Hussein, Manuel Noriega—seem to have been quite self-satisfied. The trouble with such people is not that they lack self-esteem but that they feel themselves accountable to no outside law or standard. It's not even necessary to consult history books. Any pimp, con artist, or drug pusher will prove the point. As a rule, they enjoy what they do and seem to have few, if any, self-doubts.

It is important to have self-esteem—but for the right reasons. The concept of it that is currently fashionable in education circles, however, is extraordinarily naive. When combined with equally simplistic notions about choices, it can easily lead a youngster to the conclusion that his choices can never be wrong. In Coulson's words, "If I'm really quite wonderful . . . then whatever I decide to do must be wonderful, too." Within the limited framework of affective education, it would be a reasonable conclusion to make. In the end everything is subjective. There are no standards outside the self to which to repair—no "right or wrong answers." One's feelings must be one's guide.

Ideas of this sort are understandably novel and intoxicating to an inexperienced youngster, but why they should be considered so by teachers is another question. Both Quest and Here's Looking at You, the two largest programs, are seventeen years old. Carl Rogers's *Freedom to Learn* was published twenty-two years ago. At a drug education fair a few years ago, a representative of Decide began her presentation with, "I would like to introduce you to an exciting and innovative drug education program." But, as Coulson comments, "the time when it was 'innovative' is long gone."

These programs are by now more "establishment" than innovative. They build on a conceptual framework that was introduced in the sixties and they share much of the spirit of the sixties. The emphasis on spontaneity, self-expression, rejection of authority, and emotionalism that one finds in these programs should be familiar to anyone who grew up in that decade. The quest for the true inner self which is the heart of Rogerian therapy was also the heart of the sixties youth revolt.

And this inner quest was at the heart of the explosion in drug use that began in the sixties. As psychologist Joseph Adelson writes, "No one will want to argue that the antinomian outlook 'caused' the [present] drug epidemic; but there is little question that it rationalized its early stages and beyond that helped undo the immune system which had kept drugs—and much else—at bay." One good reason to question curriculums of the Quest variety is that the philosophy that inspires them seems indistinguishable from the philosophy that inspired the original outbreak of wide-scale drug experimentation. That philosophy didn't prevent drug use then; why suppose it will prevent it now?

Many curriculum writers seem to be stuck in that earlier era. Thus, in *Health Education: The Search for Values,* a book still marketed to drug and sex educators, the reader is invited to contemplate the wonders of risk taking: "By risk taking we mean the chance one often takes when one ventures out of one's pattern of behavior . . . It is safe to say that regardless of the risk involved, the greatest risk would come from not exercising the opportunity to risk—and possibly to grow from it."

For an overly cautious adult with firmly established patterns of behavior and an adult's awareness of consequences, this might be advice worth considering. But where do educators get the right to take risks with other people's children? Research on the group method shows that even with adults it is a hazardous undertaking capable of disrupting healthy as well as unhealthy controls. This is the case even when groups are run by trained therapists. But Quest facilitators have only three days of training. An additional problem is pointed out by Dr. Harold Voth, chief psychiatrist at the Veterans Hospital in Topeka. He writes, "There is no assurance that all teachers are free of psychopathology. Exposing the child to the broad issues introduced by the Quest exercises and orchestrated by teachers of unknown mental health and stability places the child in a position of great risk." Shortly after reading Dr. Voth's comments, I came across a news item about Pamela Smart, the New Hampshire teacher who was convicted of having seduced three of her students into murdering her husband. Parents of two of the boys had initiated a suit against the school administration which "knew or should have known that Smart had formed 'inappropriate relationships' with the boys in a drug and alcohol awareness program she led." An extreme case? Of course. But it does suggest that the damage a disturbed individual can do is greatly magnified in the feeling-centered classroom. And it points to a related and more widespread problem.

A far more common type than the deviant teacher is the deviant student—the one who takes drugs, breaks the law, engages in early and promiscuous sex. One by-product of affective drug education is that it gives the users and risk takers in the class an undue influence—one they wouldn't normally have. In the normal course of events "traditionalists"—nonusers—avoid the users. They choose their friends from among peers like themselves and shy away from the others. The group process, however, throws users and nonusers together in intimate contact in a way that the traditional classroom does not. And in the upside-down world of in-depth sharing, the nonuser finds himself at a disadvantage. Why? Because the influence in such groups flows from user to abstainer. A 1976 study of teenage smokers conducted by the research team of Yankelovich, Skelly, and White suggests why:

> The profile of the teen-age girl smoker counters the image of a socially ill-at-ease youngster turning to cigarettes as a means of being thought of as more sophisticated or as a needed prop for handling social situations. Instead, it is the teen-age girl smoker who is at ease socially, very put together, and with full confidence in herself. Parties and social gatherings are her metier.

The smokers were also far more likely to use marijuana, binge-drink, and be sexually experienced. The nonjudgmental classroom discussion is tailor-made for youngsters like these, and they tend to set the tone. In one sense they are models of what such classes are meant to encourage. They are risk takers par excellence, and they have no trouble talking about their feelings and experiences. To top it off, they are often quite entertaining. Considering that the other students are duty bound, as one guidebook puts it, "to demonstrate tolerance for each other's points of view," the users have all the advantages.

Coulson observes:

Under this induction, drugs become no longer something on the edge of an inexperienced student's awareness, no longer a report-on-the-evening-news-but-personally-unthinkable. Having been "energized" (Quest's term) by one psychological classroom exercise and another and then placed in a circle for heart-to-heart discussion with peers; having exchanged feelings and found that, deep down, the users among his classmates are persons with feelings, too, the inexperienced student will be said to have "grown"—and in the process lost the fear of offending against the prohibitions of his home and the commandments of his church.

In 1978 and 1985 Professor Stephen Jurs at the University of Toledo was contracted by Quest to test the results of its programs. He found that program participation was followed by an increase in drug experimentation. Quest did not publish the results, but instead in 1988 began a new study of its Skills for Adolescence program. This study was not published either, but Dr. Coulson was able to obtain a Quest research memorandum on the preliminary findings. The study compared Quest students to a control group on smoking, marijuana/hashish use, cocaine/crack use, and alcohol use. In all cases the Quest group showed greater increases than the controls, who either remained "stable" or decreased their use. For cigarette smokers there was a "much greater increase," and for alcohol, a "striking increase." In addition, the Quest students showed a lower perception of risk; they had acquired a more relaxed attitude toward drug use. The results, states the memorandum, are "not what Quest would like to see."

Four years prior to this discouraging report, Howard Kirschenbaum, coauthor of the best-selling book *Values Clarification* and author of the initial Quest curriculum, had spoken in glowing terms of the promise of Quest before the 1984 Convention of the Association for Supervision and Curriculum Development:

We have a program called the Quest program . . . It's now being used and taught to 300,000 high school students a year in this country: 300,000! It's a humanistic education curriculum . . . It has lots of values clarification in it . . . lots of communication skills . . . lots of self-talk. . . . It's . . . a really fine synthesis of alive humanistic education.

In another part of his speech to the delegates, Kirschenbaum explained that terminology isn't important: ". . . humanistic education, holistic education, experiential education, whatever we may call it . . . We've got to connect them with the mainline concerns of the average American." Moreover, added Kirschenbaum, "I think we need to tie in humanistic education to whatever current fads or movements are taking place."

Quest's audience is now estimated to be about 2 million students per year, and it is just one of many humanistic drug education programs. But all the evidence is that humanistic education, holistic education—"whatever we may call it"—doesn't work. The failure of these programs is mirrored in the statistics. While educators have been busy helping youth to explore values and decide for themselves, the drug problem has continued unabated.

- Nearly six out of ten high school seniors say they have used illegal drugs (not including alcohol).
- The percentage of children using drugs by the sixth grade has tripled since 1975.
- One in fifteen high school senior boys has used steroids.
- One in twelve high school students admits to using LSD.
- More than half of high school seniors say they get drunk at least once a month. Two out of five get drunk at least once a week.
- The average age of first alcohol use has dropped to 12.3 years.
- A 1985 study showed that ten times as many twelve-year-old girls were smoking in comparison to a decade earlier.

In 1988 the U.S. Department of Education published a guide to selecting drug prevention curriculums. Consumers, it says, should watch for "outdated theories" and should avoid curriculums that emphasize "open-ended decision making," "values clarification," and "therapeutic educational strategies." Instead, curriculums should "maintain adult authority in the classroom . . . A classroom is not a 'bull session' and real damage can be done when teachers attempt to curry students' favor by revealing their own past indiscretions." Moreover, the report continues, "it is important that these choices [children's] be informed by parental and community standards of right and wrong, and by respect for the law . . . Decision making is never value free, nor should it rely on the students' personal good instincts." The cautionary section concludes: ". . . if a curriculum has only minimal material on substance abuse, and is mainly a social skills or self-esteem package, then it is not a real prevention curriculum."

To its credit Quest has responded to criticisms of this sort with revisions that have made its programs less affective and more directive. It has stopped publishing the Skills for Living program developed by Howard Kirschenbaum, and it now insists that it is not a values clarification program. In its current programs it balances decision-making exercises with a "no use" stance toward drugs, and it supplements self-esteem activities with a list of school service projects. Quest also invites family and community participation in its program.

Quest is by no means the worst of the drug education programs. I have focused on it because it is the largest program and also because of its clear historical link to the human potential movement. Despite its attempts to distance itself from its past, however, Quest remains a feelings-based program. It still operates on the dubious assumption that morality is a by-product of "feeling good about yourself," and it still advertises itself as a child-centered approach. If Quest's *A Guide to Leading Parent Meetings* is a reliable indicator, even the parent meetings are conducted on the child centered model. One introductory exercise asks parents to "group together according to their favorite flavor of ice cream." In other sessions parents are expected to play out the same juvenile exercises assigned to their children. The laudable parts of the Quest message (e.g., "parents are still the authorities in their households") tend to be undercut by this compulsion to keep things on the level of "have a nice day."

On the elementary school level this commitment to niceness

and fun activities is exemplified by the Quest mascot, a stuffed animal named Q-Bear ("his soft fur and warm smile make him great for hugs") who is used to lead children through the course activities. Quest is not alone in this Toys "R" Us approach to education. Other widely marketed life-skills programs feature similar animal friends. In DUSO (Developing Understanding of Self and Others) Duso the Dolphin leads children through "guided fantasy activities." Not to be outdone, the PUMSY program features Pumsy, "a loveable young dragon" puppet who helps children overcome "negative 'self-talk' " and learn "positive thinking skills." The Department of Education's guide to prevention curricula displays considerable charity when it notes that over-reliance on such "props" and "gimmicks" "may trivialize the message."

Defenders of Quest who point to the various skills it attempts to develop—listening skills, communication skills, decision-making skills—miss a larger point. These skills are presented in the context of a cultural vacuum. Except for references to popular culture (students read an article by Bill Cosby), the usual sources of important values such as myth, religion, history, and literature are altogether absent. Quest is a life-skills program that offers no profound or inspiring conception of life. What's more, the considerable time required to implement the extensive Quest curriculum leaves that much less time for the academic subjects that might acquaint students with sources of value other than the self.

What does work? One promising approach is to have drug education presented by authoritative models. For example, the DARE program (Drug Abuse Resistance Education) puts a police officer in each classroom for seventeen one-hour sessions. In class the officers teach students how to refuse drugs and how to handle peer pressure. At recess they spend time getting to know children on an individual basis. Above all, they act as positive role models.

Here is a Michigan teacher describing the effect of the DARE program on his fifth-grade class:

The children loved these police officers and respected their wisdom . . . the kids knew he [Officer Norris] cared about them and that they could trust him. By the time he was done, my students thought that anyone using drugs was ignorant, and, to use their term, "scum." My point is that Al Norris changed the norms within our school. He gave drug use the disreputable and inacceptable reputation it deserves. He truly set the standards for behavior amongst my students.

Unfortunately, not all officers are as effective as Officer Norris. The problem is that DARE insists on mixing authoritative guidance with decision making, self-esteem exercises, and other techniques of therapeutic education. Once again, we have an example of a program in which some elements work to undermine others. Research on the effectiveness of DARE shows only modest positive effects.

In any event, drug use prevention is not simply a matter of developing good curriculums. As the Department of Education guide points out, a more important factor is the school's atmosphere of expectations: "A strong school policy against substance abuse—clearly articulated, consistently enforced, and broadly communicated—is the foundation upon which any program should be built."

Among the more effective programs studied by Coulson and his team is one called Building Drug Free Schools. Not a particularly catchy title as prevention programs go, but it's one program that seems to live up to its billing. Northside High School in Atlanta, at one time known to its students as "Fantasy Island," used the program to rid itself of a serious drug problem and dramatically improved academic achievement as well.

Asked to describe his "program," principal Bill Rudolph replies, "that's very difficult to do because we don't really have a 'drug and alcohol program' here. What we have is a school that has very, very clear expectations for its students; and among those expectations is that they not break the law nor come to school under the influence of alcohol and drugs. . . . But it also means some more important things. It means you go to class, you go on time, you try hard; it means that you're going to get two to three hours of homework every night. It means that we're going to put you in the most challenging courses that we can find for you.

. . . We don't really have a 'drug program' here. What we're having is school, and we think what we're having is quality education, which *precludes* drug use."

Other successful programs create a similar climate of expectations. One such example, cited in *Schools Without Drugs,* a Department of Education publication, is Samuel Gompers Vocational-Technical High in the South Bronx. According to a 1977 *New York Times* article, students at Gompers smoked marijuana and sold drugs inside the building with the result that the police had to be called daily. At that time Gompers had a reputation as a "war zone." In 1979 a new principal, Victor Herbert, took steps to turn the school around:

- He established a drug awareness program for teachers, students, and parents.
- He stationed security guards and faculty outside bathrooms and organized "hall sweeps" in the middle of class periods. Students were no longer allowed to leave school during lunchtime.
- In cooperation with the police, Herbert arranged for the same two officers to respond to all calls from Gompers. These officers came to know the students and were eventually trusted by them.
- He persuaded IBM to hire students for after-school and summer work. Students had to be drug-free to participate.

As a result of this no-nonsense policy, Gompers became virtually drug-free. In 1986, the year the Department of Education conducted its survey of exemplary schools, there were no known incidents of Gompers students using drugs or alcohol in school or on school grounds.

The most successful schools don't limit themselves to providing drug education courses. Their first priority is to create a drug-free environment and a sense of pride in achieving and maintaining a drug-free school. Such schools also take academics seriously and assign significant amounts of homework. In addition, they emphasize extracurricular activities. The attempt is to create a school atmosphere rather than a group therapy atmosphere. The focus is on science, history, art class, and the marching band rather than on the self. Beyond that, such schools seek to enlist the help of families, businesses, police, and other groups in the community.

This combination of high expectations, serious purpose, and attention to the total environment requires considerably more work than having students sit in circles and talk about their feelings; it does, however, have the distinct advantage of making a real difference in the lives of children.

3.

SEX EDUCATION

There are two basic approaches to sex education. One view is that teenagers "are going to do it anyway" and the only thing adults can do is to encourage them to have sex safely (avoiding disease) and responsibly (avoiding pregnancy). The other view is that abstinence is the only appropriate course for unmarried teens and the only 100 percent safe approach to sex.

Until the late 1980s there was really no choice about which model a school would adopt. No abstinence-based curriculums had been developed before that point. Ever since the introduction of sex education on a large scale in the 1960s, the "responsible sex" approach had had the field all to itself. Let's start, then, by taking a look at that method and at the reasons why it came to be challenged.

The Day America Told the Truth, a 1990 survey of American beliefs and values, contains this scene from a California high school:

It's Friday afternoon and the students are leaving a class in "social living." The teacher's parting words are, "Have a great weekend. Be safe. Buckle up. Just say 'No' . . . and if you can't say 'No,' then use a condom!"

The teacher explains her philosophy: "I try to give support to everyone's value system. So I say, 'If you're a virgin, fine. If you're sexually active, fine. If you're gay, fine.'"

Although the teacher in this example gives a nod in the direction of abstinence, her approach is basically of the "responsible sex" variety. Abstinence is fine, but so is sexual activity. So is gay sex. The teacher is committed to respecting and supporting whatever choices the students make. She just wants to encourage them to make their choices "responsibly."

If this sounds like an echo of the affective/nonjudgmental approach to drug education, there is no mistake. The type of sex education that has dominated the schools from the late sixties to the present is a product of the same nondirective school of thought. Like affective drug education, it serves up a blend of facilitation, values clarification, self-esteem, and choices. Students are encouraged to question, to explore options, and to develop more tolerant attitudes toward the sexual behavior of others. This approach also supplies information about pregnancy, venereal diseases, and birth control in the belief that informed students will make better decisions. Although this informational aspect is much stronger now than in the days before AIDS, decision making remains the key ingredient. Students have to decide for themselves what is right. Teachers, parents, and churches do not have the right to tell a youngster what to choose. *Changing Bodies, Changing Lives,* one of the most widely used texts in high school and junior high sex education, tells its readers: "If you feel your parents are overprotective . . . or if they don't want you to be sexual *at all* until some distant time, you may feel you have to tune out their voice entirely." Religious teachings come in for the same treatment. "Many Catholics, Protestants, Jews, and Muslims believe sex outside marriage is sinful," says *Changing Bodies.* "You will have to decide for yourself how important these messages are for you." In sex education, as in drug education, right and wrong is what you say it is.

How well has the nondirective approach worked?

In 1986 *Family Planning Perspectives,* a publication of Planned Parenthood's Alan Guttmacher Institute, published the results of two large studies, both of which failed to show any reduction in sexual activity for teenagers who had taken sex-education courses. The larger of the two studies found that for fifteen- and sixteen-year-old girls, participation in sex education slightly increased the odds of initiating sexual activity. In the same year (1986) a Lou Harris poll commissioned by Planned Parenthood revealed that teenagers who had had comprehensive sex education had significantly higher rates of sexual activity than their peers who had not had sex education. As a result of these and numerous other studies, proponents of "responsible" sex education no longer bother to claim that their programs reduce sexual activity. The *best* that is claimed is that the programs do not increase it.

How about pregnancies? In 1988 Douglas Kirby, research director of Education, Training and Research (ETR), an offshoot of Planned Parenthood, reported to the National Family Planning and Reproductive Health Association on the "Effectiveness of School-Based Clinics": "We find basically that . . . there is no measurable impact upon the use of birth control, nor upon pregnancy rates or birth rates. This is all based upon the survey data. There is no measurable impact." A subsequent study by the Guttmacher Institute showed that condom use had, indeed, increased among teens, but so also had the rate of sexual activity. The effect of these competing trends is that the overall pregnancy rate has remained the same, with one of every ten teenage girls becoming pregnant each year.

Compared to other assessments, however, these findings are on the optimistic side. In Virginia, for example, school districts that instituted comprehensive sex education showed a 17 percent increase in teen pregnancies, while schools that were *not* teaching it had an average 16 percent *decrease* during the same time period. Dr. Jacqueline Kasun of Humboldt State University found that in Humboldt County, California, with several model programs and higher than average funding of family planning, teenage pregnancy had increased at a rate of ten times the national average. At the same time, the increase in teenage abortions was fifteen times the national average.

One of the chief goals of "safe sex" education was to reduce the number of sexually transmitted diseases—STD's for short. Yet over the last two decades, the incidence of STD's has dramatically increased—and nowhere more than in the teen population. Although AIDS has received the most attention, it actually represents only a small part of the problem.

- In 1950 genital herpes was a rare disease. It is now estimated to infect about 30 million Americans, with half a million new cases each year. The virus can cause problems during pregnancy and poses a serious threat to infants during childbirth. Herpes has no cure.
- *Chlamydia trachomatis,* an organism that is a major cause of pelvic inflammatory disease and sterility, infects about 2 million new victims each year. Girls fifteen to nineteen years old appear to have the highest infection rate.
- There are an estimated 1 million new cases of genital warts each year in the United States. Some studies suggest that a third of all sexually active teenagers have them.
- The risk of cervical cancer is dramatically increased by two factors: multiple sex partners and early involvement in sexual activity. According to an article in *Medical Aspects of Human Sexuality,* women who have venereal warts are 1,000 to 2,000 times more likely to develop cervical cancer than uninfected women. Physicians now talk about "an epidemic of cervical cancer."
- The incidence of gonorrhea has declined among teenagers over the last fifteen years, due largely to a national gonorrhea control program. Among young blacks, however, the infection rate increased dramatically in the 1980s.
- The rate of syphilis infection for teens aged fifteen to nineteen climbed 67 percent between 1984 and 1988.
- Each year more babies are born with birth defects caused

by STD's than all the children stricken with polio in the decade of the fifties.

Linus Wright, former under secretary of education, had the following comments on these trends: "The permissiveness of American society over the past twenty years has exposed a generation of teenagers to a variety of medical dangers that were known in an earlier time only to the most jaded and irresponsible of adults."

The ironic fact is that a good deal of this permissiveness has been fostered in American classrooms.

Why has sex education been unable to curb sexual activity among American teens? One simple but often overlooked answer is that it never intended to do so. Nonjudgmental sex education does *not* frown on early sexuality—not in any way that a youngster would take seriously. The fact is, most classroom sex education is based on the expectation that youngsters *will* be sexually active.

A good example of the climate of expectancy can be found in a demonstration video produced a few years ago by the Massachusetts Department of Public Health and intended to serve as a model of exemplary AIDS education. Let's fast-forward to the last ten minutes.

Shoshona, a young nurse dressed in casual clothes, is nearing the end of her presentation to a small group of suburban high school students. She has already covered a lot of ground. In the short space of forty minutes Shoshona has laid out the various sexual options, including man to man, woman to woman, woman to man, anal, oral, oral-anal, and vaginal. In addition, she has discussed several precautionary measures, including condoms, dental dams, and Nonoxynol-9—although, as Shoshona helpfully points out, "if you're using it for oral sex, you don't want to use a lubricated condom with Nonoxynol-9; it would taste pretty awful." With Shoshona's encouragement, the students have also discussed the best type of condoms (latex, not natural) and other highly practical matters such as who should pay for them and who ought to go to the pharmacy.

Shoshona's classroom manner is relaxed and friendly. Her rapport with these teens is at a level most parents could only envy. The discussion appears to be completely free and unscripted. One obvious advantage is her youth: Shoshona looks to be in her early twenties. Another advantage is her thoroughly nonjudgmental approach. Most parents would have difficulty in granting equal legitimacy to all sexual options. But Shoshona is above prejudice. Only when she speaks of society's "fear and oppression of gay people" does a judgmental tone come into her voice.

So far, the discussion has taken the prescribed nondirective path. Shoshona has encouraged the students to think about all the options, and she has been able to make most of her points in response to their questions. She has created an atmosphere in which, it seems, the discussion could go in any direction.

Some things, however, can't be left to chance. During the last ten minutes, Shoshona gives each student a large card—the kind that kindergarten teachers refer to as a flashcard. Unlike the kindergarten variety, however, each one of these cards denotes one of the fourteen steps of condom use. Shoshona asks the students to stand up, look at one another's cards, talk it over, and then try to line themselves up in the proper sequence. The cards in their proper order read: "talk with partner," "decision by both partners to have sex," "buy the condom," "sexual arousal," "erection," "roll condom on," "leave space at tip (squeeze out air)," "intercourse," "orgasm/ejaculation," "hold on to the rim," "withdraw the penis," "loss of erection," "relaxation," "throw condom out."

The students line up, but not quite in the correct sequence; Shoshona has to rearrange them. Once they have it right, she has each student display his or her card and read it aloud. "That's great!" she tells them. She seems genuinely proud. On their part, the students seem slightly embarrassed, but they all go about the exercise in a cooperative, good-humored way. Shoshona's sensitive, nonjudgmental manner has won them over.

I've shown this film to students in my adolescent psychology class, and they respond favorably. They particularly like the way Shoshona allows her students to "think for themselves."

My own reaction is different. Although Shoshona's presentation exudes an atmosphere of nondirectiveness, it seems to me that there is no real intention of looking at all the options. One alternative that might be raised and explored in a sex education class is abstinence. In fact, it is one of the many alternatives offered by the teens in the videotape. One student mentions "not having sex" as an option. Shoshona reflects this back in good nondirective fashion and then they move on. It is all over in a matter of seconds, and the subject never comes up again during the hourlong session.

Why not?

One problem with the nondirective technique is that it can never be truly nondirective. In a counseling situation (the situation in which the technique was developed), a typical client will raise more issues than can be handled in a therapy session. Certain topics seem more fruitful than others to the therapist, and those are the ones he chooses to reinforce. If he pays more attention to issue A than to issues B, C, and D, the conversation will tend to go in the direction of issue A. Clients usually develop a sense of what the therapist is interested in, and that is the sort of material that tends to come up.

The students in this class quickly sense that Shoshona is interested not in abstinence but in safe sex, and so the discussion goes in the latter direction. One boy who mentions "massage" as a possible way of having body contact while avoiding AIDS gets a good deal more attention than the girl who mentioned abstinence. "That's a really good suggestion," says Shoshona of the massage prescription, and she refers to it favorably again five minutes later.

Just how nondirective is this?

When I bring up this objection, my students concede that I have a point. Maybe it's not as nondirective as they first thought. Still, they think it's a fairly open classroom (of the kind, I suspect, they wish I would conduct). I can usually win them over to my point of view, however, by posing a question. Do they think Shoshona has come prepared with an alternative set of flashcards displaying the proper sequence for practicing abstinence, in case the discussion should go in that direction? At this point they are usually willing to admit that the discussion is never intended to go very far in that direction.

Like most teachers in most parts of the world, Shoshona is

doing what teachers have always done. She is creating a set of expectations. However, Shoshona's expectations are not those of a teacher in China or Japan or the Philippines. She expects youngsters to have sex and she expects them to use condoms when they do. The same expectation is created in sex education classrooms around the country where safe-sex instruction has become the order of the day. In addition, many schools are now establishing clinics where students can come for contraceptive information and devices. These "school-based clinics" are supposed to be only for the sexually active students, but it is difficult to imagine that their presence won't send a powerful message to the other students—namely, that the school accepts and sanctions sexual activity for teens. It is sometimes argued in defense of the clinics that students don't have to make use of them. But that seems beside the point. The courts, for example, have decided that school prayer is not permissible even if students are not required to participate, because the very presence of prayer at school constitutes an implied endorsement of religion. In similar fashion, the presence of school-based clinics that pass out condoms would seem to lend legitimacy to sexual activity.

As the statistics show, American teenagers are living up to expectations. They are having more sex and they are using more condoms. Unfortunately, for those who believe that fewer pregnancies will result, the two activities cancel each other out. As the number of teens engaging in sex increases, the number who will "make mistakes" also increases.

Not that defenders of the safe-sex/nonjudgmental approach don't have a ready answer. They claim that without their curriculums, the situation might be much worse, and besides, they say, in what has become the most common defense of safe-sex education, "you have to be realistic."

The claim of realism, however, needs some examination.

It rests, in the first place, on the assumption that all teens are having sex. But the Lou Harris/Planned Parenthood poll of late 1986 revealed that of the twelve- to seventeen-year-olds sampled, 72 percent of the girls had not engaged in intercourse. A lot of teens are having sex, but a great many are not. And of those who are "sexually active," many are a long way from being habituated to sex. Statistics on sexually active teens include adolescents who in reality are not very active at all. For example, a national survey by Zelnick and Kantner found that 20 percent of "sexually experienced" teenagers aged fifteen to seventeen have had intercourse only once. According to Douglas Powell, chief of psychology services at Harvard and author of the book *Teenagers,* "it is not unusual for normal teenagers to become celibate after their initial sexual encounters." The question that then arises is whether schools should take the tack that teenage sex is inevitable or whether they should reinforce those who are trying to resist sexual involvement.

Another lapse in realism was revealed when, in the late 1980s, the term "safe sex" had to be scuttled in favor of the more realistic term "safer sex." Medical research simply would not support the original formulation. For example, a number of studies have shown that the rate of condom failure—that is, the rate of unplanned pregnancies when using condoms—is 10 percent for all age groups and 18 percent for women under eighteen (the failure rate for diaphragms for this age group is 32 percent; for spermicide, 34 percent). But these figures are only for the first year of use. Extrapolated over time, they mean that a sexually active fourteen-year-old girl who relies on condoms has a more than 50 percent chance of becoming pregnant before she graduates from high school, and a 70 percent chance before finishing college.

Bear in mind, however, that these statistics refer only to pregnancy rates. Condoms are much less effective in stopping the spread of the AIDS virus, which can be transmitted at any time and which is 410 times smaller than sperm. As a Department of Education position paper points out: "A women is fertile roughly 36 days a year, but someone with AIDS can transmit it 365 days a year." Furthermore, in a 1987 study of seventeen homosexual couples using condoms "especially designed for the study," 15 percent of the condoms slipped off and 11 percent ruptured. A 1985 study published in the British medical journal *Lancet* reported condom breakage rates of up to 50 percent during anal intercourse.

In light of these statistics, it would appear that the nonjudgmental/safe-sex approach can add up to a dangerous combination.

Dr. Theresa Crenshaw, a past president of the American Associa
tion of Sex Educators, Counselors and Therapists, in testimony
before a House subcommittee in February 1987, said, "To say that
the use of condoms is 'safe sex' is in fact playing Russian roulette.
A lot of people will die in this dangerous game." Yet despite
warnings like this, schoolteachers routinely present homosexuality to their students as just another option about which they must
decide for themselves.

Still another failure of realism is the failure to understand teenage psychology. One of the distinctive features of adolescent
psychology is a belief in personal invulnerability. Adolescents
believe that pregnancy and disease are things that happen to
others but "won't happen to me." Logically they know this is not
true, but they believe it anyway and act accordingly. For this and
other reasons, teens are notoriously poor users of contraceptives.
Even when "it" does happen to them, teens have a hard time
comprehending the long-range implications. Wanda Franz, a professor of child development who has worked extensively with
teens, writes, "Many adolescents report being more upset about
missing the prom because of pregnancy than of having a baby."

Many people think that the answer to this is more information.
Lack of information is not the problem, however, but rather a lack
of the ability to process it. A *New York Times* writer recounts, "I
was sitting at a table with half a dozen 16-year-old girls, listening
with some amazement as they showed off their knowledge of
human sexuality. They knew how long a sperm lived inside the
body and how many women out of 100 using a diaphragm were
statistically likely to get pregnant . . . there was just one problem
with this performance: every one of the girls was pregnant."

Even adults have problems translating information into behavior. A study of gay men in 1987 reported that although over 90
percent of them knew about the risks of contracting AIDS in anal
sex, 65 percent still engaged in anal sex. Of these,

· 62 percent "never" or "hardly ever" used condoms during
  anal intercourse.
· 72 percent reported multiple sex partners within the previous six months.

- 24 percent reported that half or more of their sexual partners were anonymous.

Instead of coming to terms with the unrealistic thought processes of adolescents, sex educators have responded to the new information about unreliable condom use with an even more unrealistic proposal. One of the latest "concepts" to be introduced into sex education is the belief that students should be encouraged to substitute "outercourse" for "intercourse." This, as the name implies, involves any and every type of sexual activity short of intercourse. Debra Haffner, executive director of the Sex Information and Education Council of the United States (SIECUS), reports that in her workshops she now recommends "teaching teens about oral sex and mutual masturbation in order to help them delay the onset of sexual intercourse." In the same article, Haffner divulges that she and her colleagues have fantasized about a national "petting project."

I came across another formulation of this concept in a video about AIDS prevention which was highly recommended to me by a sex educator. In it a middle-aged doctor—a woman—encourages teenagers to engage only in "dry sex," never in "wet sex." I emphasize her gender because my impression is that many female sex educators do not appreciate the aggressive nature of male sexuality and are still projecting a pattern of female fantasies on the males. In any event, proposals of this nature show a limited understanding both of adolescents' psychology and of their physiology. There is a certain naïveté in supposing that two teenagers in the heat of sexual passion will limit themselves to "outercourse" or "dry sex." For the same reason it is naive to suppose they can be taught to always reach for a condom at the right moment. Given the dynamics of sex and the psychology of youth, consistent condom use is probably a more difficult achievement for the average teenager than complete abstinence. And complete abstinence is certainly a more realistic goal than placing one's bets on an "outercourse" that never leads to intercourse.

But there is an even greater unreality lying at the bottom of the safe-sex approach, and that is the assumption that pregnancy and sexually transmitted diseases are the only problems. Another possibility—that one can do harm to one's personality as well as to one's health through casual sex—is largely ignored. The link between sex and character is a missing link in sex education.

Sexual activity affects the kind of person we are in deep and lasting ways. The idea that one can have sex with one person after another without becoming a different person is naive, to say the least. The traditional reference to sexual intercourse as the "act of love" recognizes that it is an action that creates a bond and implies a promise. To have sex without any such intent makes one a bit of a liar. To do it over and over with numerous partners makes one a liar several times over.

Even those with a purely "practical" approach to sex education must see the problem. As one critic of the safe-sex approach asks, "How safe is sex without character?" Increasingly less safe, it now appears. Along with condom use, one of the near universal prescriptions for safe sex is the admonition "Know your partner." But how well can you know your partner if he or she lies? And people who lack character do lie, especially about their sexual activities.

Here are some findings from a survey of over 400 college men and women published in March 1990:

- Thirty-four percent of the men and 10 percent of the women admitted they had "told a lie in order to have sex."
- Even more said they would lie in a situation where it would be to their advantage.
- Sixty percent of the women believed they had been lied to for purposes of sex.
- Forty-seven percent of the men would deliberately underestimate the number of previous partners.
- Twenty percent of the men would lie about an HIV antibody test.

The researchers add: "One can probably assume that their reports of their own dishonesty underestimate rather than overestimate the problem."

Another miscalculation of the nonjudgmental/safe-sex approach was to assume that its relativist philosophy could somehow be contained—that young men and women would take it no farther than their mentors' own liberal but not licentious boundaries. Shoshona, if we can return to her for a moment, is not about to recommend sadistic or exploitative sex, but there is a moral weightlessness in her presentation which leaves open such options. In a similar fashion, the book *Changing Bodies, Changing Lives* begins one chapter with the promise *"Our main aim in this section is for you to feel good about your sexuality and what you do with it."* But what might that be? Well, it "might be masturbation, French-kissing, oral sex, sleeping with someone of the same sex or the opposite sex . . . But when the moment comes you are the one who has to decide." "Or," continues the author, perhaps sensing that a qualifier should be added, "if you are involved with someone else, you and that person decide together." But relativism means that there are *no* binding rules. It means that everything is permissible. Or—to put it more bluntly—why not rape if that's what you want to do? From a relativist standpoint, a question like this can't be answered very satisfactorily.

This, unfortunately, is not simply a philosophical difficulty. According to FBI statistics, the incidence of rape increased by 42 percent between 1977 and 1986, making it the most rapidly growing major crime in the United States. Moreover, the problem is not restricted to street crime. The incidence of rape on college campuses has also skyrocketed in recent years. In addition, surveys of male college students show that upwards of 19 percent do not even define forcible sex as rape. The attitude of younger students is still more casual. A national study of 1,700 sixth- to ninth-grade students, conducted in 1988, revealed that 65 percent of the boys thought it was acceptable for a man to rape a woman if they had been dating for more than six months; 25 percent said it was acceptable for a man to force sex on a woman if he has spent money on her; 31 percent believed it acceptable for a boy to rape a girl if she had been sexually active before. It may be that morally neutral sex education has nothing to do with these statistics, but it's a coincidence that ought to provoke some soul-searching. Josh McDowell, an author of several books on teen sexuality, suggests that "morally neutral" sex education "leaves young people with unclear boundaries concerning rape, especially date rape." "Kids who are taught to do what feels good," he writes, "cannot discern where their own sexual freedom violates that of another."

Indeed, the boundaries have become so fuzzy that even young women are no longer certain what constitutes a rape. According to psychologist Mary Koss's extensive survey of college students, 73 percent of women who have been raped do not realize they have been. Because Professor Koss uses a rather broad definition of rape, this particular statistic is subject to interpretation, but still, it suggests a great deal of confusion about acceptable limits of behavior.

The problems I have just outlined—condom failure, failure to take account of the adolescent's sense of invulnerability, widespread lying about sex, confusion about right and wrong—are examples of what might be called a lack of short-term realism on the part of sex educators. That is, these miscalculations often have immediate consequences. But there is also a lack of long-term realism, which guarantees that current problems will never go away, and in fact, will only become more serious.

As a prime example of the lack of long-term realism, consider a feature that runs through almost all safe-sex curriculums—the copious use of desensitization techniques.

Shoshona's class provides an illustration. Much of her presentation is geared to breaking down the natural resistance boys and girls have to discussing with each other subjects such as condoms, oral sex, erections, and orgasms. Her discussion of anal sex and dental dams is as casual as a discussion of recipes in a home economics class (a setting, by the way, in which sex education is now frequently taught).

This desensitization process starts at an early stage in sex education. A fairly standard practice in fifth- and sixth-grade classrooms is for the teacher to write on the blackboard the dictionary words for various body parts and sexual practices, and then to invite the students to come up and write down all the street equivalents for these terms. Other curriculums require students working as boy-girl pairs to define terms such a "foreplay," "ejaculation," and "cunnilingus." Whether or not students are satisfied with "the size of their sex organs" is another suggested topic of discussion.

The number of "creative" techniques for breaking down inhibitions is really quite astonishing:

- One "curriculum idea" is to use a diaphragm as a puppet, "opening and closing the opening as a mouth and having it talk to the children."
- Another strategy is to require each boy in a class to say "vagina" out loud while all the girls say "penis." In one eighth-grade class, a girl who was embarrassed to do this was made by the teacher to come to the front of the class and say it loudly ten times.
- At a training session for the "Michigan Model" of health education, teachers are told to encourage students to "see, feel, smell and taste" condoms.
- At a suburban high school in Massachusetts, tenth-grade students are given a homework assignment to go home and masturbate.
- One curriculum suggests that students attend a "safer sex dance party" at which they dance to "hot music with sexual messages"; another suggests they practice fitting condoms to cucumbers.
- Wardell Pomeroy's *Boys and Sex,* a book recommended and distributed by Planned Parenthood Federation of America, blandly informs its young readers that farm boys sometimes have sex with "ponies, calves, sheep, pigs, even chickens and ducks. Dogs are also commonly used but cats rarely . . ."
- Pomeroy's book *Girls and Sex* encourages girlfriends to stimulate each other to orgasm.
- *Changing Bodies, Changing Lives,* recommended and distributed by PPFA and widely used as a textbook, offers detailed instruction on lovemaking. A sample: "If you are having intercourse with a girl and want it to last longer, you can stop thrusting for a few moments when you feel yourself getting aroused. If the girl is on top and controlling the movement, you can ask her to stop for a minute or to move more slowly." A few pages later the authors advise, "Gay men too have many ways of making love," and then proceed to describe them.

· At a high school assembly in Cincinnati, a gay speaker touts the versatility of condoms by pointing out that one could easily cover his fist.

These are not isolated examples but are representative of strategies commonly employed in sex education. They are, in fact, rather mild compared to some of the films and filmstrips that are used. For example, a filmstrip accompanying a multimedia program produced by the Unitarian Universalist Association shows a heterosexual couple having normal intercourse, anal intercourse, and performing anal-oral acts. Next, a male couple is shown performing anal and oral sex, then a female couple using a dildo. Deryck Calderwood, who designed the course and has used it with fifth-graders, cautions teachers that "it may take some time to appreciate and enjoy the beauty of the experience"—that is, the beauty of same-sex lovemaking. Other materials are equally graphic. A brochure in use at the eighth-grade level in western New York State talks about "fisting," "rimming," "vibrators," "watersports," and the benefits of "talking dirty" ("Phone sex is 100 percent safe").

The rationale for this sort of thing is that it will enable young people to take a matter-of-fact approach to sexuality. Youngsters for whom sex is not invested with romantic overtones will be better able to take the proper precautionary steps. The point is to be able to view sex as a nonmoral, nonromantic recreational activity, much the way we view such body contact sports as football or hockey. Depending on the sport, helmets, pads, masks, or condoms are worn so that no one gets hurt. Youngsters who have lost their sexual inhibitions will be able to talk with each other frankly about such things before bedding down.

Much of sex education has as its aim, therefore, the deromanticization of sex. "Sex," as one Planned Parenthood pamphlet puts it, "is too important to glop up with sentiment." Dr. Sol Gordon, who is perhaps the nation's most tireless sex educator, makes a deliberate point of trivializing the sexual experience. "What's so special about sex?" asks Gordon in one of his numerous talks. His answer? "It's greatly exaggerated." As for the idea of waiting for marriage, Gordon has nothing but ridicule for it. "If you have sex before marriage," he intones in mock seriousness, "you'll have nothing to look forward to." And then the kicker, delivered with gusto: "Ladies and gentlemen, if that's all you have to look forward to in marriage, then I say, 'Don't marry'!"

But of course, having something beautiful and special to look forward to is one of the most important incentives to abstinence. Take it away and you have only pragmatic fears about health and pregnancy—fears that are often falsely allayed by assurances about protected sex. If there is nothing worth waiting for, why wait? When educators dismiss the special nature of married love with a wink and a nod, it is almost a guarantee that youngsters will not wait.

Furthermore, none of this bodes well for marriage itself—if our well-trained youngster ever gets that far. This is where the question of long-term realism comes in. What sort of spouse will a youngster make after years of being desensitized to sex? What sort of parent? If sex isn't special before marriage, what will make it special afterwards? If there is nothing particularly special about sex, then adultery won't seem particularly bad either. And why put devotion to your wife and children ahead of your own pleasures? Why bother about getting married at all? If you get someone pregnant, she can have an abortion. If she doesn't want to, that's her problem. After all, everyone has to make their own decisions.

Although sex educators like to say that proponents of abstinence for teens are not realistic, the argument cuts two ways. One of the harsh realities that now confront us is that children from broken or single-parent homes have much higher rates of drug abuse, crime, alcoholism, school failure, and suicide. They also have a much higher rate of sexual activity, pregnancy, and out-of-wedlock births. A large part of their problem derives from the fact that their parents have been unable either to make or to keep commitments. But again, what sort of marriages will the current generation of desensitized children be able to make? In what way do courses that break down inhibitions and strip sex of any moral content constitute a preparation for a committed marriage? Or committed parenthood? Isn't it likely that youngsters trained in this way will only fuel the problem of irresponsible parenthood once they grow up? Someone no doubt will supply *their* children with condoms, but who will supply them with parents? T. S. Eliot once observed that modern thinkers have a habit of "dreaming of systems so perfect that no one will need to be good." That appears to have been the hope of Planned Parenthood and other groups involved in sex education. But in any long-term view, their technical/informational approach reveals itself to be extremely shortsighted.

At one time modesty, not a condom, was a young woman's protection against any hasty indulgence she might regret. Modesty, in turn, was linked to an understanding that the sexual act is by nature intimate, private, intensely personal, and connected to the deepest level of the soul. At the same time, it was understood that society has an interest in proper sexual conduct. The pleasure principle is not a very good rule for social order. Sooner or later, sexual irresponsibility, adulteries, diseases, neglected children, and abandoned families become everyone's problem.

One way that a breakdown of sexual restraint hurts society is in the educational sphere. There is abundant evidence that the more sexually active students do poorly in school and tend to drop out more frequently. Almost half of the teenage girls who drop out of school do so because of pregnancy. But that figure only suggests one dimension of the problem. The constant distraction caused by worries about sex and about relationships takes a toll on schoolwork. Harvard sociologist David Riesman says the problem is especially acute for girls: "I can't help thinking of all the fears girls have as teenagers, especially as young teenagers. Will they get pregnant if they sleep with a boy? Should they take precautions? If they do, will it show they were waiting for it? They have terrible anxieties about all this."

Riesman goes so far as to question the whole concept of coeducation. "If one looks over the globe, one sees very few places where boys and girls are thrown at each other the way they are here in American schools—with everything unchaperoned, unsupervised, and permissive," declared Riesman in a recent interview. He suggests that coeducation only works in societies that maintain high standards of sexual conduct. Several recent studies confirm that girls do learn better in single-sex environments on both the high school and college levels. How much of this is due to the absence of sexual distraction and how much to other factors is difficult to say, but the studies do provide correlational evidence of an inverse link between sexual stimulation and school achievement. Other evidence comes from a 1987 "Survey of High Achievers" for *Who's Who Among American High School Students*. The survey found that 73 percent of the high-achieving students had never had intercourse. In Japan, where the general level of educational achievement is much higher than ours, only 17 percent of unmarried girls below the age of twenty have lost their virginity, compared to 65 percent of American girls.

It is difficult to concentrate on one's studies in a sex-saturated society, and even more so when the schools themselves become a source of erotic stimulation. During the same years that safe-sex education expanded throughout the nation's schools, scores on reading, math, science, history, and knowledge of geography declined steadily. Nine years ago, a presidential commission studying our education system titled its report "A Nation at Risk." "If an unfriendly foreign power had attempted to impose on America the mediocre educational performance that exists today," observed the panel, "we might well have viewed it as an act of war." I don't know if the remark was also meant to refer to our system of sex education, but it might well have.

In light of the foregoing, it is not surprising that a strong resistance eventually grew up against the "going-to-do-it-anyway" school of sex education. In 1981, with the passage of the Adolescent Family Life Act, federal funds became available for the development of abstinence-based curriculums. The bill was aimed at encouraging programs that would "clearly and unequivocally" promote abstinence. It also called for greater family involvement in the development of programs, since "prevention of adolescent sexual activity and adolescent pregnancy depends primarily upon developing strong family values and close family ties."

The initial reaction to the legislation divided along liberal-conservative lines, but there were important exceptions. Eunice Kennedy Shriver defended the AFLA before a Senate committee:

> To do something helpful about teenage sex and pregnancy we do not need more money for the mechanics of birth

control or more value-free sex education. We need efforts that strengthen the family commitment and marriage and get at the problems that lead adolescents into early sexual activity.

In more recent years liberal support for abstinence has grown. One example is Virginia governor Douglas Wilder. Concerned about the effects of permissive sexual standards on black families, Wilder has been vigorously promoting premarital abstinence. "If they want to have a future," says Wilder, "it is imperative that our young—males and females alike—embrace the ultimate precaution—abstinence." Moreover, "making life-long commitments; making structured and loving families . . . these are the actions that constitute the beginning of a passage into manhood."

Though it was several years before abstinence-based curriculums became available, the AFLA appears to have been a turning point. By the late 1980s a number of such programs were in use at school systems across the country. Among the more successful are Sex Respect; AANCHOR; Responsible Sexual Values Program (RSVP); Me, My World, My Future; and Sexuality, Commitment and Family.

Unlike the current safe-sex programs, these curriculums all share a common expectation that teens and preteens can and should remain abstinent. Other common topics in the abstinence-based programs are:

- Information on anatomy, reproduction, and adolescent development.
- Communication with parents.
- Future plans.
- Emotional, physical, and social consequences of early sexual activity.
- Types of love.
- Advantages of premarital abstinence.
- Guidelines for dating, dress, behavior.
- Awareness of media pressure.
- How to cope with pressures to be sexually active.
- How to change former sexual behavior.

Some of these topics are the same as might be covered in a safe-sex program. The difference is in the perspective offered. For example, in these abstinence-based programs some decision-making skills may be taught, but they are taught in the context of family and community values, and with the understanding that some choices are better than others. Another difference is that teachers do not simply facilitate discussion; they offer clear principles and maintain high expectations. Moreover, in these programs parents are very much involved. They are provided with copies of the student workbooks as well as with guidelines of their own. Some programs include parent-teen worksheets; one sends out "parentgrams" with updates on course progress. Another major difference lies in the emphasis on marriage. The abstinence programs honor monogamous, heterosexual marriage and stress the importance of such marriages to society. The emphasis on marriage helps to answer the question "What am I waiting for?" Here is an excerpt from the Sex Respect guidebook:

> In the shelter of a good marriage, the couple experiences companionship, helping, trust and completeness, a sense of security and well-being. These benefits can then be shared with the children, who are being prepared for life, within the shelter of their parents' marriage. . . .
>
> By waiting until marriage the man can learn that sex goes with responsibility and commitment. He then has a better chance to learn what love really is. . . . A woman who waits can act in tune with her inner nature that says sex is a lifetime gift of love.

Most abstinence-based programs also provide videos that portray the benefits of saving sex for marriage, the harmfulness of sex without commitment, and the possibility of a return to abstinence for teens who have already been sexually active.

Do such programs work? Because they have only been in existence for a few years, it is difficult to say with certainty. But the preliminary evidence is encouraging. In 1984 the San Marcos school district north of San Diego was faced with one of the highest pregnancy rates in California. Nearly one in five teenage girls had become pregnant. Instead of bowing to the inevitable, however, school officials took action. They selected the Sexuality, Commitment and Family curriculum developed by Teen Aid, a Spokane, Washington, group. The program was initiated in the junior high school and was supplemented by study skills and goal-setting programs. The results were impressive. The teen pregnancy rate, which had been nearly 20 percent, dropped to 2.5 percent in 1986 and then to 1.5 percent in 1988. At the same time, grades improved as well as scores on tests of basic skills. In 1988 the San Marcos program won the California award for the lowest student dropout rate. Recently released data on the Sex Respect program show a similar trend. A five-year pilot study conducted in twenty-six schools found that the pregnancy rate for girls who had taken the program was 5 percent—44 percent less than for girls who had not participated in Sex Respect.

But abstinence education was not warmly received by established sex educators. Instead, it was met with a great deal of opposition. Planned Parenthood; the Alan Guttmacher Institute; Education, Training and Research; the Center for Population Options; and various other groups balked at the idea of abstinence. Michael Hall, a Planned Parenthood executive, spoke for many when he warned that "teens will be totally turned off." Meanwhile, just in case teens didn't react in the proper way, the AFLA was challenged almost yearly in Congress, and its programs were resisted on the state and local level. The American Civil Liberties Union even filed suit against the AFLA on the grounds that the promotion of abstinence constituted an establishment of religion.

By the late 1980s, however, it was becoming apparent even to its most ardent advocates that something was wrong with the "responsible sex" approach. Despite the threat of AIDS, despite increasingly heavy doses of safe-sex education, and despite the introduction of birth control clinics into schools, the rate of teenage pregnancy and venereal disease had not decreased. Moreover, the rate of sexual activity among teens was rising year by year. The sharpest rise was among the youngest groups. The Centers for Disease Control reported in 1988 that more than a quarter of American females have engaged in sexual intercourse by age fifteen—four times the rate that prevailed in 1970.

Accordingly, many of the groups that had criticized the AFLA now began rewriting their curriculums to include an abstinence component. They had been saying all along that students should look at all the options, and here was a chance to prove it.

The way this was done, however, emphasizes the confusion that surrounds sex education and, indeed, moral education in general. The strategy, as one critic observes, was "to graft an abstinence message onto the standard nondirective decision-making approach." Abstinence was to be promoted as a positive value, but only as one choice among many. A passage from *Teen Sexual Behavior,* published by the American Alliance for Health, Physical Education, Recreation and Dance, is representative: "Although we adults feel it's in your best interest to delay intimate sexual behaviors, you and only you will decide when you will become sexually involved." Once again, choice comes out as the premier value: not choosing the right thing but simply choosing.

Educationally, this makes no sense at all. Putting an abstinence component in what remains essentially a decision-making/safe-sex format makes for a confused and compromised message. It is as if the Marines felt obliged to include a pacifist component in basic training. One fairly consistent piece of advice now given to parents by child psychologists—now that child-centered child rearing is beginning to wane—is that if they want their children to listen, they have to say things as though they mean them. If adults aren't really serious about the abstinence message, students won't be either. On the other hand, a student is more likely to make a decision to postpone sex if the adults in his or her life show some conviction about the matter.

It is not easy to persuade young people of the wisdom of abstinence, but then it is not easy to persuade them of the wisdom of sobriety. Nevertheless, we have seen that when adults do take a firm and consistent stand, as in the recent campaigns against drugs and against drunk driving, changes begin to take place. Adults have finally realized that in dealing with the impulse to experiment with powerful substances such as drugs and alcohol, the message must be unequivocal. Unfortunately, until recently, teachers have been reluctant to discuss sex in absolute moral terms, leaving students with the impression that it's purely a subjective matter. Indeed, it turns out that when teens are confronted by adults over sexual misbehaviors, a frequent response is simply, "I didn't know it was wrong."

Is abstinence a realistic expectation? Yes and no. No, if the expectation is that all youngsters will wait until marriage before having sex. Yes, if it means that a majority can be persuaded that postponing sex is the right thing to do. It is true that some will "do it anyway," no matter what. It is also true that actual behavior tends to fall below the cultural ideal. What this means in practice, however, is that the higher the cultural standard is set, the farther actual behavior rises to meet it. In turn, the lower the culture sets its standard, the farther below it actual behavior will sink.

If the culture upholds sex within marriage as the norm, it doesn't mean that everyone will wait until marriage, but it does mean that many will at least wait until they're engaged—a situation that seems to have prevailed in our culture until recent decades. But if society decides it has to be "realistic" and lowers the standard to "sex with commitment," actual behavior tends to fall to the next lowest level—let's call it "sex within the context of love." "We're not engaged," a couple will maintain, "but it's okay because we love each other." If society then decides it has to adjust to the new reality of many couples not waiting for engagement and lowers the norm to "sex with love," actual behavior again falls—this time to the level of what we might call "sex with like." Once the standard falls to the level of recreational sex about where it is now—we shouldn't be surprised to find that exploitative sex has become the norm for many or that date rape has become a major problem.

We are all, to a great extent, creatures of our culture. By and large, we tend to conform to cultural expectations, even if not perfectly. Our present culture sends out confused and misleading messages about sex—messages that, in the long run, threaten our survival. But it's not inevitable that we remain in this state. Key cultural institutions—such as the schools—can make a difference if they are willing to take a clear stand. Some will say that you can't take such stands in a pluralistic society. And it's true that some people will undoubtedly take offense, as did a group of parents in Wisconsin who, together with the ACLU, recently filed a discrimination suit against the Sex Respect program because of its emphasis on two-parent, heterosexual families. It's futile to hope to please everyone. Most people, however, do not call for their lawyer when they hear the words "marriage" or "teen abstinence"—certainly not most parents. As William Bennett observed at the time he was secretary of education, "I have never had a parent tell me that he or she would be offended by a teacher telling a class that it is better to postpone sex. Or that marriage is the best setting for sex, and in which to have and raise children. On the contrary, my impression is that the overwhelming majority of parents would gratefully welcome help in transmitting such values."

A lot depends on marriage—not least the moral health of a society. And marriage, as we are once again coming to understand, depends to a large extent on a code of chastity outside of marriage. With the coming of the sexual revolution, men began to flee their homes in droves, leaving women with the children, with double the work, and with little time or energy to provide discipline or moral guidance. Many men, of course, never bother to get married in the first place, since there is little incentive to do so. But that doesn't prevent them from fathering children. The "safe sex" approach to sex education doesn't do anything to alleviate this situation; it only intensifies it. It should be obvious by now to all but the most obtuse that women are going to continue to have babies, safe sex or no. The trouble with safe sex is that it accustoms young men to the idea that sex is something that can be had without commitment. And if they can have it without commitment, that is the way they would rather have it.

I've heard teachers complain that creating an expectation of abstinence and self-control would require going back to old-fashioned methods of education. But this is really a false premise; the fact is, teachers fall back on those "old-fashioned" methods all the time. Consider Shoshona's use of the flashcards. When it comes to teaching something she feels strongly about, she drops her nonjudgmental stance and switches to a highly directive method. It is only the values she regards lightly—such as premarital chastity—that can safely be left up to the "whatever-feels-right-for-you" process.

In trying to promote ideas about safe sex or to raise the students' consciousness about homosexuality, sex educators have no hesitation at all in using traditional methods. In the service of those causes, they are willing to employ rote learning, repetition, memorization, absolute and authoritative statements, posters, school assemblies (in which, for example, condoms are demonstrated and distributed), campaigns ("National Condom Week"), instructional films, "pregnancy prevention" fairs, pamphlets, essay contests, and yes, even flashcards.

In so doing, of course, they are paying an unintended compliment to the methods traditionally used in character education. All of which suggests there may be more to that approach than educators are currently willing to concede.

4.

HOW NOT TO
TEACH MORALITY

"It ought to be the oldest things that are taught to the youngest people," quipped G. K. Chesterton in 1910. If that guarded approach applies anywhere, moral education would seem to be the place. In learning right from wrong, young people ought to have the benefit of ideas that have been around for a while. After all, when researchers experiment with new treatments in medicine, the policy is to ask for adult volunteers, not to round up children. Common sense would seem to suggest a similarly cautious approach to experiments in teaching values.

For a long time that was the guiding policy in American schools. Teachers understood their main task to be the transmission of the culture: passing on to each new generation the lessons—some of them costly—that had been learned about right and wrong.

The 1960s, however, saw Chesterton's formula turned on its head. In that decade and the next, educators vied to outdo one another in rushing the newest developments and techniques into the classroom and into young heads. Nowhere was this done more avidly than in the field of moral education. The oldest ideas were, in effect, banished from the classroom. Almost overnight, concepts such as virtue, good example, and character formation fell out of favor with educators. We have already examined some of the concepts that took their place.

In view of what was at stake, it was a surprisingly bloodless revolution. Teaching right from wrong has as much bearing on a culture's survival as teaching reading, writing, or science. Yet the radical innovations met with little resistance. For the most part they were embraced.

What accounts for this willing acceptance by the schools?

One possibility is that good behavior on the part of young- sters—aside from the normal quotient of rebellion and mis- chief—was something that educators were able to take for granted. Many educators at the time believed strongly in the idea of natural morality. And the relatively well-behaved youngsters in their classrooms seemed to prove the point. If their charges were, perhaps, somewhat more restive than students of the previous decade, that could be explained by the difficulty of adjusting to the new climate of freedom. What was generally ignored, of course, was the possibility that morality has more to do with culture than with nature: the possibility, that is, that character education had done its job well, and that the relative calm they enjoyed was not the fruit of nature but the lingering benefit of an earlier educational culture. Whatever the case, educators appar- ently felt they could afford to experiment.

Another explanation for this bloodless coup is simply that the time was ripe for it. Those were the days of the free speech movement, of flower children and campus sit-ins and Wood- stock. It was also a time of violence—the murder of civil rights workers, the assassination of King and the Kennedys, the Vietnam War. Something was radically wrong with our culture—or so it seemed to many. And the revelations about Watergate in the early seventies did not help matters. The main sentiment—and it was a sentiment widely shared by educators—was that the culture was something to be ashamed of, not transmitted. It would be better if students started from scratch and developed their own ideas about society.

This was the atmosphere into which the so-called decision-making model of moral education emerged. It was a model that relied on students to discover values for themselves, and it promised that this could be done without indoctrination of any sort. Students would be given tools for making decisions, but the decisions would be their own. The idea gained ready acceptance in schools. Decision making was exactly what educators were looking for, and they rushed to embrace it.

The decision-making model developed along two different lines. One approach, called "Values Clarification," emphasized feelings, personal growth, and a totally nonjudgmental attitude; the other, known as the "moral reasoning" approach, emphasized a "critical thinking" or cognitive approach to decision making. Although both shared many assumptions and methods, it is important to understand the differences.

Values Clarification got its start in 1966 with the publication of *Values and Teaching* by Louis Raths, Merrill Harmin, and Sidney Simon—all professors of education. What the authors offered was not a way to teach values but a way for students to "clarify" their own values. The authors took pains to distance themselves from character education and traditional methods of teaching values. In fact, Simon once expressed a wish that parents would stop "fostering the immorality of morality." It was Simon, also, who took the lead in popularizing the new method. His *Values Clarification: A Handbook of Practical Strategies for Teachers and Students* was published in 1972, and quickly became a best-seller among teachers. According to the promotional blurb on the book's back cover, Values Clarification makes students "aware of *their own* feelings, *their own* ideas, *their own* beliefs . . . *their own* value systems."

But Values Clarification was not exactly a new idea. In reality, it was an outgrowth of human potential psychology. The developers of Values Clarification had simply taken Carl Rogers's nondirective, nonjudgmental therapy technique and applied it to moral education. Indeed, the authors of *Values and Teaching* were so committed to therapeutic nonjudgmentalism that they felt obliged to note that "it is entirely possible that children will choose not to develop values. It is the teacher's responsibility to support this choice also."

True to its origins in the human potential movement, Values Clarification also puts a heavy emphasis on feelings—so much so that it virtually equates values with feelings. That this is the case is indicated in the very first strategy in the *Values Clarification* handbook. It is titled "Twenty Things You Love to Do." This exercise is not a prelude to deeper thought ahead. Rather, it sets the tone for the whole book. A value is essentially what you like or love to do. It is not an ought-to but a want-to. In his book *Educating for Character,* Professor Thomas Lickona relates the story of an eighth-grade teacher who used this strategy with a low-achieving class only to find that the four most popular activities were "sex, drugs, drinking, and skipping school." The teacher was hamstrung. The Values Clarification framework gave her no way of persuading them otherwise. Her students had clarified their values, and they were able to justify their choices with answers they found satisfactory ("Everyone drinks and smokes dope"; "Sex is the best part of life").

Another problem with Values Clarification is that, despite its claim of being value-neutral, it actually conditions children to think of values as relative. This is apparent in strategy number three, "Values Voting." The exercise starts off innocuously enough with questions from the teacher such as, "How many of you like to go on long walks or hikes?" "How many enjoy going on a picnic?" "How many like yogurt?" and so on. But before long, questions of a weightier nature begin to appear in the list: "How many of you approve of premarital sex for boys? for girls?" "How many think we ought to legalize abortions?" "How many would approve of a marriage between homosexuals being sanctioned by priest, minister or rabbi?"

No effort is made to set these loaded questions apart. They are simply interspersed with the innocuous questions in random fashion, as if no significant differences existed among them. In the context of picnics and long walks, however, some of these "items in life's cafeteria," as Simon once called them, seem wildly out of place—like a guest appearance by Madonna on *Mister Rogers'*

Neighborhood. At least it would seem that way to a thoughtful adult. But Values Clarification is about getting in touch with feelings, not thoughts. The exercises are designed so that a young student will come away with the impression that all values are simply a matter of personal taste—like eating yogurt. Reading through the *Values Clarification* book of strategies, one is forced to conclude that its authors are more interested in circumventing the rational mind than in stimulating it.

Values Clarification has suffered some setbacks in the last decade. The anti-intellectual bias is hard to ignore; so is the research, which shows Values Clarification to be ineffectual at best and potentially harmful. Moreover, Values Clarification has come under attack from parents' groups in dozens of states. Despite these difficulties, however, Values Clarification has shown amazing powers of survival. Those who favor the approach have adopted the simple tactic of changing the name while retaining the method. Values Clarification often shows up under the guise of drug education, sex education, and life-skills courses. Although I have put these curriculums first in this book, in actual point of time they came after the introduction of Values Clarification, and relied heavily on its techniques. For example, years before writing drug education curriculums for Quest, Howard Kirschenbaum had coauthored the *Values Clarification* handbook with Sidney Simon. Although his newer curriculums contain different exercises, the old message—a value is what you like to do—still comes through clearly.

The moral reasoning approach—the other strand within the decision-making model—seemed to offer a good alternative to Values Clarification. It was the brainchild of Harvard psychologist Lawrence Kohlberg, a man who was, in many ways, the opposite of Sidney Simon. Whereas Simon was a laid-back popularizer with a mind singularly tuned to the changing moods of the sixties, Kohlberg was a serious scholar whose ideas were buttressed by philosophical arguments, and whose research was highly regarded. Although Kohlberg, like Simon, rejected character education (he called it the "bag of virtues" approach), he had something other than feelings to offer in its place. Kohlberg wanted to turn children into moral thinkers, to teach them a valid process of moral reasoning. Children would still make their own decisions, but their decisions would be based on reason.

How could students be brought to higher levels of moral reasoning? Kohlberg felt that the Socratic dialogue—the method used by Socrates and Plato—was ideal. The Socratic dialogue provided a way of drawing out ideas without imposing values or moralizing. Moreover, the dialogue seemed to create an atmosphere of equality between student and teacher—a goal that at the time seemed highly desirable.

Accordingly, Kohlberg and his colleagues developed a curriculum based on the discussion of ethical dilemmas. Like Socrates or Plato, the teacher poses one of these dilemmas and then encourages an exchange of ideas and opinions while keeping his own values in the background.

Here is an example of one such dilemma:

Sharon and Jill were best friends. One day they went shopping together. Jill tried on a sweater and then, to Sharon's surprise, walked out of the store wearing the sweater under her coat. A moment later, the store's security officer stopped Sharon and demanded that she tell him the name of the girl who had walked out. He told the store owner that he had seen the two girls together, and that he was sure that the one who left had been shoplifting. The store owner told Sharon that she could really get in trouble if she didn't give her friend's name.

The dilemma, of course, is to decide what Sharon should do.

A skilled teacher could get quite a bit of mileage out of a quandary like this. Some of the issues that might come up would be lying versus loyalty, self-sacrifice versus self-protection, the cost to the public of shoplifting versus the cost to the girl if she's arrested.

In addition, the teacher may further complicate the situation by asking hypothetical questions: "Suppose Jill comes from a poor family and can't afford to buy new clothes?" or "Suppose you knew that other children had been making fun of Jill because of her unstylish clothing?" or "What if Sharon offers to pay for the sweater herself? Should the store agree to drop the matter?" The teacher may go a step further and have students get the feel of the predicament by role-playing the various parts in the shoplifting scenario.

Here's another dilemma:

> Suppose a ten-year-old boy is hit by a car and brought by ambulance to the emergency room of a hospital. He needs surgery right away but the doctor needs the parents' permission. When the parents arrive they refuse consent for an operation. They are Christian Scientists and believe in the power of prayer rather than medicine to heal. The doctor could get a court order to override the parents but that might take too long. Should the doctor go ahead and operate despite the parents' objections?

You can see why the dilemma approach became popular. In the hands of any moderately capable teacher, it's a surefire formula: the educational equivalent of a roller-coaster ride. Opinions go back and forth, up and down; the argument takes sudden, unexpected turns. Does the class favor an immediate operation? Then the teacher can play devil's advocate. He can say, "So you don't really care about freedom of religion. How would *you* like it if *your* freedom to practice *your* faith was taken away? Suppose your religion forbids you to salute the flag, and you are expelled from school for not saluting? Would that be right?" Or he may switch the focus to parental rights: "How would *you* feel if *you* were a parent and doctors operated on *your* child without your permission?" At any moment the discussion can go spinning off in a new direction.

Like a roller-coaster ride, the dilemma approach can leave its passengers a bit breathless. That is one of its attractions. But like a roller-coaster ride, it may also leave them a bit disoriented—or more than a bit. That, as a growing number of critics are suggesting, is one of its drawbacks.

The question to ask about this admittedly stimulating approach is this: Do we want to concentrate on quandaries or on everyday morality? Not many children will grow up to face the doctor's dilemma described above. More to the point, it is not a dilemma any of them currently face. A great deal of a child's moral life—or an adult's, for that matter—is not made up of dilemmas at all. Most of our "moral decisions" have to do with temptations to do things we know we shouldn't do or temptations to avoid doing the things we know we should do. A temptation to steal money from her mother's purse is a more common problem for the average girl than deciding whether or not to turn in a friend who is shoplifting. It is certainly more common than deciding whether to perform surgery on an injured child.

The Jill and Sharon dilemma is actually a rather mild example of the form. Dilemmas about homosexuality, wife swapping, extramarital sex, abortion, and even cannibalism are routine on the junior high and high school levels and often make their way into elementary classrooms. The Donner Party dilemma, for example, tells the story of westward-bound settlers trapped by snow in the Sierra Nevada Mountains and faced with the alternatives of death by starvation or cannibalism. Another Kohlberg dilemma concerns a mother who must choose between the lives of her two children. A Values Clarification dilemma places the student in the position of a government bureaucrat who must decide which of several people are to survive in a fallout shelter and which are to die of radiation poisoning.

The danger in focusing on problematic dilemmas such as these is that a student may begin to think that all of morality is similarly problematic. After being faced with quandary after quandary of the type that would stump Middle East negotiators, students will conclude that right and wrong are anybody's guess. They will gain the impression, as Cornell professor Richard Baer has pointed out, "that almost everything in ethics is either vague or controversial . . ."

Youngsters are often much more perceptive than adults in sensing where this line of reasoning leads. As one teacher admits, "I often discuss cheating this way, but I always get defeated because they will argue that cheating is all right. After you accept the idea that kids have the right to build a position with logical arguments, you have to accept what they come up with."

What Chesterton said about teaching "the oldest things" seems to apply here. Classroom time might be better spent in talking about the virtues of friendship, loyalty, and honesty, and how to practice them, rather than in dredging up situations where honesty might not be the best policy or where loyalty and honesty conflict or even where cannibalism might be a legitimate course of action.

Why isn't it done that way? The answer is that the developers of these curriculums are proceeding on the basis of a dubious assumption. They seem to assume that such things as honesty, property rights, and human life are already highly valued by youngsters and, therefore, the only difficulty is to choose among these values when they conflict. That is, they assume a sort of natural goodness and integrity in the child, whereby he or she will always want to do the right thing. If there is a problem, it's only a problem of getting in touch with one's feelings or of learning to reason things out. The old idea that many of us suffer not from a defect in reasoning but from a defect in character is not considered. Thus, in the Jill and Sharon dilemma, it is assumed that boys and girls have already mastered the ABC's of morality, that the kinds of dilemmas they are grappling with are of the higher-order kind that faces Sharon ("Shall I be loyal to my friend or truthful to the authorities?") rather than the lower-order kind that faces Jill ("Shall I take this sweater?"). But what if stealing a sweater is not a dilemma at all for me but my habitual mode of action?

Some of what is wrong with this assumption is revealed in a conversation Kohlberg had with Edwin Delattre shortly before Kohlberg's death. Delattre, who is professor of applied ethics at Boston University, tells it this way:

He [Kohlberg] expressed perplexity about the ineffectiveness of his methods in prisons where he had been working. He told me that he posed for inmates one of his favorite dilemmas: "Your wife suffers from an incurable and potentially terminal disease for which she must take regular doses of a very expensive medicine. The medicine is manufactured by a single company, and you have exhausted all of your financial resources in past purchases of the medicine." The question he posed is whether you should let your wife die or steal the drug.

The convicts were unperplexed. To a man, and without hesitation, they said, "Steal it." "But why," Larry Kohlberg asked them, "would you do that?" Laughing, they answered, "Because we steal things. *We wanna know why the stupid husband didn't steal it in the first place.*"

The point is that the decision whether or not to steal is only a dilemma for those who already think stealing is wrong. As Delattre observes, "no one can really *have* a dilemma or moral problem without already caring to be the kind of person who behaves well, the kind of person who wants to discover the right thing to do and to have what it takes to do it."

At issue here is the very nature of the moral life itself. Kohlberg's conception seems to be that morality has to do with solving difficult ethical problems. His tendency to view it this way may stem in part from his own experience. As a young man he was involved in the struggle to establish a Jewish homeland in Palestine. He and the men and women he worked with were constantly faced with difficult, unprecedented, and dangerous dilemmas involving the lives and freedom of others.

The superheated atmosphere in which Kohlberg worked may help to explain the system he later developed. The question remains, however, whether his emphasis on dilemmas is rightly placed. As one of Kohlberg's critics points out, "Not all of what constitutes one's morality consists of responding to problematic social situations . . . a person's morality is an ongoing quality of life and not disjointed responses to isolated situations."

In fact, as Delattre suggests, it is the kind of person one is in the first place that determines what will and will not be a "dilemma" in one's life. For a person of good character a temptation to cheat on one's spouse or to cheat a business partner will be recognized as just that—a temptation and not a dilemma. On the other hand, for those lacking character interesting "dilemmas" are always arising. For example, one Kohlberg exercise—the "swapping" dilemma—concerns a number of married couples who want to exchange partners for sexual purposes. Quite obviously, however, this is a dilemma only for people who allow themselves to entertain such possibilities.

"This approach," as Delattre observes of Kohlberg's model,

"obscures the fact that relatively few of our moral failings are attributable to inept reasoning about dilemmas. Many more arise from moral indifference, disregard for other people, weakness of will, and bad or self-indulgent habits." The hard part of morality, in short, is not *knowing* what is right but *doing* it. And if this is so, the remedy lies not in forming opinions but in forming good habits.

This is not to say that the dilemma approach should never be used. If used judiciously and in an age-appropriate way, it can be a useful teaching tool—particularly in discussing policy issues or current events in the upper grades or in college. But as the first line of approach for developing values, it is woefully inadequate. It involves young people in repeatedly questioning values that may never have taken hold for them in the first place.

In short, it's a strange way to teach morality. An analogy would be an American history course in grade school that concentrated on the ambiguities rather than the achievements—for example on Jefferson's ownership of slaves rather than his authorship of the Declaration of Independence, or on Martin Luther King, Jr.'s adulteries rather than his leadership of the civil rights movement. There is a time and place for learning such facts, but to put them first in a child's experience and then expect him to develop much loyalty to the nation or its values would be foolish.

The same holds true for moral education. Debunking moral values before they are learned is not a good policy. Before students begin to think about the qualifications, exceptions, and fine points that surround difficult cases they will seldom or never face, they need to build the kind of character that will allow them to act well in the very clear-cut situations they face daily. The basics ought to come first. "We should not," as former secretary of education William Bennett points out, "use the fact that there are indeed many difficult and controversial moral questions as an argument against basic instruction in the subject. We do not argue . . . against teaching biology or chemistry because gene splicing and cloning are complex and controversial."

But what about Socrates? And what about Kohlberg's claim to be following in his path? There is certainly much to be admired in Socrates' calm, reasonable method of inquiry and in his patience and goodwill, but Kohlberg seems to have missed a key point about the Socratic method: it was not meant for youngsters. No one speaks more authoritatively about the Socratic method than Plato, and Plato maintained that it was to be reserved for mature men over the age of thirty. "One great precaution," said Plato, "is not to let them [students] taste of arguments while they are young"—the danger being that they would develop a taste for arguments rather than a taste for truth. Young minds, like young puppies, said Plato, would only "pull and tear at arguments." Such a method might keep youngsters entertained but it would certainly not make them virtuous. For Plato it was much more important for young people to learn a love of virtue than to argue about it. The dialogue was for those for whom the love of virtue was already in place.

This is the problem with using the dialogue method prematurely. Another problem is that not everyone using it has the wisdom, integrity, or maturity of a Socrates.

I occasionally used a dialogue/dilemma approach when I was teaching eighth grade in the mid-sixties. Though Kohlberg hadn't come along with his curriculum at that time, it was easy enough to find dilemmas or make them up. I thought I was allowing my students to think for themselves, but I can see now that I was more interested in having them think like me. That was not difficult to accomplish using the dilemma approach. It tended to knock my students off base. I could see that it sometimes also had the effect of alienating them from their parents' beliefs—particularly if their parents had traditional or conservative views. That didn't bother me at the time, but it bothers me now. (By the way, both Socrates and Plato were charged with leading youth away from their parents. I think most scholars of the classics would agree that the charge was not entirely without merit.)

In order to make reparations for my past misuse of the dilemma approach, I make a point each semester of telling my college students what is wrong with it. I find I can get the point across by making an analogy to television talk shows, the kind hosted by Phil Donahue and Oprah Winfrey. Such shows have a lot in common with current moral education classrooms: They thrive on the exchange of ideas and opinions, and they have the same ground rule—all views are to be respected. Moreover, the tendency of these programs to concentrate on the more unusual arrangements that crop up in life (swapping clubs, the Man/Boy Love Association, mothers and daughters who date the same man) parallels the focus on thorny and rarely encountered dilemmas in the moral education class.

What is the cumulative effect of shows like this on the home viewer? Is he or she converted to swapping or to the cause of man-boy love? Probably not. But there is another effect. Watching the shows makes for increased tolerance for differing viewpoints and behaviors. The viewer may not adopt such viewpoints but he now sees that there is something to them, or at least, that they can be defended in an articulate way. Living in a pluralistic society, we tend to think this is a desirable outcome. It is not stretching the point very much to say that in our culture, tolerance and open-mindedness have become the chief virtues.

It may be important to recall, however, that "tolerance" was not included in the four classical virtues or in the three Christian virtues that were later added to them. The notion that all ideas are to be respected is a fairly recent one—and not an easy notion to defend. Do the values of the Ku Klux Klan deserve respect? How about the values of the Mafia or the Colombian cocaine cartels? Do we owe respect to the values of the pornography industry? Christina Hoff Sommers, a professor of philosophy at Clark University, notes that this cultivation of tolerance also occurs in moral education classrooms. "But," she adds, "when tolerance is the sole virtue, students' capacity for moral indignation, so important for moral development, is severely inhibited." Whether in classrooms or on TV, a constant parade of alternative "values" tends to undermine the virtuous instinct that some things are and ought to be repugnant.

My question to my students about the talk show and the dilemma-centered classroom alike is whether such discussions can do more than develop a generalized—and sometimes excessive—tolerance. More precisely, can a person develop good moral character through participation in a talk show? through classroom rap sessions? Is this the way to develop traits such as courage, self-restraint, perseverance, or integrity? Students grasp the point immediately. Character is not about your skill in debate, it's about the kind of person you are.

Why then is the dilemma approach still in widespread use? One answer is that although it won't do much to develop a love of virtue or a hatred of vice, it will often do a lot for a teacher's popularity. Neil Postman, a professor of communications at New York University, suggests in a recent article that in order to compete with television, teaching has been reduced to a form of popular entertainment:

> Consequently, drawing an audience—rather than teaching—becomes the focus of education, and that is what television does. School is the one institution in the culture that should present a different worldview: a different way of knowing, of evaluating, of assessing. What worries me is that if school becomes so overwhelmed by entertainment's metaphors and metaphysics, then it becomes not content-centered but attention-centered, like television, chasing "ratings" or class attendance. If school becomes that way, then the game may be lost, because school is using the same approach, epistemologically, as television. Instead of being something different from television, it is reduced to being just another kind of television.

Kohlberg himself was quite serious about education; he never tried to be an entertainer. Nevertheless, his projects tended to produce educational fiascoes. In 1974, in an attempt to create not just a curriculum but a whole school based on his principles, Kohlberg founded the experimental Cluster School in Cambridge, Massachusetts. The "just community" school, as it was sometimes called, lasted only five years. According to Professor Sommers's account,

> these student-citizens were forever stealing from one another and using drugs during school hours. These transgressions provoked a long series of democratically conducted "town meetings" that to an outsider look very much like EST encounter groups. The students were frequently taken on re-

treats . . . where many of them broke the rules against sex and drugs. This provoked more democratic confrontations where, Kohlberg was proud to report, it was usually decided that for the sake of the group the students would police one another on subsequent retreats and turn in the names of the transgressors.

None of this worked, however, and serious problems with drugs, theft, sex, and racial division continued unabated. And this despite the fact that the school had only thirty students, who were tended to by six specially trained teachers, dozens of consultants, and Kohlberg himself. In 1978, writing in *The Humanist,* Kohlberg said:

> Some years of active involvement with the practice of moral education at Cluster School has led me to realize that my notion . . . was mistaken . . . the educator must be a socializer teaching value content and behavior, and not only a Socratic or Rogerian process-facilitator of development . . . I no longer hold these negative views of indoctrinative moral education and I believe that the concepts guiding moral education must be partly "indoctrinative." This is true, by necessity, in a world in which children engage in stealing, cheating and aggression.

But, as with Maslow, followers and enthusiasts of the Kohlberg approach seemed to tune out these second thoughts and reassessments. Since the failure of the Cluster School, sixteen school systems have instituted "just community" schools—thus confirming Sommers's observation that "in American professional education nothing succeeds like failure." *Newsweek* recently described one such school in New York City:

> West Indians snub the Bronx blacks, Dominicans won't eat with Puerto Ricans. Today's meeting verges on chaos. Tessa, a sophomore from Belize, has the chair and the attention of perhaps a third of the kids there. The question: should RCS [Roosevelt Community School] make community service a

requirement for graduation? Five sullen boys talk steadily in the rear. Kids wander to the sandwich table, chat, write in their diaries. Debaters shout: "Hey, Tiffany, why you opposed, ya dumb bitch?" Allan Sternberg, the history teacher who runs the program, struggles to maintain order.

In the end the students vote against mandatory community service. "Sternberg," reports *Newsweek,* "tries a plaintive note of regret, but they cut him off. 'You asked us, we said "no," now it's over with,' says one member." Somehow *Newsweek* manages to find a vague "fragmentary" progress in all this. But it's not, I think it safe to say, the sort of progress parents would like to see.

I have a question that I sometimes pose to groups of parents. It goes as follows:

Suppose your child's school was instituting a course or curriculum in moral education at the fifth- to seventh-grade level. As a parent which of the two models below would you prefer the school to use?

A.   The first approach encourages students to develop their own values and value systems. This approach relies on presenting the students with provocative ethical dilemmas and encouraging open discussion and exchange of opinion. The ground rule for discussion is that there are no right or wrong answers. Each student must decide for himself/herself what is right or wrong. Students are encouraged to be nonjudgmental about values that differ from their own.

B.   The second approach involves a conscious effort to teach specific virtues and character traits such as courage, justice, self-control, honesty, responsibility, charity, obedience to lawful authority, etc. These concepts are introduced and explained and then illustrated by memorable examples from history, literature, and current events. The teacher expresses a strong belief in the importance of these virtues and encourages his/her students to practice them in their own lives.

The vast majority of parents will choose B—the character education option. But when I ask groups of teachers and teachers-in-training which of the two models they would choose to teach, they invariably prefer model A. Many teachers say they would not use the second approach under any circumstances.

Parents and teachers in America have been on different wavelengths for quite some time, but I don't think it's necessarily the parents who need to make an adjustment. I believe they prefer character education over the experimental model not because of some knee-jerk conservatism, or because of their limited knowledge of theory, but because they have a better grasp of what is at stake, and because it is their own children who are in question.

A colleague who administered this "questionnaire" to parents in a working-class neighborhood overheard one of them say in reference to the decision-making model, "Make up his own mind? Are they serious?" Not very articulate, but I would wager that what she said was based on a lot of practical knowledge.

Sooner or later, each person does have to make up his or her own mind. However, a person who has learned something of courage, respect for truth, and concern for others, who has begun to put these ideals into practice, and who cares about doing the right thing is better equipped to reach sound moral judgments than one who has been schooled only to exchange opinions. To introduce a child to the complicated and controversial issues of the day without some prior attempt at forming character is a formula for confusing him, or worse. To do it in a format that suggests there are no right answers compounds the confusion and amounts to a loading of the deck. One doesn't have to be exclusively liberal or conservative, religious or nonreligious to be troubled by this scheme.

Like the talk show, the dilemma approach leaves a boy or girl no objective criteria for deciding right and wrong. The only criterion is "what feels right to me," or—in the case of the better-managed classes—"what I can rationally defend." But, as we know from the talk show, rationality is an all-purpose tool that will serve any master. Morality seems to require acquaintance with something more basic which, for want of a better term, we can call "moral premises." Moral premises are not reasoned to but are seen or grasped by an intuitive act. And being able to grasp them, as Aristotle suggested, may well be a factor of being virtuous in the first place—or at least, beginning to practice the virtues. There are many things in life that can't be understood from the outside. We don't really understand tennis or chess, for instance, until we begin to play them. In the same way, we can't understand the rightness of charity until we begin to practice it. "Objective," noncommittal discussions of other people's moral behavior allows students to stay outside the "game" while misleading them to believe they are in it. In the absence of deeper foundations, it seems likely that students will simply become adept at "pulling and tearing at arguments" like Plato's young puppies. At the same time, they will gain a facility for rationalizing whatever it is they have an inclination to do. Nothing more is being asked of them.

5.

A HISTORY LESSON

I've been arguing that much of our moral confusion can be explained in terms of a shift away from character education. But what exactly is character education? And how does it differ from the approaches we've discussed?

It differs in the first place by not being reducible to a classroom method. "Moral upbringing" would be a better term to describe it than "moral education." Character formation is Pip learning kindness from Joe Gargery (in *Great Expectations*) or Harvey Cheyne learning integrity from Manuel (in *Captains Courageous*). Or—to use two examples from recent television programs—character formation is growing up in a family like the Waltons or the Ingallses. In short, it is a more comprehensive thing—more like an initiation into life than a debate about life issues.

This comprehensive approach is based on a somewhat dim view of human nature. Indeed, one of the main differences between character education and the decision-making model is disagreement over the degree of difficulty involved in being moral. Character education wants to stack the deck in favor of good conduct, on the assumption that good conduct is not our natural first choice. From the character education perspective, goodness is not an easy project. And it's not, for the most part, an intellectual project. University of Illinois professor Edward Wynne, who has made a study of character education, observes that "its underlying philosophy assumed that 95 percent of the time we know what is the right thing to do; the problem is that we lack the will or determination to do it." An example is John Dean, who, when asked whether taking an ethics course in college would have averted his participation in the Watergate cover-up, replied that it would not, since he knew beforehand that what he was doing was wrong. Even the saints were taken aback by the difficulty of the project. "The good that I want to do, I don't," wrote Saint Paul; "the evil that I don't want to do, that is what I do."

From a traditional point of view, the chief way to counter our lack of will and determination is through the development of good habits. An effective moral education would be devoted to encouraging habits of honesty, helpfulness, and self-control until such behaviors become second nature. The idea is that we could then respond to tempting situations in an automatic way, much as an expert tennis player responds automatically to a hard serve. If we become persons of a certain kind, we won't need to debate our course of action, we will know "instinctively" how to act.

This is how the ancient Greeks and Romans understood moral education, except that instead of talking about "habits," they used the word "virtues." In its original sense, the word meant something like our word "strength." If you had a virtue such as courage, you not only had an idea about what constitutes courageous behavior, you also had the strength to act accordingly. And like muscular strength, you could lose it if you didn't keep in practice. Aristotle said that a man becomes virtuous by performing virtuous acts; he becomes kind by doing kind acts; he becomes brave by doing brave acts.

If Aristotle was right about this, it means, of course, that much of our modern talk about "choices" and "decision making" is rather shallow. An individual can't choose to do something if he lacks the capacity for it. For example, running the Boston Marathon is not a choice for those who are out of shape. It only becomes a choice for those who are willing to put in many months of training. In similar fashion, a child's freedom to choose altruistic behavior over self-centered behavior is severely limited if he has never formed a habit of helping others in need. Far from stifling our freedom to choose, habits actually enhance it. They give us command and control of ourselves.

Such a view is useful in understanding the failure of decision-making education. Sex educators, for example, claim that students are free to choose any option; but that seems a bit disingenuous when we consider that one of the options requires a great deal more discipline than the others. Youngsters might be able to make much freer decisions about sex if it were not for the fact that training in modesty and self-control is withheld from them. All previous cultures, by contrast, have felt that the virtuous path was always the more difficult one. Consequently, they were willing to do the hard work of preparing youngsters for it—a sort of affirmative action on behalf of the virtues.

This discussion of choices and habits may also help to explain a curious irony in American culture. For a society that babbles incessantly about choices, ours seems to be able to exercise precious little freedom when it comes to making them. Judging by statistics, this may be the most compulsive and addictive society ever to have stepped onto the stage of history. The list of addictions not only includes alcohol, tobacco, and drugs but extends to gambling, eating, shopping, and sex. Whole sections of bookstores are now devoted to manuals that promise to break us of our compulsions.

None of this would have surprised Aristotle. A culture that neglects to cultivate good habits, he would have observed, will soon find itself the prisoner of bad habits.

How did the Greeks—and for that matter, all other civilized societies—go about teaching good habits of behavior? The best way for a young person to learn them was by identifying with and imitating someone who already practiced them. Even the philosophers learned this way. In a letter to a young friend, Seneca wrote: "Plato, Aristotle, and the whole throng of sages . . . derived more benefit from the *character* than from the words of Socrates."

But the Greeks, and the Romans, did not rely entirely on the power of good personal example. Worthy models, after all, are not always evenly distributed among the population; and some people have the bad luck to be born among thieves. In addition, even the best people are on occasion weak, fallible, and inconsistent. Traditional societies recognized this, and they compensated for it with a generous supply of models drawn from history and legend. A child might be surrounded by crass and uncaring adults, but he could always catch a glimpse of another vision from the storyteller in the marketplace or in the pages of a book. Thus it was no accident that character education placed so much reliance on story and history. Long before the Greeks learned about virtue from Aristotle, they learned about it from the *Iliad* and the *Odyssey,* from Achilles and Hector, from Odysseus, Telemachus, and Penelope.

This idea of molding or forming one's character according to the example of outstanding men and women—whether from history or legend—prevailed until fairly recent times. The study of the humanities as it was originally conceived by Petrarch in the fourteenth century was, in its essence, the study of the lives of the noble Greeks and Romans. And this goal of drawing strength and inspiration from them remained a goal for a long time. Even eighteenth- and nineteenth-century Americans were profoundly influenced by Plutarch's *Lives.* Others turned to the Bible, to Foxe's *Book of Martyrs,* or to the lives of the saints. It was a simple but profound concept: a life based not on principle or precept but on other lives.

It was also an indispensable concept for those living in a democracy. John Adams wrote that our form of government was only meant for a virtuous people, and Jefferson, Madison, and Washington concurred. A government of the people would work only as long as the people were good people. Schools did their part by explicit instruction in the importance of honesty, hard work, altruism, and patriotism, but also by presenting stories of virtue to children. The *McGuffey Reader,* which by 1919 had the largest circulation of any book except the Bible, contained readings from Aesop, Shakespeare, and the Bible as well as stories about Lafayette, Washington, and Wilberforce (the Englishman who almost single-handedly brought an end to the slave trade).

How well did character education work? Not perfectly, by any means. The Greeks and Romans owned slaves; so did some of the founding fathers. Women were excluded from public life. Compassion was not always extended to those outside one's family or group. By our standards, much of what was accepted behavior in the past seems harsh and unfair. But we should remember that our standards have been built on theirs. Our present enlightened ideas about equality and justice didn't come out of the blue. And once again, it's one thing to have enlightened views and another thing to really practice fairness and consideration in daily life. The real test is not whether a child of the nineties will have more advanced ideas about race and gender than, say, a child of the thirties or forties. He will. The test is how he actually behaves.

We do have ways of making such behavior comparisons, because someone has been keeping score. FBI statistics show startling increases in crimes committed by children and teens over the last five decades. The difference can also be seen in the differing concerns of teachers then and now. Compare what classroom teachers identified as the greatest threats to the educational process in 1940 and today. First on the list in 1940 was talking out of turn; today it is drug abuse. The number-two concern in 1940 was chewing gum; today it is alcohol abuse. Number three in 1940 was making noise; number three today is pregnancy. The fourth most pressing problem in 1940 was running in the halls; today it is suicide. Fifth, sixth, and seventh on the list in 1940 were getting out of line, wearing improper clothing, and not putting paper in the wastebasket; today they are rape, robbery, and assault.

None of this, however, was foreseen by early critics of character education. Instead, they were convinced that a rosier future lay in store once character education and other traditional forms of schooling were dispensed with. The first attempt to undo character education came with the progressive education movement in the twenties and thirties, and was only partially successful. The second attempt three decades later was a complete rout; by the late sixties the decision-making model of moral education was in full possession of the field.

How did we get from one to the other? What happened to this idea of the Greeks and Romans—an idea that persisted even into the twentieth century—that goodness could be reliably cultivated in boys and girls? The immediate causes, as we have seen, lay in the social upheavals of the sixties. But the groundwork had been set down centuries earlier.

The philosophical origins of the "choose-your-own-values" approach which dominates education today can be found in two systems of thought that arose in the seventeenth and eighteenth centuries. "Systems of thought" is a mild way of putting it. Rationalism and Romanticism can more properly be considered historical *forces*. They swept away centuries-old habits of thought, and they swept the Western world into the modern age.

Rationalism is the theory that the exercise of reason is the only basis for belief and action. It was the philosophical core of the Enlightenment—the seventeenth- and eighteenth-century intellectual movement characterized by faith in the power of intellect, a keen interest in science, and the pursuit of political freedom. The term "Enlightenment," of course, implied a prior darkness. Enlightenment thinkers—the *philosophes*—were eager to shake off past ignorance and superstition, and many of them wanted to shake off religion as well. The *philosophes* believed that the human mind could be liberated from the hold of custom, religion, and all nonrational belief. They hoped to establish a way of freeing thought from the narrow limitations of "this time" and "this place." They believed that reason (spelled with a capital *R* during the French Revolution), together with science, could both comprehend human problems and solve them. In view of the rapid strides science was making in solving technical problems, it did not, at the time, seem an unreasonable belief. The sentiments of the Enlightenment are nicely summed up by a character in Flaubert's novel *Madame Bovary*. "My God," he proclaims, "is the God of Socrates, of Franklin, Voltaire, and Béranger!"

One of the chief Enlightenment projects was the attempt to establish morality on a rational basis. The project was to find principles of ethics which could be agreed to by all men and women, no matter what their class, culture, or religion. These principles, because they were founded on reason, would be able to stand on their own without the assistance of church or commandments. The philosopher who is most closely associated with this attempt is Immanuel Kant. Kant wanted to show that moral order could be based on self-regulation (his own life was so well regulated that the people of Königsberg are said to have set their clocks by his afternoon walks). Once individuals could see the reasonableness of certain moral principles, they would, he argued, voluntarily behave lawfully instead of having to be coerced by the threat of punishment. It was Kant who introduced "autonomy" as a technical term in ethics. Those who had a base of autonomous reason for their behavior would have a more solid allegiance to morality than those who conformed through habit or custom or fear of the law.

Professor Kohlberg's moral reasoning approach stands in this Enlightenment tradition. Following Kant's lead, Kohlberg argued that, given the right classroom conditions, children would figure out the important ethical principles for themselves. Moral development would not be a factor of one's culture, family, or faith: the key, rather, would be rationality.

Kohlberg brought Kant into the modern classroom. But along with this enlightened approach came some interesting questions. For example, does the theory imply that morality depends on intelligence? In many places, Kohlberg seems to be saying that it does. He postulated six stages of moral development which are, in turn, linked to stages of cognitive development. On this scale, individuals whose morality is motivated by religion or custom are consigned to either stage three or stage four. Stage six, the highest level, is only for those who can reason autonomously. Kohlberg realized that moral reasoning skills don't always translate into good behavior, but he seemed convinced that most of the time, they do. He wasn't quite saying, "The smarter you are, the better you are"—but he was skating close to that conclusion.

A second implication—one with explosive ramifications—has to do with sex differences. Psychologists (including many feminist psychologists) are generally agreed that boys are better at abstract reasoning than girls. Does this imply that boys are also better at moral reasoning? That would seem to be the import of Kohlberg's theory. Professor Carol Gilligan, one of Kohlberg's colleagues at Harvard, addressed the issue head-on. Kohlberg's theory, she said, was primarily a description of the reasoning process of males. She noticed that boys consistently scored higher than girls on Kohlberg's moral judgment tests, and concluded that the whole theory was biased in favor of males. Gilligan proposed that females had a separate and equally valid way of arriving at moral decisions. For females moral questions were approached from an orientation to caring and relationships rather than (as for males) an orientation to abstract principles of justice. Given one of Kohlberg's dilemmas, a typical boy, says Gilligan, sees it as "a math problem with humans," whereas a typical girl sees it as "a narrative of relationships that extend over time." Unwilling to ignore the human factor, the girl scores only a stage three on Kohlberg's moral maturity scale to the boy's stage four.

Gilligan's criticisms deserve more discussion, and will be taken up later, but for the time being let us note that she touches on a third question that can be raised concerning the whole Kantian/ Kohlbergian enterprise: Just how abstract can moral reasoning become before it loses touch with the human side of morality? Just how reliable is rationality when it is divorced from considerations of the heart? G. K. Chesterton, the English essayist, made an acute observation about such a loss of perspective. He said that insanity does not mean losing your reason, it means losing everything else except your reason. Had Kohlberg carried moral decision making too far into the realm of analysis and abstraction? Did his approach suffer from a serious loss of human perspective? Was it all head and no heart? These were the sort of charges Kohlberg soon found himself faced with. From a historical perspective, they were exactly the criticisms one would expect.

The original Enlightenment provoked a similar reaction. There was a limit to people's appetite for science, abstraction, and impersonal reason. When the limit was reached, a revolt set in. We now call it Romanticism. The Romantic movement rediscovered art, mystery, and irrationality. And it rediscovered emotions. In fact, it elevated emotion to a position it had never before held in the history of thought. And with this new emphasis on the emotional self came a whole new way of defining morality.

The chief prophet of the Romantic movement was the Swiss-born philosopher Jean Jacques Rousseau. It was Rousseau who developed the doctrine of natural goodness in its most attractive form. The theory proposed that in a natural state children could be counted on to develop natural virtues. This would happen in an almost automatic way, like the process that occurs when a bud unfolds into a flower. Since all individuals are different, each child would develop differently. But all would unfold in a positive direction: that is, into roses, marigolds, and sunflowers—not into poison ivy or skunkweed. The idea had enormous appeal in Rousseau's time. Benjamin Franklin, for example, sported a beaver cap when he visited France, to demonstrate his affinity with nature and with Rousseau, who had initiated the style. And this despite the fact that the prescriptions found in Rousseau's work had little in common with the precepts of *Poor Richard's Almanack.* At the same time, the voyages of Cook and de Bougainville to the South Seas were inspired, at least in part, by the hope of finding the "Noble Savage" Rousseau had postulated.

Nevertheless, the theory was a radical break with the past. The difference can be illustrated by comparing two books with the same title: Augustine's *Confessions* and Rousseau's *Confessions.* In the earlier work, Augustine confesses that he has failed and fallen short of the mark. And Rousseau? Rousseau confesses how interesting he feels himself to be. In typical passages, he writes: "What could your miseries have in common with mine? My situation is unique, unheard of since the beginning of time . . ." "The person who can love me as I can love is still to be born." "Show me a better man than me, a heart more loving, more tender, more sensitive . . ." ". . . if there were a single enlightened government in Europe, it would have erected statues to me."

It would be an understatement to say Rousseau lacked humility. He appears to have been one of history's great egomaniacs— although he would not have called it egomania but honesty. The contrast with Augustine and, for that matter, with the whole of the classical and Christian tradition was marked. The difference between Augustine and Rousseau is the difference between imitation and self-expression. In the tradition to which Augustine belonged, individuals did not look to themselves for guidance and strength, they looked outside. Greeks and Romans looked to the warrior-hero or to the statesman as a model; Christians looked to Christ or the saints. In either case, one's personal self was considered too weak and unreliable. "To thine own self be true" would have seemed utterly foolish advice not only to Augustine but to Cicero and his contemporaries. Even in Shakespeare's play, these words are put into the mouth of an old fool.

But for Rousseau it was the sum and substance of wisdom. Since each person was a font of goodness, it was unnecessary to look to others; and—since each person was splendidly unique—it made no sense. "I am made unlike anyone I have ever met; I will even venture to say that I am like no one in the whole world," declares Rousseau in the *Confessions*. Rousseau, as we would say, "broke the mold." In his view, there was no mold. It followed, then, that one becomes virtuous not by following the example of others but by expressing one's own self.

This doctrine—"To thine own self be true"—made sense to a whole succession of thinkers after Rousseau: to the Romantic poets in England and on the Continent; to Emerson, Thoreau, and Whitman in America ("Who can there be more wonderful than myself?" asked Whitman); and in the twentieth century to anthropologists like Margaret Mead, psychologists like Carl Rogers, and educators like John Dewey. It was in education particularly that Rousseau had his greatest influence, although, ironically, he was to have little impact on French education. Perhaps the French were too well aware of the shabby way he had treated his own children (he abandoned all five of them to orphanages). In any event, French schooling is still conducted in much the same way it was during the time of the Bourbons. But for American education Rousseau's theory was a time bomb. It began to tick loudly in the twenties, and in the sixties it exploded.

In that decade a host of educational critics such as A. S. Neill, John Holt, Paul Goodman, Herbert Kohl, George Leonard, and Carl Rogers took up the cause of the free-flowering child. "The basic nature of the human being, when functioning freely, is constructive and trustworthy," said Rogers, speaking more or less for the others, and in language that echoed Rousseau. Teachers and others should stand back and let these natural processes go to work.

If the moral reasoning approach comes out of the rationalist tradition, the Values Clarification approach is the heir of the Romantic tradition. "What feels right is right" was not a new idea when the values clarifiers installed it into school curriculums. The only difference is that the idea had previously been confined to a handful of bored aristocrats, poets, artists, and, to use the nineteenth-century term, "beautiful souls."

The Rousseauian explosion of the sixties was not, of course, confined to the schools. Rousseau's celebration of natural instincts had its counterpart in a number of preoccupations that arose in the sixties, and are still with us. "Feeling good about yourself," "getting in touch with your feelings," "letting it all hang out"—these are simply less articulate expressions of Rousseau's own approach to life. Some other lineal descendants of the Romantic/Rousseauian tradition are the current concern over "the child within," the nostalgia for primitivism, and, on the part of some, a near worshipful attitude toward nature.

A further influence of Rousseau is reflected in our ambivalent attitude toward heroes. Whereas earlier ages engaged in unabashed hero worship, ours prefers to cut them down to size. Instead of pointing to the noble qualities of public figures, we feel compelled to point out their feet of clay. Not surprisingly, a number of surveys indicate that contemporary boys and girls have few if any heroes. When they can think of someone they would like to identify with, it will quite often be a high-salaried entertainer—a Michael Jackson or an Eddie Murphy. Many if not most of these figures are admired not for their virtues but for their success. It is also instructive to note that no sort of unpleasant revelations about these stars will do much to harm their standing. In fact, they will usually improve it (as Rousseau's show of boorishness increased his own popularity with his patrons). This is an age that feels more comfortable with the confessional mode than the heroic one.

It is doubtful that Rousseau could have foreseen a Michael Jackson or the outpouring of confessions one can now hear any day on a talk show, but the recent turn away from heroism would have been to his liking. A major goal of his educational plan was to discredit the importance of imitation and all the moral effort it involved. Consequently, in *Emile,* one of the most influential books on education ever written, he sets down the astonishing dictum that children shouldn't read books. He particularly didn't want Emile reading books about heroes. Among other things, such looming models might engender inferiority feelings. Rousseau strikes a very modern note here: one shouldn't have to compare oneself.

Once again, the full effect of his ideas seems to have been delayed by some two centuries. Rousseau's contemporaries sensibly ignored his recommendations. But in the decades following the 1950s a major shift took place. Children didn't exactly stop reading books, but to a large extent they stopped reading heroic literature. Why? Partly because it was no longer being written, but partly also, I think, because teachers and librarians were becoming embarrassed by that sort of thing. It didn't fit in with the tenor of the times. When I was in seventh grade, our teacher read aloud for about twenty minutes every day from Marie McSwigan's *Snow Treasure* until she had read the whole book. I was captivated by this tale of Norwegian boys and girls who helped smuggle gold bullion out from under the noses of their Nazi occupiers. They were brave and trustworthy and quick-witted, and hearing about them made me want to be like them. For a period of about three weeks I actually looked forward to school.

By the decade of the seventies such an event would have been a rare occurrence in a seventh-grade classroom. For one thing, a progressive teacher would not be caught dead reading aloud to seventh-graders; for another, a new type of story was coming into vogue. Psychologist David Elkind refers to it as the "therapeutic" story:

> Previously in much of children's literature, the goals were often to help or to please others—parents, friends, pets— who were needy or endangered. A boy took risks to save a dog or a girl worked hard to get a desired gift for a sick friend. In children's fiction today, however, the goals are often therapeutic and rehabilitative. Heroes and heroines are healing themselves rather than helping others.

Healing themselves—or increasingly, it appears, simply accepting themselves. The best examples of this literature of self-acceptance are the stories of Judy Blume. Blume, far and away the most successful author of books for young adults, writes: "When I was young I could never find any books about kids like me, and that's what I wanted to read about." The "kids like me" she writes about are self-obsessed, sexually absorbed, shallow, sullen, emotionally numb, contemptuous of adults, and relentlessly materialistic. Youngsters of this sort have, of course, appeared before in fiction: the character of Nellie from *Little House on the Prairie* comes to mind. The novel thing about the Blume books is that her non-judgmental prose contains no suggestion that such children should mend their ways. The main characters in stories such as *Blubber* and *Then Again Maybe I Won't* are nasty and mean-spirited—but "so what?" as they might say. "That's the way kids are, and it's okay" seems to mark the limit of the Blume philosophy. There is in her stories no encouragement to look outside the self, and thus, as Michelle Landsberg, a Canadian writer, observes of Blume, no "enlargements of the self." Rather, her books consistently endorse narcissistic self-centeredness. Children didn't exactly stop reading books in the seventies and eighties, but more and more of what they were reading resembled nothing so much as junior versions of Rousseau's *Confessions*.

If children were having difficulty finding good models in books, it was also getting hard to find them in reality. Setting a good example is not easy work. It means that adults may have to force themselves to behave better than they might otherwise be inclined. Rousseauian doctrine provided several reasons why they shouldn't have to bear that burden. The idea that all values come from within was one reason for letting adults off the hook. Another was Rousseau's notion that, in the last analysis, we are *all* fellow children.

For someone who laid such a heavy burden of blame on society, Rousseau was all too willing to let society do all the hard work in life. In his ideal form of government, the State would be recast as a benevolent parent while actual parents would be free to enjoy an extended childhood. The writer George Sand referred to him reverently as "Saint Rousseau." He might well have been the patron saint of the baby boom generation as it grew up and began to grow older. Not that many actually read Rousseau. It was easier to pick up the Rousseauian gospel from the pages of self-help books where one could get advice on discovering "the child within." This preoccupation with remaining a child or becoming one again was, of course, bound to clash with the duty of role modeling. In *Children Without Childhood*, Marie Winn recounts the story of two apparently not untypical parents of the seventies who carried the new equality to its logical conclusion:

> Betsy was thirteen, I guess, the summer she began to smoke dope with us. We always smoked openly at home, but we never let Betsy or her friends smoke at our house. We didn't think it would be fair to the other parents. But that summer we smoked a lot, and she'd be there sitting with us, and we knew that she had already smoked with her friends—all her friends started in seventh grade—and so we just included her when we turned on.

The story nicely illustrates the seventies conviction that being honest about one's behavior was vastly more important than the behavior itself. Equally revealing is the mother's reaction when, two years later, Betsy's behavior has gotten completely out of hand, and they are forced to crack down:

> There we were, put in the role of old-fashioned, repressive parents, that was what was so bizarre. Because we're just the opposite really . . . I kept saying, "I'm being put in a role and I don't want to play it! I hate this role!" But I *had* to take on that role.

This feeling of resentment, of being put upon by having to play a role, be a model, is characteristic of recent generations but it also echoes the resentment of Romantic spirits down through the ages whenever they are called upon to be other than just themselves. The story of Betsy and her parents, however, has an unromantic but happy enough conclusion:

> Finally we all went to a family therapist . . . We went about eight sessions, and it was really very helpful. Betsy was ready

for a change. She was worn out. It's hard to tell what the therapist did that made us all change. But among other things, she told my husband and me to stop smoking dope. And we did.

This conclusion—that example really does matter—is one that more and more adults are coming to. But it is not an easy lesson to absorb. It violates the Romantic faith that children will do fine on their own, and—more to the point—it puts limits to adult self-expression.

It is a lesson that both parents and educators need to relearn. Before education entered its Romantic phase in the late sixties, "good character" was a primary consideration in hiring teachers. The requirement assumed that if "example is the best teacher," students ought to have the best examples as teachers. When the Romantic revolution hit the schools, that idea lost credence. Teachers, like everyone else, could just be themselves. In retrospect, it seems unsurprising that when educators cast about for a new type of moral education in the late sixties, they would hit on a scheme like Values Clarification—a scheme that requires no modeling on the part of the teacher, and no evidence of personal character.

But this neglect of good example is not confined to the Romantic movement in education. Kohlberg's moral reasoning approach doesn't bother with good example either. The Enlightenment tradition provided plenty of reasons why children should think for themselves, but precious few why they should follow the example of others. This observation leads to a final point. It would be inaccurate to think that rationalism and Romanticism were entirely distinct. Although the two movements differed in many ways, they also shared common ground. Both had little use for custom or religion (rationalists replaced religion with reason, Romanticists replaced it with nature). Both movements, moreover, prized individual autonomy over any other goal. The modern world is, in a sense, the child of both parents. In fact, the modern world may be understood as an alliance between rationalism and Romanticism in the service of the autonomous person. This is why critics of contemporary culture have a hard time deciding whether ours is an anti-intellectual age governed by the Romantic impulse, or a rational/technical society that has lost track of its humanness. Actually, it is both.

In this respect, education is a microcosm of the larger society. Rationalism and Romanticism almost define the world in which educators now operate. They tend to shuttle back and forth between these two poles as though there were no other alternative. Almost any new development or method in education will turn out, on examination, to be a variation of one or the other. New versions of Romantic naturalism crop up every few years. Values Clarification is one example; we will look at some others in future chapters. Each swing of the pendulum in that direction then provokes a counterswing in the other direction—toward critical thinking, problem solving, and other "cognitive" approaches.

As far as moral education is concerned, however, these swings of the pendulum actually have little effect. Neither do attempts to combine the two styles. Despite the fact that the Values Clarification approach and the moral reasoning approach stem from different systems of thought, their net effect is remarkably similar. In both cases, we see a complete neglect of habit formation. The concept of virtue is alien to both. Both place a higher value on autonomy than morality. Both approaches seem to assume that moral education can be carried on without any reference to the culture or to cultural knowledge.

With all these swings of the pendulum, there is no forward motion, only a further retreat from the tradition of character education—a tradition that does not lie somewhere between the poles of rationalism and Romanticism but somewhere completely outside that arc. Moral education will continue to go nowhere unless it can turn off its limited track and move toward a wholly different mode of understanding human action.

MORAL ILLITERACY

Martin Luther once described the human race as being like a drunk who falls off one side of his horse, gets back on, and promptly falls off the other side. This is a good description of what happened to moral education in the late sixties, except that it might be more accurate to picture two drunks on horseback. The first falls off the right side of his horse, and the second, taking note, avoids that calamity only to fall off the left side. Kohlberg avoided the lurch toward feelings only to tumble off on the other side—the side of "critical thinking." But perhaps I ought to explain more fully why I think that was a mistaken direction.

It is becoming increasingly clear that we can't base moral education on a "follow-your-feelings" basis, but the critical thinking alternative still has broad appeal. A great many educators remain convinced that salvation can be found along the path of reason. What many of them fail to realize is that reason is on shaky ground when it stands alone. Aristotle emphasized the impor-

tance of acquiring good habits of thinking, but he also emphasized habits of feeling and habits of acting; and as we have seen,
he stressed the importance of good upbringing. Plato, he believed, relied too much on the power of unaided reason.

Yet one of the main thrusts of recent moral education has been
to set reason up on its own: to create, in effect, a culture-free
morality. Kohlberg, for example, thought that children should
become autonomous ethical agents, independent of family,
church, and state. And he employed some powerful arguments in
making his case.

The trouble with character education, with the whole "cultural
transmission ideology," as he called it, was its potential for serving
totalitarian causes. The methods sometimes employed in forming
character were also the methods regularly used by tyrants in
indoctrinating the masses. Flags and oaths and patriotic songs
could stir noble sentiments, but they could just as easily stir base
ones. And in the wrong hands, habit formation could be used to
induce a habit of blind obedience. The Hitler Youth were uncom-
fortably similar to the Boy Scouts. Education, particularly moral
education, should be free of all such emotional conditioning. It
should respect the child's autonomy and his ability to make judgments independent of his culture. Who would be a good example
of such autonomous moral reasoning? Kohlberg frequently cited
Martin Luther King, Jr. (incorrectly, as I will explain).

Because it is such a persistent and influential theme in American education, this effort to make children into autonomous ethical thinkers deserves close examination. Ironically, some of the
evidence against it comes from an extensive study of individuals
who rescued Jews in Nazi-occupied Europe. The study, conducted by Samuel and Pearl Oliner and reported in their book *The
Altruistic Personality,* showed that only a small minority of the
rescuers were motivated by "autonomous" or "principled" ethics.
The rescuers referred much more frequently to the way they were
brought up, to the example of parents, or to the influence of
religion. As the Oliners make clear, these people were not "moral
heroes, arriving at their own conclusions about right and wrong
after internal struggle, guided primarily by intellect and rationality." On the contrary, "what most distinguished them were their

connections with others in relationships of commitment and care." In addition, these were people who, more than most, had internalized community and family norms. It was the bystanders and nonrescuers who were motivated by concerns about their independence and autonomy.

Why did the rescuers help? Here are some typical answers from those surveyed:

> I cannot give you any reasons. It was not a question of reasoning. Let's put it this way. There were people in need and we helped them.

> They taught me discipline, tolerance and serving other people when they needed something. It was a general feeling. If somebody was ill or in need my parents would always help.

> When you see a need you have to help. Our religion was part of us. We are our brother's keeper.

> The basic morality in this little homogeneous country is such that we have been told for generations to be nice to your neighbor, be polite, and treat people well. It came through during the war.

> My father taught me to love God and my neighbor, regardless of their race or religion.

> At my grandfather's place, when they read the Bible, he invited everybody in. If a Jew happened to drop in, he would ask him to take a seat. He would sit there too. Jews and Catholics were received in our place like everybody else.

Another finding of the Oliners is of equal interest. Most of the rescuers hardly deliberated before acting: "Asked how long it took them to make their first helping decision, more than seventy percent indicated 'minutes.'" The astonishing rapidity of their decisions is far different from the endless debates that take place now in American classrooms, and suggests that helping others had become a *habitual* mode of response. Their behavior, in short, seems to constitute an argument for traditional ideas about culture and character rather than a case for critical thinking.

How about Martin Luther King, Jr., as an example of moral autonomy? In some respects Kohlberg couldn't have chosen a less apt example. King was able to successfully resist and overcome the entrenched culture of Jim Crow in the South not because he had invented a new set of principles but because he appealed to a tradition that both preceded and transcended the tradition of Jim Crow. A minister and the son of a minister, he was steeped in Bible stories and the messianic traditions of the black church, along with its hymns and spirituals. When he attended Crozer Theological Seminary, he immersed himself in the writings of Plato, Aristotle, Mill, and Locke. In his speeches, he referred to Lincoln, to the Declaration of Independence, to Negro spirituals, to Moses and the Promised Land. His "Letter from Birmingham Jail" even included a citation from the medieval theologian Thomas Aquinas on the difference between just and unjust laws.

King was, in short, the bearer of a tradition. He was able to mobilize white as well as black Americans because he was successful in reminding them of what they already believed about justice and common human decency. His demand was not that America create a new morality but that it live up to its best traditions and beliefs.

Nevertheless, the ideal of the culturally autonomous ethical thinker is not easy for educators to abandon. Just the other day I read the following in a college textbook: "Morally autonomous people think independently and critically and make their own decisions about right and wrong . . . Martin Luther King's struggle for civil rights is an example of moral autonomy."

The critical thinking advocates are right to worry about the dangers of mindless patriotism and unthinking conformity. Where they go wrong is in their one-sided emphasis on the process of thinking. As Mortimer Adler points out, "There is no such thing as thinking in and of itself. All the thinking any of us do is thinking about one subject matter or another . . ." The question is this: Does freeing children from their cultural heritage really free them to think for themselves? Or only to think from within some other context—such as the context provided by television? Once you deprive children of the content of serious culture, do they become their own persons or simply more in thrall to popular culture? How can we keep young people from being manipulated? One answer is to teach them critical thinking. But a better answer might be to teach them history—along with literature, biography, and yes, scripture. Then they might have something with which to compare and contrast and judge—something by which to call others, and themselves, to account.

One of the basic problems in moral education is to find the proper balance between content and process. Where should the emphasis be placed: on the content of the Judaeo-Christian-Western moral heritage, as was done in the past, or on independent thinking processes, as Kohlberg, Simon, and others would have it? The stress in recent decades has, of course, been on the second. Like the Cheshire cat, moral content has been in the process of disappearing from moral education. Not much of substance is left except, perhaps, for a ghostly smile.

But is content really that dispensable? Can we count on individuals to find out what they need to know about right and wrong once they've mastered certain processes? Should each generation of youngsters have to reinvent the moral wheel? Can they?

This controversy about moral education is really part of a larger controversy in American schools and colleges. A look at that larger dispute may help provide some perspective on the smaller. For a long time the general curriculum has been under the same pressure as the moral education curriculum—that is, pressure to shift from an emphasis on content to an emphasis on process. Thus, it is argued, children don't need to learn to calculate so much as they need a process for thinking about math; they don't need historical facts so much as they need ways of thinking critically about the historical process. And the same applies to science, literature, and geography: the facts are not nearly as important as strategies for thinking about them.

Process-centered learning has been the rage now for several decades. What has been the result? One main effect is that students coming out of American high schools simply don't know many facts. Surprisingly large numbers of them can't locate the United States on a map of the world, can't distinguish World War I from World War II, can't identify Winston Churchill or Joseph Stalin. As for critical thinking, a 1989 survey of *college seniors* found that one quarter of them could not distinguish between the thoughts of Karl Marx and the United States Constitution.

One of the people who have written most cogently about this topic is Professor E. D. Hirsch of the University of Virginia. Hirsch's book *Cultural Literacy* created a stir and became a bestseller largely because he dared to make a list of 5,000 things that people in a literate society ought to know. Unfortunately, many of his critics tended to concentrate on the list and ignore the argument of the book. Hirsch's argument was basically this: Communities and cultures depend for their existence on shared knowledge. Without such specific knowledge and a shared ethos, it becomes difficult for members of a community to communicate and cooperate. Those without this knowledge will always be condemned to the margins of society. If the knowledge deficit becomes widespread, the culture will collapse.

A good deal of past and current history supports this hypothesis. Contrary to the claims of advocates of "cultural diversity," the actual history of culturally diverse societies is one of discord and bloodshed. Unless there exists a common language, common religion, or common traditions to bind them, people in such societies tend to be at each other's throats. By contrast, a country with many racial and ethnic groups can remain relatively peaceful for decades if these groups share the same language or values.

Such stability is endangered, says Hirsch, when educators neglect specific content in favor of critical thinking skills. And ironically, critical thinking itself will be one of the first casualties. A youngster won't learn to think critically if he doesn't have anything to think about. He won't learn to read or write very well either, nor will he have much grasp of history or current events.

Hirsch blames Rousseau for this state of affairs, Rousseau and John Dewey, who translated Rousseau's content-neutral ideas into American educational practice. Rousseau's name is on Hirsch's list, by the way, and we can use it here to illustrate his point. A literate person would not have to be told who Rousseau was. He would know that he was a Swiss philosopher who wrote about nature and Noble Savages and had some influence on the French Revolution. And he wouldn't have to know any more than that. That would be sufficient to follow the author's argument and ensure easy communication with him. Not knowing Rousseau's identity would not in itself, of course, limit someone's life (unless he happened to teach philosophy), but if enough of these content deficits existed in an individual, he would have difficulty entering the American mainstream. If he did not know North from South, or couldn't read directions on a package, or wasn't familiar with the law, he would be severely handicapped. Unable to participate in society, he would lose the sense of having a stake in it.

Just as it is important for a community to have a common literate culture, it is equally important for it to have a common moral culture. America *has* had a common moral culture for most of its history. In the past most people would have known of Adam and Eve's disobedience, the loyalty of Penelope and Telemachus, Abe Lincoln's honesty, the treachery of Benedict Arnold, the generosity of the couple in "The Gift of the Magi," the selfishness of Scrooge, the Ten Commandments, and the Twenty-third Psalm. None of this knowledge would ensure decent behavior, but it would be a good start. It would at least guarantee that people were speaking the same language. Like a common stock of knowledge, a common set of ideals seems necessary to any society that hopes to socialize its young.

But, as is the case with factual content, there now appears to be a decline in shared moral content. Let me give three examples from my own experience with college students.

The first incident happened five or six year ago during an exam. One of the questions concerned sex education and contained the word "abstinence." It was a poor choice of words. In a few minutes a student came up to my desk. "What's abstinence?" she asked. I thought for a moment, then said, "Oh, just substitute the word 'chastity.'" There was a brief pause, then . . . "What's chastity?" she asked.

I mentioned the incident the next semester to another class, thinking that it might amuse them, but I was wrong again. Half of them had never heard of "chastity" either. I was reminded of Orwell's observation about the difficulty of practicing a virtue or principle when one lacks the very words for expressing it.

The second incident took place about a year later, this time in a graduate class of about twenty students. For some reason the topic of the Ten Commandments came up, and I decided it would be helpful to the discussion to list them on the board. I asked for some help from my students, only to find that they were unable to come up with the complete list. I don't mean that single individuals in the class were unable to do the task, I mean that the entire class working in concert couldn't do it.

The third incident occurred only recently in an undergraduate class. I was trying to draw a contrast between moral education that emphasizes process and moral education that emphasizes content. I used Values Clarification as an example of the process approach because it offers a list of seven processes to use in forming values. The first guideline is "prizing and cherishing your values"; the second is "publicly affirming your values"; the third is "choosing from alternatives"; and so on. It's an appealing list until you stop to realize that because of its lack of content, it can be used to arrive at any value position. Hitler "cherished" his values, and "publicly affirmed" them. He could have subscribed to the whole list. I then suggested that a good example of a list with moral content would be the Ten Commandments or the Corporal Works of Mercy. But the latter term met with blank stares. No one in this class of forty or so had ever heard of the Seven Corporal Works of Mercy. This would be understandable in a public institution, but I happen to teach at a Catholic university, and until recently, any student from a Catholic grade school would have known the Works of Mercy by heart. The list is:

1. Feed the hungry.
2. Give drink to the thirsty.
3. Clothe the naked.
4. Shelter the homeless.
5. Comfort the sick.
6. Visit those in prison.
7. Bury the dead.

The list was drawn up on the assumption that if you were going to practice the virtue of charity, you ought to know what it involved. Of course, the list is based on incidents in the Bible, and if you knew your Bible stories, you wouldn't need to memorize the list. Perhaps that was the reason for dropping it from the curriculum. The problem is, not many of today's college students seem to have much familiarity with Bible stories either. It is not uncommon to encounter students who don't know the story of the Good Samaritan or the Blind Man at the Well or Joseph and His Brothers. Charles Sykes, in his book *The Hollow Men,* recounts an anecdote about two university students who, though they were majoring in art history and studying Leonardo's *The Last Supper,* had no idea what the Last Supper was all about.

On the elementary and high school level the stock of knowledge about right and wrong has dwindled even more drastically. In 1985 Professor Paul Vitz of New York University reported the results of a comprehensive study of ninety widely used elementary social studies texts, high school history texts, and elementary readers. What Vitz discovered was a "censorship by omission" in which basic themes and facts of the American and Western experience had been left out. Of the 670 stories from the readers used in grades three through six, only five dealt with any patriotic theme; moreover, "there are no stories that feature helping others or being concerned for others as intrinsically meaningful and valuable." "For the most part," writes Vitz, "these are stories for the 'me generation.'" More seriously, religion and marriage—institutions that have traditionally provided a context for learning morality—are neglected: None of the social studies books dealing with modern American social life mentioned the word "marriage," "wedding," "husband" or "wife."

In one story by Isaac Bashevis Singer, a boy prays "to God" and later says "thank God," but in the sixth-grade version, the words "to God" are omitted and the expression "thank God" is changed to "thank goodness." Although many Americans pray and go to church, hardly anyone does in these ninety books which are supposedly representative of American life. The importance of Christianity and Judaism in world history is similarly slighted. So are the religious motivations of the colonists and founders. Contemporary religious motivation is also almost nonexistent. For example, although Martin Luther King, Jr., is mentioned in many texts, only one bothers to note that he was a pastor and that black churches played a key role in the civil rights struggle.

This is a question not of asking textbooks to support or endorse religion or marriage or altruistic behavior but simply of asking them to recognize their existence and their social and historical importance. Since television presents a similarly skewed version of the world and because so many families are in shambles, many young people today have only the vaguest acquaintance with a common moral culture that was once available to all.

How does this lack of background knowledge affect the everyday lives of young men and women? That's difficult to say. But we do know that many young people no longer realize that rape is wrong, and there are indications that much greater numbers are unaware that drunkenness is wrong. In his book *Educating for Character,* Thomas Lickona relates a Catholic university chaplain's observation that "college students rarely confess, as students once did, the sin of getting drunk (always considered a grave sin in Catholic moral theology)." Lickona continues, "It's not that today's students at this university never get drunk, many do. But apparently they do not think, as their predecessors did, that getting drunk is a serious moral wrong." Student drunkenness, as might be expected, is on the rise on college campuses across the country. On many campuses, it is *the* major problem. Along with the increase in drunkenness, there has been a corresponding increase in vandalism. Colleges spend hundreds of millions annually in repairing dorms that have been trashed by students.

Parents tend to blame schools for this state of affairs; schools tend to blame parents. Lickona quotes a fifth-grade teacher in a Boston suburb:

> About ten years ago I showed my class some moral dilemma filmstrips. I found they knew right from wrong, even if they didn't always practice it. Now I find more and more of them don't know. They don't think it's wrong to pick up another person's property without their permission or to go into somebody else's desk. They barge between two adults when they're talking and seem to lack manners in general. You want to ask them, "Didn't your mother ever teach you that?"

The question of whether schools or parents bear most of the blame is not an easy one to resolve; it's a chicken-and-egg dilemma: Parents influence the children first before they go to school, but schools shape the children before they become parents. In any event, one thing is clear: When both fail to hand on the stock of knowledge, experience, and example that constitutes a culture's moral capital, children are in trouble. They begin to resemble not Noble Savages but simply savages. We can see the effects of moral illiteracy in the increasingly casual nature of crime. Police report that growing numbers of young lawbreakers seem to have no sense of human community, no point of contact. Many young murderers and muggers sincerely do not understand what they have done wrong or why they should be punished. They are outside the common moral culture. The cool, blank stare one sometimes encounters among young criminals is blank in part because the light of civilization has gone out of it.

This phenomenon is not simply a matter of insufficient education—if by education we mean years of school completed. An illiterate and uneducated person can still be in touch with the moral inheritance of his culture. In *The Moral Life of Children,* Robert Coles shows how, even in the slums of Rio or in a sharecropper's shack in the rural South, children continue to learn the common ideals through church attendance, Bible stories, or the example of committed adults. In most societies, these informal attempts at inculcating moral culture are supplemented and complemented by the formal educational system. The two reinforce each other.

But when the schools stop contributing to the fund of shared moral knowledge, the informal systems are put under enormous strain. And when they start to break down, we begin to get a picture of what a society looks like when each person makes up his own "morality." By withholding the culture from a whole generation of youth, we are not helping them to "think for themselves," but only forcing them to patch together crude codes of behavior from the bits and pieces they pick up on television or in the streets.

What has been the reaction of educators to the decline of cultural literacy? One group, represented by people like Diane Ravitch, Chester Finn, and William Bennett, has called for a renewed emphasis on the unifying themes of Western culture and history. Another, considerably larger group continues to argue that critical thinking is more important than cultural content. In addition, there is a third group. The argument of this group—the multiculturalists—is that a multiracial, multiethnic society such as ours deserves a multicultural curriculum. In one version of multiculturalism, this means enriching the common culture by looking at the contributions of many groups; in another version, it means that black students study black history, literature, and culture while Hispanic students study Hispanic culture—and so on, down the line. Multiculturalists also favor greater "diversity" in the curriculum but, once again, there is disagreement over what this entails. For some it means paying attention to a greater diversity of ethnic groups; for others it means giving more consideration to homosexuals and other "neglected" minorities. Several states are now considering revisions that would make their curriculums more diverse, and in colleges and universities, courses are already being monitored for diversity. It is, depending on how you look at it, education's latest crusade or its latest fad.

Being against multiculturalism is a little like being against motherhood—indeed, opposition to it is a much more serious offense than opposition to motherhood. It is a difficult position to be in because, of course, there is a lot to be said for knowing your roots and understanding other cultures. In addition, America *is* a multiethnic society fed by many streams and tributaries. The more American students can know about this complex mix, the better.

For one group of multiculturalists—sometimes referred to as "pluralists"—that is what multicultural education means: a greater appreciation for the many strands that make up our common heritage. But many of the multiculturalists have staked out a more radical agenda. They don't want a richer common culture. Instead, they insist that no common culture is desirable. Critics of this "separatist" brand of multicultural education claim that its real mission is to discredit and destroy the common culture altogether. That was certainly the import of the much publicized affair at Stanford University in 1988 when students chanted, "Western culture's gotta go," and the administration responded by immediately watering down the Western Civilization Program. Since then, the attack on our so-called "Eurocentric" culture has been stepped up. It is widely criticized as being inherently racist, sexist, classist, and homophobic. More and more high schools, as a result, are dropping their European history offering and cutting back on American history until the textbooks can be rewritten.

What does this mean for moral education and for the common moral culture? According to historian Arthur Schlesinger, Jr., "if separatist tendencies go unchecked, the result can only be the fragmentation, resegregation and tribalization of American life." I fear that the loss of unifying moral ideals—moral illiteracy—will mean the same thing. We can see the effect of racial and ethnic separatism in the Soviet Union, in Yugoslavia, India, Sri Lanka, Iraq, Cyprus, Lebanon—all over the world. It's a formula for violence. In *Illiberal Education,* Dinesh D'Souza makes a convincing case that the ideology and practice of multicultural separatism have already led to a marked increase of racial tension and hostility on university campuses. That, I suspect, is nothing compared to what will happen once the idea hits the schools and the streets.

Given the fractured nature of present-day American society, it seems the height of folly to think that what we need is an experiment in more fractionalization. In the extreme form of diversity education—the form that now seems ascendant—there are no transcendent themes or common commitments, just a plurality of groups fighting to establish their individual identities and claims. It is the opposite of the historic American goal of assimilation and integration.

It is also—and this I believe is its central purpose—simply another way of introducing relativism into American schools. After the fall of the Berlin Wall, journalists discovered that most American teenagers could not understand the significance of the event. For them the Communist bloc was just another culture with its own way of doing things. A substitute teacher in a Virginia suburb who polled his students in three advanced government classes a few years ago found that fifty-one out of fifty-three of them saw no moral difference between the American system of government and that of the Soviet Union. The two who could see a difference were both Vietnamese boat children.

From the extreme multiculturalist point of view, all cultures are created equal and no system of values is less valid than another—except, of course, traditional Western values, which are highly suspect. Back in the mid-sixties the National Science Foundation funded—at a cost of $7 million—a series of textbooks for fifth-graders called *Man: A Course of Study* (MACOS). The title is a bit odd in view of the fact that most of the units in the curriculum discuss animals. The one unit that deals with humans concentrates on the Netsilik Eskimos and pays much attention to their practices of cannibalism, wife sharing, and abandonment of the aged. In the words of one MACOS critic, these practices "are consistently portrayed as plausible and natural responses to the social situation."

MACOS was the social studies equivalent of Values Clarification. It was the philosophy of nonjudgmentalism writ large: in other words, who is to say that what this group or that group of people does is right or wrong? Many of those who call themselves multiculturalists appear to be engaged in another, though far more comprehensive, attempt to install both cultural and ethical relativism into the heart of the curriculum. Teaching the language, art, and history of other societies seems to be the last thing on their minds. When one reads through the reports and recommendations of various committees on diversity, one experiences a strong sense of déjà vu: the language of the reports is not the language of history and culture but the language of therapeutic education. A task force on minority education appointed by the New York State commissioner of education recommended in 1990 that Western civilization be deemphasized so minority students "will have higher self-esteem and self-respect." In a similar vein, exponents of "Afrocentric" education have begun to fabricate new versions of black history that will serve as a form of therapy for young blacks. Self-acceptance, rather than accurate knowledge, sets the agenda.

Such tampering with historical facts is not a problem for many advocates of diversity, since the notion of objectivity is seen as an imposition of Western culture. For some this applies not only to historical accuracy but also to scientific and mathematical accuracy. According to Professor Peggy Means McIntosh of Wellesley College, "exact thinking" is no longer desirable in science. Indeed, according to another educator, there may be "no right or wrong answer" to the question "How much is one subtracted from four?" That is the conclusion of "The Challenge of Multiculturalism," an article that appeared in *American Counselor,* and was highly recommended by some of my colleagues.

This is not reassuring. These ideas are taken far more seriously in educational circles than can be imagined by those outside the field. It is especially disturbing when we ask what such relativism might mean for moral education. If advocates of diversity think there is no right and wrong when it comes to simple math, what will they say about simple morality? Does cultural diversity imply moral diversity?

That appears to be the case for many influential diversity advocates. For example, one of the four preferred approaches to multicultural education identified by the American Association of Colleges for Teacher Education is "the support of explorations in alternative and emerging lifestyles." Likewise, "skills for values clarification" is one of the four objectives for multicultural education listed by the National Council for Accreditation of Teacher Education. The buzzwords of humanistic psychology flow like a leitmotif through the literature of multiculturalism. One article states that "it is wrong to assume that one set of values is superior to any other," and that "nonjudgmental diversity is our strength as a nation." A book titled *Schooling for Social Diversity* invokes the phrase "tolerance for diversity" over and over. Other spokespersons for the movement speak of "holistic processes," "many realities," "multiple perspectives," and that old standby, the danger of "imposing values." Many multiculturalists also want to include sexual orientation as a form of diversity—a tactic that removes homosexuality from the universe of moral judgment, and makes being gay equivalent to being Jewish or Chinese. Still other multiculturalists embrace a mystical primitivism. Wade Nobles, one of the featured speakers at the National Conference on the Infusion of African and African-American Content in the High School Curriculum, described the superiority of black Africans in the following terms: "We are the creative cause . . . Black folk *be.* We *be.* We be doin' it. And our bodies tell us our physical essence and we don't listen."

This Atlanta-based conference, which included shell horns, drums, dancing girls, and bare chested men in sashes, was not exactly a fringe event. The conference was sponsored by major publishers and was attended by more than a thousand teachers and administrators. Thomas Sobol, the New York State commissioner of education, addressed the meeting. Asa Hillard, a member of his task force, organized it. Its guiding document, *The Portland African-American Baseline Essays,* is, according to a recent *Time* article, "radically changing the curriculums of school systems all over the country."

The Atlanta conference is instructive. The reporter who covered it for the *New Republic* notes that Western philosophy was described as "vomit," and "all the major religions of the world" were dismissed as "male chauvinist murder cults." He reports that "Plato and Aristotle were vilified" regularly during the two days of seminars. Plato and Aristotle are, of course, intimately tied to the tradition of teaching the virtues. Although most of Aristotle's science has been superseded, his ethical theory remains a key source of our present laws and moral codes. One wonders what it is about him that so rankles a conference of high school teachers. Is character also a Western cultural invention? Is virtue?

From the point of view of reestablishing cultural and moral literacy, these developments within the multicultural movement are not promising. The answer to the problem of cultural illiteracy is not to teach bits and pieces of other cultures while devaluing the Western tradition. Students are far more in need of simple perspective than they are of multiple perspectives. To assign equal validity to all cultures, customs, and values is to create the educational equivalent of a Tower of Babel. The result is bound to be both cultural and moral confusion.

Few cultures are free of racial or ethnic antagonisms. In many parts of the world, women are almost totally subject to men. Clitoridectomies are still performed among some African tribes. Wife beating is considered a minor matter in India and in some Latin societies. Child prostitution is not uncommon in some parts of the world. Slavery reportedly still exists in Mauritania and the Sudan. Infanticide is practiced in parts of China. In dozens of societies, civil rights and free speech are only words. What is a child supposed to make of these multicultural items? What *can* he make of them if he is taught that there are no right or wrong ways, just different ways? What he needs is some way of making sense of such facts, of ordering and judging them. That is the point of transmitting a whole culture. Otherwise the child is adrift on a sea of relativism with no compass.

The Western tradition provides such a standard of judgment. And more than other traditions, it provides a standard for judging its own sins. As Arthur Schlesinger, Jr., points out, "The crimes of the West have produced their own antidotes. They have provoked great movements to end slavery, to raise the status of women, to abolish torture, to combat racism . . . to advance personal liberty and human rights." It is to the Western standard that groups and individuals in other societies appeal when they seek to redress injustices within their own borders. It makes no sense to deprive our own children of that standard.

It is by no means a narrow standard. The Western tradition— and in particular, the American tradition—is open to a wide diversity of peoples, creeds, and cultures. "Paradoxical though it may seem," writes Diane Ravitch, "the United States has a common culture that is multicultural." No doubt there is room for improvement. And no doubt there is much to be learned from other cultures. But what needs to be asked is whether that is the sort of thing that anti-Western multiculturalists really want. One can look at the multicultural movement as an exciting and much needed new step in education, or as another, perhaps tragic, misstep. It takes a long time to build up a tradition of shared ideals and civilized habits, but it can be torn down in a surprisingly short time. Once it is gone, it is not easily restored.

VISION AND
VIRTUE

One way to counter moral illiteracy is to acquaint youngsters with stories and histories that can give them a common reference point and supply them with a stock of good examples. One of the early calls for returning stories to the curriculum was made by William Bennett in a speech before the Manhattan Institute:

> Do we want our children to know what honesty means? Then we might teach them about Abe Lincoln walking three miles to return six cents and, conversely, about Aesop's shepherd boy who cried wolf.
>
> Do we want our children to know what courage means? Then we might teach them about Joan of Arc, Horatius at the Bridge, Harriet Tubman and the Underground Railroad.
>
> Do we want them to know about kindness and compassion, and their opposites? Then they should read *A Christmas Carol* and *The Diary of Anne Frank* and, later on, *King Lear*.

It's a long list and one that no doubt would have horrified Rousseau. Among the reasons Bennett puts forward in arguing for the primacy of stories are that "unlike courses in moral reasoning," they provide a "stock of examples illustrating what we believe to be right and wrong," and that they "help anchor our children in their culture, its history and traditions. They give children a mooring." "This is necessary," he continues, "because morality, of course, is inextricably bound both to the individual conscience and the memory of society . . . We should teach these accounts of character to our children so that we may welcome them to a common world . . ."

Bennett is not liked in teachers colleges and schools of education. He wasn't liked when he was secretary of education, and the legacy he left makes him unpopular still. As education secretary he stood for all those things progressive educators thought they had gotten rid of once and for all. He wanted to reemphasize content—not just any content but the content of Western culture. And he wanted to return character education to the schools. His emphasis on stories of virtue and heroism was an affront to the Rousseau/Dewey tradition that had dominated education for years. Furthermore, by slighting "moral reasoning," Bennett also managed to alienate the party of critical thinking. Educators reacted angrily. Bennett was accused of being simplistic, reactionary, and worst of all, dogmatic. William Damon of Brown University, himself the author of a book on moral development, wrote that "Bennett's aversion to conscious moral decision making is itself so misguided as to present a threat to the very democratic traditions that he professes to cherish. Habit without reflection is adaptive only in a totalitarian climate."

Yet Bennett's concern over character was not simply a conservative phenomenon. Liberals too were having second thoughts about a moral education that relied only on moral reasoning. In a 1988 speech that could easily have been mistaken for one of Bennett's, Derek Bok, the president of Harvard University, stated:

> Socrates sometimes talked as if knowledge alone would suffice to ensure virtuous behavior. He did not stress the value of early habituation, positive example and obedience

to rules in giving students the desire and self-discipline to live up to their beliefs and to respect the basic norms of behavior essential to civilized communities.

Bok went on to call for "a broader effort to teach by habit, example and exhortation," and unlike Bennett, he was speaking not of the elementary or high school but of the university level.

Nevertheless, one still finds a resistance among educators toward the kind of stories Bennett recommends—stories that teach by example. I don't mean this in a conspiratorial sense. I find this reaction in student teachers who have never heard of Bennett. Moreover, as far as I know, no committee of educators ever came together to promulgate an antistory agenda. It has been more a matter of climate, and of what the climate would allow. In my conversations with teachers and would-be teachers, one of the most common themes I hear is their conviction that they simply don't have the right to tell students anything about right and wrong. Many have a similar attitude toward literature with a moral; they would also feel uneasy about letting a story do the telling for them. The most pejorative word in their vocabulary is "preach." But the loss of stories doesn't strike them as a serious loss. They seem to be convinced that whatever is of value in the old stories will be found out anyway. Some are Rousseauians and believe it will be found out through instinct; others subscribe to some version or other of critical thinking and believe it will be found out through reason.

The latter attitude is a legacy of the Enlightenment, but it is far more widespread now than it ever was in the eighteenth century. The argument then and now is as follows: Stories and myth may have been necessary to get the attention of ignorant farmers and fishermen, but intelligent people don't need to have their ethical principles wrapped in a pretty box; they are perfectly capable of grasping the essential point without being charmed by myths, and because they can reach their own conclusions, they are less susceptible to the harmful superstitions and narrow prejudices that may be embedded in stories. This attitude may be characterized as one of wanting to establish the moral of the story without the story. It does not intend to do away with morality but to make it more secure by disentangling it from a web of fictions. For example, during the Enlightenment the Bible came to be looked upon as an attempt to convey a set of advanced ethical ideas to primitive people who could understand them only if they were couched in story form. A man of the Enlightenment, however, could dispense with the stories and myths, mysteries and miracles, could dispense, for that matter, with a belief in God, and still retain the essence—the Christian ethic.

Kohlberg's approach to moral education is in this tradition. His dilemmas are stories of a sort, but they are stories with the juice squeezed out of them. Who really cares about Heinz and his wife (the couple in the stolen drug dilemma)? They are simply there to present a dilemma. And this is the way Kohlberg wanted it. Once you've thought your way through to a position on the issue, you can forget about Heinz. The important thing is to understand the principles involved. Moreover, a real story with well-defined characters might play on a child's emotions and thus intrude on his or her thinking process.

But is it really possible to streamline morality in this way? Can we extract the ethical kernel and discard the rest? Or does something vital get lost in the process? As the noted short story writer Flannery O'Connor put it, "A story is a way to say something that can't be said any other way . . . . You tell a story because a statement would be inadequate." In brief, can we have the moral of the story without the story? And if we can, how long can we hold it in our hands before it begins to dissolve?

The danger of such abstraction is that we quickly tend to forget the human element in morality. The utilitarian system of ethics that was a product of the English Enlightenment provides a good illustration of what can happen. It was a sort of debit-credit system of morality in which the rightness or wrongness of acts depended on their usefulness in maintaining a smoothly running social machine. Utilitarianism oiled the cogs of the Industrial Revolution by providing reasonable justifications for child labor, dangerous working conditions, long hours and low wages. For the sake of an abstraction—"the greatest happiness for the greatest number"—utilitarianism was willing to ignore the real human suffering created by the factory system.

Some of the most powerful attacks on that system can be found in the novels of Charles Dickens. Dickens brought home to his readers the human face of child labor and debtor's prison. And he did it in a way that was hard to ignore or shake off. Such graphic "reminders" may come to us through reading or they may come to us through personal experience, but without them, even the most intelligent and best-educated person will begin to lose sight of the fact that moral issues are human issues.

I use the words "lose sight of" advisedly. There is an important sense in which morality has a visual base—or, if you want, a visible base. In other words, there is a connection between virtue and vision. One has to see correctly before one can act correctly. This connection was taken quite seriously in the ancient world. Plato's most famous parable—the parable of the cave—explains moral confusion in terms of simple misdirected vision: the men in the cave are looking in the wrong direction. Likewise, the Bible prophets regarded moral blindness not only as a sin but as the root of a multitude of sins.

The reason why seeing is so important to the moral life is that many of the moral facts of life are apprehended through observation. Much of the moral law consists of axioms or premises about human beings and human conduct. And one does not arrive at premises by reasoning. You either see them or you don't. The Declaration of Independence's assertion that some truths are "self-evident" is one example of this visual approach to right and wrong. The word "evident" means "present and plainly visible." Many of Abraham Lincoln's arguments were of the same order. When Southern slave owners claimed the same right as Northerners to bring their "property" into the new territories, Lincoln replied: "That is to say, inasmuch as you do not object to my taking my hog to Nebraska, therefore I must not object to your taking your slave. Now, I admit this is perfectly logical, if there is no difference between hogs and Negroes."

Lincoln's argument against slavery is not logical but definitional. It is a matter of plain sight that Negroes are persons. But even the most obvious moral facts can be denied or explained away once the imagination becomes captive to a distorted vision. The point is illustrated by a recent Woody Allen film, *Crimes and*

Misdemeanors. The central character, Judah Rosenthal, who is both an ophthalmologist and a philanthropist, is faced with a dilemma: What should he do about his mistress? She has become possessive and neurotic and has started to do what mistresses are never supposed to do: she has begun to make phone calls to his office and to his home, thus threatening to completely ruin his life—a life that in many ways has been one of service. Judah seeks advice from two people: his brother Jack, who has ties to the underworld, and a rabbi, who tries to call Judah back to the vision of his childhood faith. The rabbi (who is nearly blind) advises Judah to end the relationship, even if it means exposure, and to ask his wife for forgiveness. Jack, on the other hand, having ascertained the woman's potential for doing damage and her unwillingness to listen to reason, advises Judah to "go on to the next [logical] step," and he offers to have her "taken care of." The interesting thing is that Jack's reasoning powers are just as good as the rabbi's; and based on his vision of the world, they make perfect sense. You simply don't take the chance that a vindictive person will destroy your marriage and your career. And indeed, Jack finally wins the argument. In an imagined conversation, Judah tells the rabbi, "You live in the Kingdom of Heaven, Jack lives in the real world." The woman is "taken care of."

Jack's reasoning may be taken as an example of deranged rationality or—if you change your angle of vision—as the only smart thing to do. Certain moral principles make sense within the context of certain visions of life, but from within the context of other visions, they don't make much sense at all. From within the vision provided by the rabbi's faith, all lives are sacred; from Jack's viewpoint, some lives don't count.

Many of the moral principles we subscribe to seem reasonable to us only because they are embedded within a vision or world-view we hold to be true—even though we might not think very often about it. In the same way, a moral transformation is often accompanied by a transformation of vision. Many ordinary people describe their moral improvement as the result of seeing things in a different light or seeing them for the first time. "I was blind but now I see" is more than a line from an old hymn; it is the way a great many people explain their moral growth.

If we can agree that morality is intimately bound up with vision, then we can see why stories are so important for our moral development, and why neglecting them is a serious mistake. This is because stories are one of the chief ways by which visions are conveyed (a vision, in turn, may be defined as a story about the way things are or the way the world works). Just as vision and morality are intimately connected, so are story and morality. Some contemporary philosophers of ethics—most notably, Alasdair MacIntyre—now maintain that the connection between narrative and morality is an essential one, not merely a useful one. The Ph.D. needs the story "part" just as much as the peasant. In other words, story and moral may be less separable than we have come to think. The question is not whether the moral principle needs to be sweetened with the sugar of the story but whether moral principles make any sense outside the human context of stories. For example, since I referred earlier to the Enlightenment habit of distilling out the Christian ethic from the Bible, consider how much sense the following principles make when they are forced to stand on their own:

> Do good to those that harm you.
> - Turn the other cheek.
> - Walk an extra mile.
> - Blessed are the poor.
> - Feed the hungry.

"Feed the hungry" seems to have the most compelling claim on us, but just how rational is it? Science doesn't tell us to feed the hungry. Moreover, feeding the hungry defeats the purpose of natural selection. Why not let them die and thus "decrease the surplus population" as Ebenezer Scrooge suggests? Fortunately, the storyteller in this case takes care to put the suggestion in the mouth of a disagreeable old man.

Of course, there are visions or stories or ways of looking at life other than the Christian one, from which these counsels would still make sense. On the other hand, from some points of view they are sheer nonsense. Nietzsche, one of the great geniuses of philosophy, had nothing but contempt for the Christian ethic.

In recent years a number of prominent psychologists and educators have turned their attention to stories. In *The Uses of Enchantment* (1975), child psychiatrist Bruno Bettelheim argued that fairy tales are a vital source of psychological and moral strength; their formative power, he said, had been seriously underestimated. Robert Coles of Harvard University followed in the 1980s with three books *(The Moral Life of Children, The Spiritual Life of Children,* and *The Call of Stories)* which detailed the indispensable role of stories in the life of both children and adults. Another Harvard scholar, Jerome Bruner, whose earlier *The Process of Education* had helped stimulate interest in critical thinking, had, by the mid-eighties, begun to worry that "propositional thinking" had been emphasized at the expense of "narrative thinking"—literally, a way of thinking in stories. In *Actual Minds, Possible Worlds,* Bruner suggests that it is this narrative thought, much more than logical thought, that gives meaning to life.

A number of other psychologists had arrived at similar conclusions. Theodore Sarbin, Donald Spence, Paul Vitz, and others have emphasized the extent to which individuals interpret their own lives as stories or narratives. "Indeed," writes Vitz, "it is almost impossible not to think this way." According to these psychologists, it is such narrative plots more than anything else that guide our moral choices. Coles, in *The Moral Life of Children,* observes how the children he came to know through his work not only understood their own lives in a narrative way but were profoundly influenced in their decisions by the stories, often of a religious kind, they had learned.

By the mid-eighties a similar story had begun to unfold in the field of education. Under the leadership of Professor Kevin Ryan, Boston University's Center for the Advancement of Character and Ethics produced a number of position papers calling for a reemphasis on literature as a moral teacher and guide. Meanwhile, in *Teaching as Storytelling* and other books, Kieran Egan of Canada's Simon Fraser University was proposing that the foundations of all education are poetic and imaginative. Even logico-mathematical and rational forms of thinking grow out of imagination, and depend on it. Egan argues that storytelling should be the

basic educational method because it corresponds with fundamental structures of the human mind. Like Paul Vitz, he suggests
that it is nearly impossible not to think in story terms. "Most of the
world's cultures and its great religions," he points out, "have at
their sacred core a story, and we indeed have difficulty keeping
our rational history from being constantly shaped into stories."

In short, scholars in several fields were belatedly discovering
what Flannery O'Connor, with her writer's intuition, had noticed
years before: "A story is a way to say something that can't be said
any other way . . ."

This recent interest in stories should not, however, be interpreted as simply another Romantic reaction to rationalism. None
of the people I have mentioned could be classified as Romanticists. Several of them (including Flannery O'Connor) freely acknowledge their indebtedness to Aristotle and Aquinas—to what
might be called the "realist" tradition in philosophy. Although
literature can be used as an escape, the best literature, as Jacques
Barzun said, carries us back to reality. It involves us in the detail
and particularity of other lives. And unlike the superficial encounters of the workaday world, a book shows us what other lives are
like from the inside. Moral principles also take on a reality in
stories that they lack in purely logical form. Stories restrain our
tendency to indulge in abstract speculation about ethics. They
make it a little harder for us to reduce people to factors in an
equation.

I can illustrate the overall point by mentioning a recurrent
phenomenon in my classes. I have noticed that when my students
are presented with a Values Clarification strategy and then with a
dramatic account of the same situation, they respond one way to
the dilemma and another to the story. In the Values Clarification
dilemma called "The Lifeboat Exercise," the class is asked to
imagine that a ship has sunk and a lifeboat has been put out from
it. The lifeboat is overcrowded and in danger of being swamped
unless the load is lightened. The students are given a brief description of the passengers—a young couple and their child, an
elderly brother and sister, a doctor, a bookkeeper, an athlete, an
entertainer, and so on—and from this list they must decide whom
to throw overboard. Consistent with current thinking, there are

no right and wrong answers in this exercise. The idea is to generate discussion. And it works quite well. Students are typically excited by the lifeboat dilemma.

This scenario, of course, is similar to the situation that faced the crew and passengers of the *Titanic* when it struck an iceberg in the North Atlantic in 1912. But when the event is presented as a story rather than as a dilemma, the response evoked is not the same. For example, when students who have done the exercise are given the opportunity to view the film *A Night to Remember,* they react in a strikingly different way. I've watched classes struggle with the lifeboat dilemma, but the struggle is mainly an intellectual one—like doing a crossword puzzle. The characters in the exercise, after all, are only hypothetical. They are counters to be moved around at will. We can't really identify with them, nor can we be inspired or repelled by them. They exist only for the sake of the exercise.

When they watch the film, however, these normally blasé college students behave differently. Many of them cry. They cry as quietly as possible, of course: even on the college level it is extremely important to maintain one's cool. But this is a fairly consistent reaction. I've observed it in several different classes over several years. They don't even have to see the whole film. About twenty minutes of excerpts will do the trick.

What does the story do that the exercise doesn't? Very simply, it moves them deeply and profoundly. This is what art is supposed to do.

If you have seen the film, you may recall some of the vivid sketches of the passengers on the dying ship as the situation becomes clear to them: Edith Evans, giving up a place on the last boat to Mrs. Brown, saying, "You go first; you have children waiting at home." Harvey Collyer pleading with his wife, "Go, Lottie! For God's sake, be brave and go! I'll get a seat in another boat." Mrs. Isidor Straus declining a place in the boats: "I've always stayed with my husband, so why should I leave him now?"

The story is full of scenes like this: Arthur Ryerson stripping off his life vest and giving it to his wife's maid; men struggling below-decks to keep the pumps going in the face of almost certain death; the ship's band playing ragtime and then hymns till the very end;

the women in boat 6 insisting that it return to pick up survivors; the men clinging to the hull of an overturned boat, reciting the Lord's Prayer; the *Carpathia,* weaving in and out of ice floes, racing at breakneck speed to the rescue. But there are other images as well: the indolence and stupidity of the *California*'s crew who, only ten miles away, might have made all the difference, but did nothing; the man disguised in a woman's shawl; the panicked mob of men rushing a lifeboat; passengers in half-empty lifeboats refusing to go back to save the drowning.

The film doesn't leave the viewer much room for ethical maneuvering. It is quite clear who has acted well and who has not. And anyone who has seen it will come away hoping that if ever put to a similar test, he or she will be brave and not cowardly, will think of others rather than of self.

Not only does the film move us, it moves us in certain directions. It is definitive, not open-ended. We are not being asked to ponder a complex ethical dilemma; rather, we are being taught what is proper. There are codes of conduct: women and children first; duty to others before self. If there is a dilemma in the film, it does not concern the code itself. The only dilemma is the perennial one that engages each soul: conscience versus cowardice, faith versus despair.

This is not to say that the film was produced as a moral fable. It is, after all, a true story and a gripping one, the type of thing that almost demands cinematic expression—hardly a case of didacticism. In fact, if we were to level a charge of didacticism, it would have to be against "The Lifeboat Exercise." It is quite obviously an artificially contrived teaching exercise. But this is didacticism with a difference. "The Lifeboat Exercise" belongs to the age of relativism, and consequently, it has nothing to teach. No code of conduct is being passed down, no models of good and bad behavior are shown. Whether it is actually a good or bad thing to throw someone overboard is up to the youngster to decide for himself. The exercise is designed to initiate the group into the world of "each man his own moral compass."

Of course, we are comparing two somewhat different things: a story, on the one hand, and a discussion exercise, on the other. The point is that the logic of relativism necessitates the second approach. The story of the *Titanic* was surely known to the developers of "The Lifeboat Exercise." Why didn't they use it? The most probable answer is the one we have alluded to: The story doesn't allow for the type of dialogue desired. It marshals its audience swiftly and powerfully to the side of certain values. We feel admiration for the radio operators who stay at their post. We feel pity and contempt for the handful of male passengers who sneak into lifeboats. There are not an infinite number of ways in which to respond to these scenes, as there might be to a piece of abstract art. Drama is not the right medium for creating a value-neutral climate. It exerts too much moral force.

Drama also forces us to see things afresh. We don't always notice the humanity of the person sitting next to us on the bus. It is often the case that human beings and human problems must be presented dramatically for us to see them truly. Robert Coles relates an interesting anecdote in this regard about Ruby Bridges, the child who first integrated the New Orleans schools. Ruby had seen *A Raisin in the Sun,* and expressed to Coles the wish that white people would see it: "If all the [white] people on the street [who were heckling her mercilessly] saw that movie, they might stop coming out to bother us." When Coles asked her why she thought that, she answered, "Because the people in the movies would work on them, and maybe they'd listen." Ruby knew that whites who saw her every day didn't really see her. Maybe the movie would make them see.

Admittedly, I have been mixing media rather freely here, and this raises a question. Films obviously have to do with seeing, but how about books? The paradoxical answer is that the storyteller's craft is not only a matter of telling but also of showing. This is why writing is so often compared to painting, and why beginning writers are urged to visualize what they want to say. So, even when a writer has a moral theme, his work—if he is a good writer—is more like the work of an artist than a moralist. For example, C. S. Lewis's immensely popular children's books have strong moral and religious themes, but they were not conceived out of a moral intent. "All my seven Narnian books," Lewis wrote in 1960, "and my three science fiction books, began with seeing pictures in my head. At first they were not a story, just pictures.

The Lion [The Lion, the Witch and the Wardrobe] all began with a picture of a faun carrying an umbrella and parcels in a snowy wood."

Stories are essentially moving pictures. That is why they are so readily adaptable to the screen. And a well-made film, in turn, needs surprisingly little dialogue to make its point. When, in *A Night to Remember,* the shawl is torn away from the man's head, we do not have to be told anything. We *see* that his behavior is shameful; it is written on his face.

On the simplest level the moral force of a story or film is the force of example. It shows us examples of men and women acting well or trying to act well, or acting badly. The story points to these people and says in effect, "Act like this; don't act like that." Except that, of course, nothing of the kind is actually stated. It is a matter of showing. There is, for instance, a scene in *Anna Karenina* in which Levin sits by the side of his dying brother and simply holds his hand for an hour, and then another hour. Tolstoy doesn't come out and say that this is what he ought to do, but the scene is presented in such a way that the reader knows that it is the right thing to do. It is, to use a phrase of Bruno Bettelheim's, "tangibly right."

"Do I have to draw you a picture?" That much used put-down implies that normally intelligent people can do without graphic illustration. But when it comes to moral matters, it may be that we do need the picture more than we think. The story suits our nature because we think more readily in pictures than in propositions. And when a proposition or principle has the power to move us to action, it is often because it is backed up by a picture or image. Consider, for example, the enormous importance historians assign to a single book—*Uncle Tom's Cabin*—in galvanizing public sentiment against slavery. After the novel appeared, it was acted out on the stage in hundreds of cities. For the first time, vast numbers of Americans had a visible and dramatic image of the evils of slavery. Lincoln, on being introduced to author Harriet Beecher Stowe, greeted her with the words "So this is the little lady who started the big war." In more recent times the nation's conscience has been quickened by photo images of civil rights workers marching arm in arm, kneeling in prayer, and under police attack. It is nice to think that moral progress is the result of better reasoning, but it is naive to ignore the role of the imagination in our moral life.

The more abstract our ethic, the less power it has to move us. Yet the progression of recent decades has been in the direction of increasing verbalization and abstraction, toward a reason dissociated from ordinary feelings and cut off from images that convey humanness to us. "At the core of every moral code," observed Walter Lippmann, "there is a picture of human nature." But the picture coming out of our schools increasingly resembles a blank canvas. The deep human sympathies—the kind we acquire from good literature—are missing.

Perhaps the best novelistic portrait of disconnected rationalism is that of Raskolnikov in *Crime and Punishment*. Raskolnikov has mastered the art of asking the question "Why not?" What is wrong with killing a repulsive old woman? he asks himself. What is wrong with taking her money and using it for a worthy cause— namely, to pay for his own education? With that education, Raskolnikov eventually plans to bring his intellectual gifts to the service of mankind. It is good utilitarian logic.

In commenting on *Crime and Punishment*, William Barrett observes that in the days and weeks after the killing, "a single image breaks into this [Raskolnikov's] thinking." It is the image of his victim, and this image saves Raskolnikov's soul. Not an idea but an image. For Dostoevsky the value of each soul was a mystery that could never be calculated but only shown.

The same theme recurs in *The Brothers Karamazov*. At the very end of the book, Alyosha speaks to the youngsters who love him: "My dear children . . . You must know that there is nothing higher and stronger and more wholesome and useful for life in after years than some good memory, especially a memory connected with childhood, with home. People talk to you a great deal about your education, but some fine, sacred memory, preserved from childhood, is perhaps the best education. If a man carries many such memories with him into life, he is safe to the end of his days, and if we have only one good memory left in our hearts, even that may sometime be the means of saving us."

There is no point in trying to improve on this. Let us only

observe that what Dostoevsky says of good memories is true also of good stories. Some of our "sacred" memories may find their source in stories.

We carry around in our heads many more of these images and memories than we realize. The picture of Narcissus by the pool is probably there for most of us; and the Prodigal Son and his forgiving father likely inhabit some corner of our imagination. Atticus Finch, Ebenezer Scrooge, Laura Ingalls Wilder, Anne Frank, David and Goliath, Abraham Lincoln, Peter and the servant girl: for most of us these names will call up an image, and the image will summon up a story. The story in turn may give us the power or resolve to struggle through a difficult situation or to overcome our own moral sluggishness. Or it may simply give us the power to see things clearly. Above all, the story allows us to make that human connection we are always in danger of forgetting.

Most cultures have recognized that morality, religion, story, and myth are bound together in some vital way, and that to sever the connections among them leaves us not with strong and independent ethical principles but with weak and unprotected ones. What "enlightened" thinkers in every age envision is some sort of progression from story to freestanding moral principles unencumbered by stories. But the actual progression never stops there. Once we lose sight of the human face of principle, the way is clear for attacking the principles themselves as merely situational or relative. The final stage of the progression is moral nihilism and the appeal to raw self-interest—the topics of the next chapter.

8.

MORALITY MAKES
STRANGE
BEDFELLOWS

Professor Carol Gilligan seems, at first glance, a likely candidate
for establishing moral education on a better footing. Her theory
makes room for the apparent fact that men and women have
different cognitive styles. She sees the danger of abstract ethics—
the danger of forgetting about real people. She emphasizes the
importance of care and connectedness. She recognizes, as Kohlberg did not, the importance of myth and story, and she takes care
to illustrate her ideas with examples from legends and novels.
Finally, one sees in her work none of the simpleminded relativism
of Values Clarification. Gilligan is aware that moral decisions call
for a balancing of individual needs and social needs—something
that never seems to have occurred to the developers of Values
Clarification.

In some educational circles, Gilligan is looked upon as a savior
who will deliver children from the cold, lifeless world of male
morality and into a warm network of caring relationships. Along
with a handful of other psychologists, she is credited with discov-

ering that women have a different way of knowing, and a different orientation toward morality. Gilligan says that women are interested in relationships, not rules: consequently, they base their moral decisions on those relationships, not on abstract notions of right and wrong. Gilligan suggests that because education is largely in the hands of women, women teachers have it within their power "to bring a new order of living into the world"—an order of caring.

Gilligan has not produced a curriculum toward this end, and neither, as far as I know, has anyone else. But she has introduced a hopeful note. Here, it seems, is the theory that can put the heart back into moral education. As promising as it seems, however, there are some jarring notes in the theory, which suggests a less happy outcome. Both Johnny and Jill may have to await another savior.

The first of these difficulties is that Gilligan, like Kohlberg and Simon, is not interested in moral content but in process—in her case, the process by which women arrive at moral decisions. Professor Gilligan built her theory by focusing on the decision-making process of twenty-nine women who were contemplating having abortions. Though the women themselves agonize over the decision, Gilligan does not. Either outcome (having the abortion or keeping the child) is valid as long as one can justify one's process of choosing. The only guideline Gilligan offers can be summed up in the phrase "Consider your own needs and the needs of others." At first glance, it seems like good advice, but when we see how it is actually used by the men and women Gilligan interviews, the guideline melts into air. It leaves them with an extraordinarily wide latitude. No matter what sort of behavior Gilligan's subjects engage in—having an abortion, not having an abortion, staying together, or breaking up—they are always able to rationalize it in terms of needs and relationships. And that, it seems, is all that is required. As long as you satisfy yourself that you are maintaining some sort of relationship with someone (even if only with yourself), you are in the clear. There are no external standards in Gilligan's system, any more than there are in Kohlberg's or Simon's. Nothing is right or wrong, but choosing makes it so.

The second problematic note in Gilligan's work is what might be described simply as "body faith." In a recent article, Gilligan repeatedly insists that a woman's knowledge of right and wrong comes not through the culture but through her body—"that repository of experience and desire." Then, in words that echo Rousseau's idea of the naturally wise child, she suggests that we "may also discover that we are harboring within ourselves a girl who lives in our body . . . who intensely desires relationships and knowledge." She further suggests that women teachers should not succumb to "the temptation to model perfection by trying to be perfect role models," lest by so doing they prevent adolescent girls from getting in touch with their own bodies and their own inner children.

Gilligan writes about eleven- and twelve-year-old girls as though they don't really need an education: all they need to know is what they already know from their relationships and their bodily experiences. A young girl's most dangerous enemy, it turns out, is the traditionally virtuous woman—or a junior version of her. "The mesmerizing presence of the perfect girl" suddenly "calls into question the reality which they have lived in—the moving, changing world of thoughts and feelings, relationships and people." In short, young girls who aren't careful of the company they keep run the danger of "disconnecting themselves from their bodies."

Gilligan is particularly proud of girls who speak openly of their sexual desire. She is concerned that young women are at risk for ignoring "desire or passion or pleasure." Her favorite term of approval for a young girl is "irreverent." All of this, of course, has a familiar ring. Although Gilligan insists that women speak in a different voice (*In a Different Voice* is the title of the book that established her reputation), this sounds very much like the voice of Rousseau.

This brings us to the third troublesome note in Gilligan's work—the political tone that pervades it. Gilligan says that girls who are in touch with their bodies, and who "know what they know," must inevitably become politicized because they will realize that society wants them to repress their bodies and their knowledge. What we call "morality," she strongly suggests, is simply another word for the values that men have imposed on women. Not surprisingly, her most recent article (the one I have been citing) is entitled "Joining the Resistance: Psychology, Politics, Girls and Women." It is about the "intersection between political resistance and psychological resistance" in adolescence, and how girls must resist the shaping power of Western culture. In a two-page version of the article condensed for the *Harvard Alumni Bulletin*, the word "resistance" occurs fifteen times.

The political note is even more pronounced in Gilligan's followers—those who are trying to elaborate on and extend her theories. A recent book on "the ethic of care" is a good example. It contains twelve articles by fifteen professors exploring the implications of Gilligan's work. Although the book is ostensibly about moral education, its heart belongs to radical politics. Its themes are not "character" or "virtue" but "power," "powerlessness," "racism," "sexism," "victimization," "subjugation," "state-sponsored violence," "oppressive structures," and "liberation." The word "care" is there also, but several of the authors wield it like an ax.

What is going on? To be sure, there is some overlap between morality and politics. And there is no doubt that politics affects our daily living in various degrees. Politics does matter. But to suggest to high school boys and girls (as these authors seem willing to suggest) that it is all that matters is another thing altogether. Not only does it shift the focus away from personal character, it thoroughly undermines it. If morality just boils down to politics, it means that youngsters needn't really concern themselves with developing character. Instead of reforming themselves, their job is to reform society. This is not unlike the Marxist idea that the revolution must come first, and all else will follow. And besides, who needs bourgeois morality?

Many schools are interested in Gilligan's ideas about moral education. And understandably so. It is to be hoped that schools can find ways to teach care and cooperation to students. At the same time, this particular care package needs close examination. It has unpromising precedents.

As any number of commentators have noted, universities have become highly politicized in recent years. On many campuses, the university is no longer viewed as a place where one pursues truth but as a place where one pursues power. Campuses have become divided along race, class, and gender lines. Feminist scholars, many of them influenced by Gilligan's theories, have taken the lead in this politicization and polarization; some of them look upon the classroom as akin to a political cell—a place for raising consciousness.

It would be unfortunate if these class and gender wars were introduced into elementary and high schools. But there are signs this may happen. Much of the agenda for primary and secondary schools is set in university schools of education, and such schools have not escaped the general politicization of university life. After spending two years visiting education schools across the country, author Rita Kramer concluded that the typical "ed school" is more concerned with politics than academics. She reports that an extraordinary amount of course time is spent teaching future teachers about "oppressive systems," "power structures," and "the class system" (not to be confused with the classroom system).

What may be the opening salvo in the attempt to raise gender consciousness on the elementary and secondary levels is a widely publicized report just released by the American Association of University Women, and compiled by the Wellesley College Center for Research on Women. Despite the fact that 72 percent of all elementary and secondary teachers are female, and despite the fact that girls get better grades than boys, are less likely to drop out of school, and are more likely to go on to college, the report nevertheless claims that schools are biased against girls. The authors of the report complain that after "twenty years of consciousness raising," the subject of "gender politics" is still ignored in schools.

The report calls for stricter enforcement of antidiscrimination laws, required coursework for teachers and administrators on "gender-fair" and multicultural curriculums, and evaluation of teachers and administrators based on the degree to which they promote "gender-equitable and multicultural education" (the report endorses the New York State plan prepared for education commissioner Thomas Sobol). The list of recommendations is full of "musts": "The Women's Educational Equity Act Program (WEEAP) in the U.S. Department of Education must receive increased funding." "Federal and state funding must be used to support research, development, and follow-up study of gender-fair multicultural curricular models." "Comprehensive school-based health-and-sex-education programs must begin in the early grades and continue sequentially through twelfth grade."

What kind of sex education? The report lauds school-based clinics, says that "the assumption of heterosexuality is a form of discrimination," and wants courses to emphasize "the body as a source of joy, pleasure and comfort." In the several pages devoted to teen pregnancy and sex education, not a word is said about abstinence. The report does, however, somehow manage to link the teen pregnancy problem with traditional Western values. "Western culture," it says, "has honored the role of mothers above all others for women." This, suggests the report, has been a big mistake, since such honoring creates an incentive for teen motherhood.

The tortuous logic involved in arriving at that conclusion suggests that this report on gender bias has a bias of its own—against Western culture. The truth is that Western culture has always honored *married* motherhood, but has always frowned on motherhood out of wedlock. It has also held up the ideal that sex is to be reserved for marriage. If sexually active teenagers are acting within any tradition, it is not the Western tradition but the more recent "tradition" espoused by the report of looking on the body "as a source of joy, pleasure and comfort," and not looking much beyond that.

The fact that married motherhood is less honored today than ever before suggests that the report's authors are tracking the wrong suspect. Another of their complaints is that sexual harassment of girls by boys is increasing and is tolerated by teachers and administrators. But this, along with the problem of out-of-wedlock pregnancy, is not a result of the Western cultural influence but rather a result of its decline. The Western ideal for men was embodied first in the code of chivalry and then in the code of the gentleman. However unfashionable such codes may be at present, it should be noted that they did not countenance the sexual harassment of women. Federal antidiscrimination laws or school district antiharassment policies may serve as substitutes for such internalized codes of gentlemanly behavior, but they are poor substitutes.

The real solution to the moral problems raised in the AAUW report is to address them as problems of character rather than as political problems requiring political solutions. The other solution proposed by the report—to have schools function as social agencies and therapy centers "where girls and boys can express feelings and discuss personal experiences"—is no solution either. It has already been tried. Both "solutions" only serve to divert attention away from the demanding discipline of learning virtue.

Carol Gilligan is cited throughout the report, and its political tone is in keeping with her own. But there is more to Gilligan's theory than politics. Schools could conceivably avoid the problem of politicization by simply adopting Gilligan's "care perspective" and deleting the political aspect. Even so, a problem would remain. The problem is that Gilligan's ethic of care is not grounded in any solid concept of right and wrong; rather, the whole argument for it seems to be something along the lines of "Trust us: we're women and we care."

In view of the fact that women are much less involved in crime than men are, and much more involved in caring for the young and old, this is a tempting proposition. But it still leaves a number of questions unanswered. Does it mean that all of a woman's instincts are good and caring? If not, how does she know which instincts to follow? Doesn't culture play a part in guiding our instincts? For example, while it is true that women are more involved in caring activities than men are, it is also true that church attendance is much higher among women than men. Perhaps the key to making men care is to encourage them to go to church. But that is not the kind of recommendation one hears from social scientists.

Moreover, the traditional perception of feminine goodness is associated with women's willingness to make sacrifices and put others first. Women are generally perceived to be less selfish than men. But it is precisely this aspect of women's caring that troubles Gilligan. She criticizes both the ethic of sacrifice and "conventional conceptions of feminine 'goodness.' " Gilligan notes, apparently with approval, that early proponents of women's rights equated self-sacrifice with slavery, and she quotes Elizabeth Cady Stanton's declaration "Put it down in capital letters: SELF-DEVEL-OPMENT IS A HIGHER DUTY THAN SELF-SACRIFICE." Gilligan claims that the ethic of sacrifice is an immature moral orientation and should be replaced by an ethic that takes more account of one's own needs.

Although her advice has been hailed as revolutionary, it can just as easily be characterized as redundant. There has probably never been a time in history when individuals have been more focused on their own needs, and less imbued with an ethic of sacrifice and self-restraint, than our own. Historian James Lincoln Collier's recent book *The Rise of Selfishness in America* suggests that selfishness is the chief problem of our age. What is needed, says Collier, is a recovery of the ethic of sacrifice. It is true that women have always made great sacrifices and still do, but then, so does a man when he is playing his role properly in a family. A forty-hour work week plus overtime at an uninteresting job is not exactly the fulfillment of a man's impulses and yearnings, nor is the control he must exercise over his appetite for drink or sexual indulgence or over his fantasies of adventure and escape. Sacrifices—by both women and men—are essential to the moral order and to the healthy functioning of families.

Gilligan doesn't say that you can have care without sacrifice, but she and her various coauthors manage to considerably water down the meaning of such terms as "care," "responsibility," and "commitment." For example, Gilligan's book *Mapping the Moral Domain* contains an essay by Nona Lyons in which Lyons notes, "It was only in the nineteenth century that 'responsibility' became attached to moral accountability and rational conduct." Lyons prefers the earlier definition of "answering to something."

"Something" is, of course, rather a vague term, but Gilligan and her colleagues have a penchant for vagueness. They seem to have borrowed more than a page from Simone de Beauvoir's *The Ethics of Ambiguity.* In the preface to *Mapping the Moral Domain,* Gilligan suggests that a proper orientation toward moral problems will "create a genuine sense of moral ambiguity." In fact, Gilligan seems to think that it is a good idea to maintain a sense of ethical ambiguity, although, as she admits, "the persistent error in care reasoning is vacillation and lack of clear judgment resulting from a tendency to include all possible ways of seeing."

What does become clear from a careful reading of Gilligan's work is that there is nothing binding or absolute in her care perspective. It is all situational, relational, and nonjudgmental. Does caring ever mean "for better or worse, for richer or poorer, in sickness and in health"? One does not come away with that impression. In Gilligan's comparison of George Eliot's *The Mill on the Floss* (1860) with Margaret Drabble's retelling of the tale in *The Waterfall* (1969), Gilligan seems to condone Drabble's heroine, who steals her friend's husband. I say "seems" because it is never entirely clear what Gilligan believes about anything. But she does think it worthwhile to quote one particular passage in which the heroine says, "If I cannot act without my own approbation—and I must act, I have changed, I am no longer capable of inaction—then I will invent a morality that condones me."

Are there any objective standards in the care perspective? At one point, Gilligan does say that "care can be 'principled'—governed by standards of authentic relationship." But here again, we are back in murky waters. What is an "authentic" relationship? Can't any two teenagers involved in a sexual relationship convince themselves they have an authentic relationship? Can't any man who is carrying on an affair assure himself that his relationship with his lover is more authentic than his relationship with his wife? It is precisely because of our tendency to deceive ourselves about such matters that all cultures have felt it necessary to spell out which sorts of relationships are valid and which are not. But Gilligan doesn't want relationships to be guided or bounded by cultural prescriptions. Instead, she wants to create an instant new tradition—"a new order of living"—without reference to religion or custom or culture, but simply spun out of our "web of relationships"—a web that, as she fails to realize, depends very much on the absolute proscriptions and prescriptions for which she has no use.

It is all wonderfully unspecific and full of so many relational loopholes and ambiguities that it can be interpreted almost any way the reader pleases. It is interesting to note that *Changing Bodies, Changing Lives,* the book that introduces junior high schoolers to the joy of sex, devotes four double-column pages to explaining Gilligan's concept of "voices." The remarks come at the head of a chapter entitled "Exploring Sex with Someone Else (Heterosexuality and Homosexuality)." And what follows leaves little doubt that the authors are confident that after listening to the various voices, teens will want to go ahead and explore. The rest of the chapter is taken up with explicit instruction in lovemaking interspersed with the "voices" of teenagers who have tried sex and enjoyed it immensely. As the authors well realize, Gilligan's "listen-to-the-voices" approach is just another variation of the decision-making/"choose-your-own-morality" model.

Ironically, there *is* a well-thought-out philosophy of caring in natural law theory, but the concept of natural law is rejected by the vast majority of feminist scholars. Natural law theory spells out responsibilities that are built into the nature of human relationships. For example, parents have duties of care toward their children because children are, in fact, dependent on their parents. Likewise, children owe honor and obedience to their parents because of the protection and nourishment they receive, and because their parents have given them the gift of life. Similarly, divorce is wrong because, by the very nature of family life, it is harmful to children.

But such specific familial obligations are the last thing feminist thinkers want to talk about. In fact, as Christina Hoff Sommers points out, most contemporary feminist moral philosophers feel that the only obligations we have are the ones we freely choose. On the face of it, that seems reasonable, but, as Sommers observes, the idea is "generally fatal to family morality," since most family relationships are not voluntary. Brothers and sisters do not choose each other, and children don't choose their parents ("I didn't ask to be born into this family" is a familiar complaint). Does this mean that children needn't obey their parents? According to Sommers, that is exactly what some philosophers now claim. The family, they say, is just another relationship based on power.

In short, there are no natural obligations. Rita Kramer quotes a professor at Columbia University Teachers College as telling her class: "Relativism is a good thing. Our aim should be to involve as many people with their multiple voices as possible. . . . There are no 'objective standards,' there is no such thing as 'objective norms.' " The professor next addresses Hannah Arendt's espousal of an objective moral law, the law that made possible the trial of Nazi war criminals. "There is no such law," says the professor. Apparently, everything is power politics.

It would be unfair to lump Carol Gilligan together with all feminist thinkers as though no significant differences existed among them. Nevertheless, her ideas about caring seem to be characterized by a similar lack of norms. In the final analysis, "caring" is what you say it is.

Since the notion of "caring" is such an attractive one, it is important for parents and teachers to understand that the version of it that Gilligan and other educators have in mind is bound up with some rather exotic ideas about ethics. Ironically, a good deal of feminist thought, Gilligan's included, can be traced to a thinker whose worldview was based on contempt rather than care.

The thinker I refer to is the nineteenth-century German philosopher Friedrich Nietzsche, a man whose philosophy may be summed up as the worship of power and genius. Nietzsche comes to modern feminist psychology by way of the French writer and philosopher Simone de Beauvoir. The more extreme forms of current feminist thought really begin with one book, de Beauvoir's *The Second Sex,* and de Beauvoir had a lifelong dedication to the ideas of Nietzsche. All her energies were directed to enlisting women into the ranks of those superior types celebrated by Nietzsche: those who make, and break, and recast values. As de Beauvoir insisted, however, the goal of creating new moralities would always elude women as long as they were subject to the "slavery" of marriage and motherhood.

To understand de Beauvoir is to understand much of feminist thought. But in order to understand both, we have to step back for a moment and take a closer look at Nietzsche. Once we understand him, many pieces of our current moral jigsaw puzzle will fall into place.

At its core, Nietzsche's philosophy is pure nihilism. But one hardly notices the nihilism at first. What one sees initially is the call to a higher life: a life that is lived adventurously, experimentally, even dangerously. As literary critic Terry Eagleton observes: "Much of Nietzsche's writing reads like a brochure for a youth adventure scheme." Nietzsche exalts the drama of life. He wants to see it lived to the fullest. He celebrates the body. He celebrates the irrational and "Dionysian" part of our nature. He detests hypocrisy and conformism. He is, in some senses, a Romantic, but it is not the sunny Romanticism of Rousseau. He is far more honest than Rousseau, and not at all sentimental. His criticisms of the Enlightenment go much deeper. He rips off the veil of rationalism, and shows there is nothing beneath it.

What did Nietzsche have to say about morality? Nothing that ordinary citizens could take comfort in. As far as Nietzsche was concerned, morality was good only *for* ordinary people. It was an invention of Jews and Christians. He called it "slave morality." His own interest was focused on an extraordinary type of individual: what he called the superman, or, in German, *Übermensch*. The superman does not allow himself to be fettered by conventional morality. He is even beyond the categories of good and evil. He is a law unto himself. He doesn't subscribe to a received set of values, but rather, he creates his own values out of the power of his will.

With Nietzsche, morality goes into the dustbin of history. What replaces it is not pure reason but pure will. Life in Nietzsche's view is a meaningless, chaotic void: there is no God, no purpose or plan; nature and the universe are indifferent to man. The only meaning or order life has is that which is imposed on it by strong individuals. "What is good?" asks Nietzsche. "—All that heightens the feeling of power, the will to power, power itself in man. What is bad? —All that proceeds from weakness."

Like many other men of genius, Nietzsche was not modest about his role in history. In a letter dated October 18, 1885, he writes, "I fear I am the one who will blow up the history of men into two halves." To a large extent that is a correct assessment. Nietzsche did have an explosive effect on our ideas about morality. Prior to Nietzsche, philosophers had always tried to justify moral decisions in reference to something else—either God or natural law or reason or nature. With Nietzsche, decisions become self-legitimating. An exercise of the will justifies itself just

like an exercise on the high bar. One does it because one has the
strength to do it, and because it is natural to exercise one's powers
to the fullest. Since, from the Nietzschean viewpoint, there are no
external standards, the point is not what you choose, the point is
to choose daringly and wholeheartedly. Nowadays we would call
it being "authentic." A good illustration of authentic choosing can
be found in a story about the French philosopher Jean-Paul Sartre, who was strongly influenced by Nietzsche. Sartre was once
asked by a young man whether he should collaborate with the
Nazis and thus secure his family's position, or join the Resistance
and jeopardize it. Sartre replied that either choice was legitimate
as long as it was made in a committed—that is, authentic—way.

As is well known, Jean-Paul Sartre and Simone de Beauvoir
were lifelong companions. Although de Beauvoir envied Sartre's
genius, the events of the last two decades suggest that *The Second
Sex* has turned out to be more influential than anything written by
Sartre. In spreading the Nietzschean gospel of self-created values,
de Beauvoir had no equal. In de Beauvoir are prefigured all the
curious contradictions that make up feminist ideology: the emphasis on authentic relationships and the hostility toward family
relationships, the conviction that everything must be freely chosen and the equally passionate conviction that everything must be
mandated because, having been slaves for so long, women don't
know how to choose correctly (as de Beauvoir put it: "No woman
should be authorized to stay home to raise her children . . .
Women should not have that choice precisely because if there is
such a choice, too many women will make that one").

De Beauvoir's philosophy supposedly serves the cause of
women's rights. What needs to be noticed about her scheme of
reasoning, however, is that it contains no protection for the rights
of women or anyone else. With de Beauvoir, as with Nietzsche,
the link between morality and a real moral order—a natural law
inscribed in human nature—is severed. There is no appeal here,
as there is in the Declaration of Independence, to "the laws of
nature and of nature's God." Rather, "morality" is to be defined
by those with strong wills. In practice, this means that right and
wrong are reduced to politics. Those in power decide, and the
rest go along. Or if you have the will, you can resist those in

power, and take power yourself. De Beauvoir thought it was time for women to make up some of the rules—never mind that all rules are arbitrary. But this philosophy—that values are the arbitrary creation of those in power—leaves those who are out of power no standards to which they can appeal for protection. And without any notion of intrinsic human worth, the value of out-group individuals can plummet like stocks in a market crash.

We don't have to speculate about this because that philosophy has already been put into practice on a wide scale. When Adolf Hitler first met Benito Mussolini, he presented him with a gift of the collected works of Nietzsche. It was an appropriate memento. Hitler's ideas about life and politics were largely derived from Nietzsche. Hitler subscribed to the Nietzschean idea that superior people have an inborn right to rule. He also believed they should be free of any bondage to worn-out moralities. Along with Nietzsche, he despised "slave morality"—the Judaeo-Christian ethic. Although Nietzsche was not anti-Semitic in the way Hitler was, he clearly paves the way for anti-Semitism by pointing to the Jews as the source of the inhibiting moral system that had crippled the vital impulses of European peoples. Hitler was merely echoing Nietzsche when, in a speech, he asserted, "Conscience is a Jewish invention. Like circumcision, it mutilates a man."

It is a big jump from Nazism to current feminist philosophies of education, and it is not a connection I intend to make. But there is a connection with Nietzsche. His assumption that morality is something you invent for yourself is widely shared—not only by feminists but by many artists and intellectuals who feel themselves exempt from conventional rules (for that matter, any successful person runs the risk of imagining himself, in Tom Wolfe's telling phrase, a "Master of the Universe").

Although feminist educators (among whom we can include a number of men) are bothered by much of Nietzsche's thought, they do seem to believe women have been victims of slave morality—a category into which Nietzsche lumped women along with Christians and Jews. Some of these theorists want to reject the "slavery" of sacrifice and service. Others go further and include notions such as "duty," "obligation," and "responsibility" under the category of slave morality.

Exactly where Gilligan stands on this continuum is hard to say. In keeping with her own theoretical perspective, she makes a point of speaking in different voices. At one moment she talks in the voice of a concerned and sympathetic older sister, and in the next she is the revolutionary, urging young people to cast off the chains of Western culture. Whatever voice Gilligan may employ, however, there are two reasons to doubt that any good will come of her attempt to redefine morality.

First, even though Gilligan attacks the "autonomous" approach to ethics, the intellectual framework within which she operates is intimately connected to the most autonomous and arbitrary system of ethics ever invented—to Nietzsche, Sartre, and de Beauvoir.

Second, what Gilligan and her cotheorists mean by the "web of relationships" is not what most people mean. For most people the web starts with husband or wife and then goes on to include sons, daughters, mothers, fathers, brothers, sisters, grandparents, aunts, and uncles. But Gilligan's data base consists almost entirely of interviews with single men and women, and with teenage and preteenage girls. Page after page of her books is taken up with their thoughts about their relationships.

Gilligan takes these thoughts quite seriously. I am inclined to say *too* seriously. The friendship between two fifteen-year-old girls or between a teenage girl and her current boyfriend seems to be put on a par with the relationship of married love. I have to say "seems" again because Gilligan and her coauthors almost never talk about married love. Over and over we hear about "relationships" and "connections," but hardly a word about the paradigmatic example of commitment, the relationship of marriage. One of Gilligan's coauthors, Lyn Mikel Brown, after describing the relationships of teenage girls, notes, "Standards and role obligations are terms that do not accurately describe their experience, yet they *are* often terms that describe parental, religious and societal notions of morality. These cases, therefore, illustrate how a culture and a psychology that recognize and value a narrow vision of morality may exclude the moral significance of the experience of these young women."

This constant disparagement of "role obligations" as narrow

and old-fashioned needs to be emphasized because it is basically a disparagement of the institution of marriage and therefore of the institution of the family. Yet in most of the world, it is these role obligations that hold societies together, not the friendships of boys and girls, men and women. It is significant that Gilligan and her colleagues don't point to any examples of caring societies based on "authentic" relationships. They can't, because such societies exist only in their heads.

Not that we can't find societies that seem more caring in comparison to our own. But when we examine them, we find that they are more, not less, committed to marriage and traditional patterns, more bound by mores and custom. For example, one would be hard-pressed to find a more caring culture than that of the Philippines, a country often described as "the place where Asia wears a smile." Despite great poverty in the Philippines, there is also great generosity and charity. People with barely any money of their own will manage to find some to give to those more needy, and businesses will hire two or three times as many workers as they need so everyone can have a job (needless to say, the businesses don't make much profit). Mothers and fathers work hard to put their children through college. Brothers and sisters take turns sacrificing to help each other reach educational or career goals. A family of eight or ten crowded into a tiny nipa hut will find room for a cousin from a distant village who needs a place to stay for a year or two while attending college or getting established in a job. Nursing homes are practically nonexistent. Teenage girls walk hand in hand, and with a complete lack of self-consciousness. So do teenage boys. The love and caring is quite palpable and quite genuine.

In some ways it is exactly the kind of society radical feminists want to create. Except that this particular ethos of care is intimately connected with social structures feminist educators want nothing to do with. Like other Asian peoples, Filipinos prize marriage and family. In addition, the Philippines is one of the most thoroughly Catholic countries in the world, a place where Church rules and rituals are observed quite strictly. Divorce is illegal, modesty is prized, girls are chaperoned, boys are expected to court a girl in her home under a parent's watchful eye (in much the way that young men in Victorian times courted young ladies), most girls are virgins at marriage, traditional ideas about sex roles prevail.

There are plenty of problems in the Philippines. One could, I suppose, even blame them on the ethic of self-sacrifice. But anywhere one turns in the Third World or in the primitive world—the worlds that radical feminists and multiculturalists seem to think are closest to their own mythical utopia—one finds very traditional, even rigid and hierarchical social arrangements.

But let us return to our own culture. Many of the social problems that bother feminist educators are real enough—battered women and teens, rape, abused children, the feminization of poverty. The question is, how are these problems best attacked?

Although the problems are particularly severe now, they are not entirely new, and it is instructive to see how our society addressed similar problems in the past. The late eighteenth and early nineteenth century provide a case in point. By the turn of the century puritanism existed only as a memory, and private virtue, which Adams and Jefferson saw as crucial to the republic, was at a low ebb. Church attendance was not high, but rates of premarital pregnancy and illegitimacy were; gambling was a major leisure occupation, and to quote one historian, "In the early 1800s the United States was an alcohol-soaked culture." Average alcohol consumption was twice what it is today. Husbands and fathers spent their wages in taverns. Drunken, rowdy, and rude behavior was common in cities.

In the 1830s and 1840s a reaction set in. Citizens in major cities responded with voluntary associations and church-related societies that sought to instill character and self-control in young men. And apparently with great success. Rates of alcohol consumption, drunkenness, and crime fell sharply over the next two decades. Most of this improvement came about as the result not of police force but of consent. For example, thousands of young men signed temperance pledges, church attendance increased, and a new idea of the gentleman arose: not someone born into wealth and title but any man who acted with decency, self-control, and courtesy.

This movement, which lasted through the century and paralleled a similar reform of morals and manners in England, eventually came to be known as Victorianism. In recent years historians have shown a renewed appreciation for the once maligned Victorian spirit. James Lincoln Collier describes it as follows:

> Victorianism was a revolution in thought, attitude and manner which touched virtually every aspect of ordinary life. It reversed attitudes toward pleasure and self-gratification, especially as it concerned such matters of the senses as sex, drink and dancing. It saw the rise of an aggressive women's movement, the parent of today's feminism. It brought with it a rededication to Christian religion, to honor in human relations, to a general decency in manners and expression. Underlying everything was the idea that human beings could not live solely to gratify themselves, but must in every sphere of life—in politics, in philosophy, in social commerce—take into account the needs of the family, the community, the country, or even the whole of mankind. When choices were being made, not merely must others be thought of, they must be given first consideration.

As with today's feminist movement, women were seen as the key to changing society, because they were thought to be more caring and more spiritual. But that is where the similarity ends. Caring meant creating homes and schools with a high moral tone where children were raised to respect others, to learn social codes, to be polite and mannerly, to control their impulses. The idea that a more caring society could somehow be achieved by encouraging boys and girls to "get in touch with their bodies," or by encouraging them to listen to various "voices" and then decide morality for themselves, would have been rejected out of hand. Victorian women did not want a "transvaluation of all values," they wanted a return to Christian values of charity and duty.

Collier makes a convincing case that the Victorians, both men and women, were more caring and less selfish than we are. The Victorian age had no federal welfare system, but the nineteenth century saw an extraordinary growth of organizations that were dedicated to improving the condition of the poor. Here again, the ethic of care was linked to an ethic of character. Sobriety, self-control, obedience to the law, and industry were seen as the way out of poverty. So was family structure. Ironically, the early Chinese immigrants were often pinpointed as a chief source of vice and crime in the cities. The reason? Because of immigration policies, there was little or no family life among the Chinese. By 1890 there were about twenty-seven Chinese men for every Chinese woman. Jacob Riis, the author of the influential reform book *How the Other Half Lives,* was severe with the Chinese but also offered a realistic solution:

> Rather than banish the Chinaman, I would have the door opened wider—for his wife; make it a condition of his coming or staying that he bring his wife with him. Then, at least, he might not be what he now is and remains, a homeless stranger among us. Upon this hinges the real Chinese question in our city.

The attempt to improve the moral environment of the poor as a way of helping them out of poverty later came to be seen as a form of condescension and an imposition of middle-class values. But in some ways the modern view is less respectful. Victorian reformers felt that the poor also wanted more orderly and civil conditions, and that with the proper encouragement and help, the poor were as capable as anyone else of meeting high standards of personal conduct. Our own attitude seems much more condescending: it says, in effect, that the poor can't possibly meet the moral standards of the rest of society; hence, let's lower the standards for them and accommodate whatever practices and social arrangements happen to prevail in the worst environments. Thus, if the poor have webs of relationships rather than intact families, moral language must be reworked accordingly, and thus, if any changes are to be made to the environment, they must be governmental changes, and must not involve self-reformation.

This same condescension characterizes many of today's educators. Feminist moral educators seem anxious to teach children that they are victimized by unfair social and political structures, and that therefore their problems are the fault of someone else.

There is an element of truth here, of course: social and political structures are never entirely fair, and many of our personal problems are not of our making. But it is exactly the opposite of the message that young people, of whatever social class, need to hear. It means they have a claim to victim status, and so to the nonresponsibility we accord to the victim. This is what students need least. It shortcuts the hard work of forming character which is what they really need, and which schools should be about.

As Neil Postman observes in his book *Teaching as a Conserving Activity*, "The classroom is a nineteenth-century invention, and we ought to prize what it has to offer. It is, in fact, one of the few social organizations left to us in which sequence . . . social order, hierarchy, continuity, and deferred pleasure are important." Moreover, adds Postman, "poor people still regard the schools as an avenue of social and economic advancement for their children and do not object in the least to its being an orderly and structured experience." It can provide such advancement to the extent that it teaches discipline, self-control, and what Postman calls "a standard of civilized interaction."

The poor do not want their children to have a raised consciousness so much as they want them to have a good education and to learn good habits of behavior. When Professor Gilligan says women must move from psychological resistance to political resistance, and calls for "a recovery of anger as the political emotion par excellence," she is not speaking for the poor but for an intellectual elite. If anger is called for in the schools, it should not be misdirected at forms of political oppression visible only to the eagle eyes of the politically radicalized; rather, it should be directed at the culture of self-gratification, sexual permissiveness, and irresponsibility visible everywhere. The elite philosophy that people can get along splendidly without cultivating personal virtue works fine—for the elite. They generally have enough resources to cover a multitude of experiments, at least for a good long time. For the poor and working class such experiments with new moralities have more immediate and devastating consequences.

Those moderate feminists who think of feminism in terms of equal opportunities for women should realize that in academia and in educational circles, feminism means something entirely different. It is an esoteric mix of Nietzschean philosophy, Marxist social analysis, and even mystery cult religions. This brand of feminism, moreover, is based on the rejection of the principles that made it possible for women to achieve equal status with men in Western societies. Furthermore, it rejects the natural law and common law standards that provide protection to society's most vulnerable members. Finally, it is not particularly interested in marriage or in traditional concepts of the family or in the formation of character. Before embarking on yet another experiment in moral education, educators ought to better acquaint themselves with that intellectual framework. Parents and teachers should not be taken in by a moral philosophy simply because it comes wrapped in the language of care.

BEAUTY AND THE
BEASTS

Having damned Nietzsche in one respect (in respect to his denial of fixed morality), let me call attention to another aspect of his thought that deserves consideration. With his penetrating psychological insight, Nietzsche saw that most people are convinced not by arguments but by aesthetics—by the force of beauty. Or more accurately, by what they perceive to be beautiful.

Imagination rules reason, and not the other way around. It also rules societies. Those individuals with the power to capture the imagination also have the power to capture governments. The greatest rulers, Nietzsche insisted, were also great artists because they imposed form on chaos. They were often cruel taskmasters, but at the same time, they gave back to their people a bold vision of destiny. The superior person, even if he is not a ruler, follows the same doctrine: the highest experience is to make one's life a work of art. One of the most startling, and also most compelling, formulations in philosophy is Nietzsche's assertion "It is only as an *aesthetic phenomenon* that existence and the world are eternally *justified.*"

As with other Nietzschean ideas, this one also contains dark possibilities. Hitler understood it and practiced it. It is well known that Hitler was an aspiring artist who was deeply wounded when his attempts to enter the Vienna Academy of Arts met with rejection. What is less known is the extent to which he conceived of Nazism as an artistic endeavor, and the extent to which he was aided by artists inside Germany. Some of it was rather impressive art, particularly the Nuremberg rallies which were designed as grand theatrical events. The architect Albert Speer, Hitler's closest friend, designed dazzling visual effects for the Nuremberg amphitheater, including a grand display of lights. The rallies themselves were carefully choreographed. Historian Modris Eksteins describes what it was like in *Rites of Spring:* "The enthusiasm was kindled by meticulous attention to detail: high precision parades, forests of banners, carefully rehearsed catechetical speeches. At the end came Hitler. His concluding oration was timed to end as night fell. The rally would close under the magical spell of Speer's 'cathedral of ice': hundreds of search lights pointing to the sky." "From first to last," Eksteins notes, "the Third Reich was spectacular, gripping theater. That is what it was intended to be."

In 1934 Hitler commissioned filmmaker Leni Riefenstahl to document the party rally at Nuremberg. The result was a masterful film, *Triumph of the Will.* Riefenstahl stood head and shoulders above other documentary filmmakers of the day, and she put her considerable talents completely in the service of the Reich. With its cast of handsome boys and girls, its torchlight parades and drum tattoos, the rally was already inspired theater. Using aerial shots, daring camera angles, and superb editing, Riefenstahl transmuted it into high cinema. With its interweaving themes of power and innocence and its generous supply of half-naked bodies, the film conveys a powerful undertone of eroticism. It also manages to convincingly present Hitler as something like an unstoppable force of nature, something destined to prevail. It leaves no doubt why Germans (and others as well) were attracted to Nazism.

Hitler's deranged attempt to "beautify" the body politic and his success in enlisting enthusiastic support for his endeavor prove

Nietzsche's point: people are more strongly motivated by aesthetic arguments than by intellectual ones. Yves Montand, the French film actor, confesses that he was converted to communism after watching Eisenstein's film *Battleship Potemkin*. It is not an uncommon type of experience. For example, converts to Catholicism are often initially attracted by the aesthetics and rituals of the Church rather than by its doctrine. To understand the point is not to give up on reason, on the one hand, or to shy away from aesthetics, on the other, but simply to recognize the power of aesthetics for good or bad.

Bruno Bettelheim suggests that aesthetic power is determinative for the moral life right from the start. In his well-known book on fairy tales, he contends that a child's choices are based less on right versus wrong than on "who arouses his sympathy and who his antipathy." "The question for a child," says Bettelheim, "is not 'Do I want to be good?' but 'Who do I want to be like?' " The hero in a fairy tale wins the child to the side of virtue because the hero is the most attractive figure in the story.

Long after childhood, our ethical behavior is still influenced by our aesthetic preferences: by what attracts our imagination. Therefore, any adequate analysis of moral behavior must look at the imagination as well as at reason and volition. Claes Ryn, chairman of the National Humanities Institute, has written extensively on the subject, and he provides some helpful observations. A good education, says Ryn, will pay attention to all three faculties—will, imagination, and reason—because the three work together, and contrary to the usual assumption, reason is not particularly strong in relation to the other two. No matter how brilliant he may be, an individual's reason tends to be pulled along by his imagination and will. For example, many intellectuals in Britain before the outbreak of the Second World War refused to see what was coming despite the warnings of people like Churchill, and despite the obvious arms buildup in Germany. As Ryn points out, they were led by an escapist imagination. Similarly, many intellectuals in both England and America refused, despite abundant evidence, to see the atrocities of Stalin's regime because their imaginations had been captured by the utopian vision of communism. Moreover, just as reason follows on the heels of imagination, imagination is strongly influenced by will. Many Germans claimed they knew nothing of the concentration camps and other Nazi horrors. Perhaps, observes Ryn, they did not *want* to see anything. These well-known examples of averted vision have their counterpart in our everyday lives. As Ryn says, "Little acts of self-deception let us glide past the facts that might force us to reconsider our ways and our outlook. We do not *want* to change."

How do we break out of the cycle of distorted will, imagination, and reason? Just as art can lead us into illusion, it can lead us back to reality. Good art—art that is faithful to the human condition, and not escapist, illusory, or cynical—can put us in touch with what Ryn calls "the ethical standard within experience." Good art provides a revelation of ethical reality.

In a sense, all art whether good or bad contains moral lessons. This is particularly true of stories: they can't help passing judgment on how people behave themselves. "Persons attempting to find a moral in [this story] will be banished," wrote Mark Twain at the beginning of *Huckleberry Finn,* and then proceeded to catch up his readers in one of the great novels of conscience. The question is not whether art deals with ethics. It does it all the time. Any adventure episode on TV is bound to raise ethical questions. As soon as they are raised, however, they are usually buried under car chases, explosions, and sex scenes. The question is whether the story treats people and problems with depth and honesty.

Schools can do better than popular culture. They are in a position to provide exposure to the best in music, in art, in literature, and in film. And this art, in turn, provides a deeper knowledge of self and others than participation in "magic circles" or peer group discussions ever can. Good literature, for example, doesn't introduce a child to "kids like me" but to others who are better than himself—who are just like he might become if he fulfills his potential for goodness. "When we read," writes novelist John Gardner, "we ingest metaphors of goodness, wordlessly learning to behave more like Levin than like Anna (in *Anna Karenina*), more like the transformed Emma (in Jane Austen's novel) than like the Emma we first meet in the book." We can easily add more examples: learning to behave more like the transformed boy in *Captains Courageous* than the boy we first meet, more like Portia than Shylock, more like the younger brother in *King of the Golden River* than the older brothers (he gives water to a thirsty man; they refuse). When fiction works for us, observes critic Wayne Booth, we have been—at least for the duration— that kind of person.

One way or the other, art is intimately related to the way we live our lives. One way or the other, some aesthetic vision of life governs our behavior. A proper education nourishes the imagination with rich and powerful, yet realistic images. From that fund the child can build a deep and adequate vision of life. The alternative is not that children will be left without images, symbols, and stories but that their perceptions of life will be colored almost totally by the commercialized dreams and illusions that come out of Hollywood and Madison Avenue.

Or their imaginations will be captured by what might be called "the aesthetics of the streets." We are frequently shocked by reports of what seem to be "random" acts of violence. Often, however, they are not random at all but expressions of an aesthetic of violence. An informative book on the subject is sociologist Jack Katz's *Seductions of Crime: Moral and Sensual Attractions of Doing Evil.* Katz points out that, strange as it may sound, aesthetics play a large part in the ritual life of gangs. Moreover, says Katz, the aesthetics they practice are Nietzschean aesthetics. Not that any of the gang members he describes have ever heard of Nietzsche; but somehow they have hit on the same themes. They think of themselves as elites ("street elites" is Katz's term), and consider themselves to be above conventional rules of right and wrong, beyond conventional notions of good and evil. They also exhibit an intuitive grasp of Nietzsche's credo that an aesthetic phenomenon is its own justification. Their attitude is that it is better to make one's life a work of art, even though a brief and flaming one, than to capitulate to the emasculating demands of school and society.

As a consequence, style is of great importance in gang life. A gang leader's status, interestingly enough, does not depend on physical strength or fighting ability. According to Katz, "Esthetic leadership appears to be the key." What is important is one's mastery of street language, one's manner of bearing, one's style of dress. The gang member sees himself as an actor who is always "on," and thus, according to Katz, much time is spent before mirrors practicing "meanness" or the rapid production of a knife or gun (as Travis Bickle does in *Taxi Driver*). Much of the time, the activities of gang life are nothing more than street theater. From time to time, however, the drama takes a deadly turn.

Of course, many factors—from poverty, to school failure, to family troubles—push youngsters into gangs. But it would be a mistake to underestimate the attractive power of such a life. In all times and in all circumstances, there is, especially for the young, a temptation to defy society and to lead a dynamic, dramatic existence—to "live dangerously," in Nietzsche's phrase. There is nothing natural about wanting to be on society's side. The natural thing when you are young is to want action.

What is needed to counter the attractions of the criminal aesthetic is a more vital aesthetic. For example, the Guardian Angels have been effective in enlisting youthful passions against crime because they pay attention to the human need for real theater. Their success is due, in no small measure, to the aesthetic aura that surrounds them. In fact, any group that hopes to deal effectively with crime has to develop an aesthetic of its own. A policeman who hopes to assert his authority over four or five members of a "street elite" has to be able to project quite a dramatic presence. By the same token, finding the right aesthetic can make a major difference in the rehabilitation of criminals. Two of the most successful approaches to rehabilitating young criminals are Outward Bound programs (which provide an adventure/challenge aesthetic) and "boot camp" prison programs (which provide a military aesthetic).

Unfortunately, the Nietzschean themes of power and assertion of will are not just themes in books or films but are increasingly being played out in city streets. In the meanwhile, schools seem unable or unwilling to take aesthetics seriously. They can do little to halt the progress of violence because they can offer no countervailing vision as schools once did. Perhaps this is an effect of becoming too pluralistic, of trying to be all things to all people. In any event, it is imperative for educators to understand that schools must be more than instructional-services institutions or multicultural shopping malls. Even the commendable goal of creating schools that are more caring is not enough. The goal should go beyond making school into a nice place, because niceness doesn't satisfy. Something more is needed.

Nietzsche asserted that men must have joy, but then, so did Thomas Aquinas. The word means "gladness," "delight," "rejoicing," "being filled." It means more than "happiness," and more than "pleasure," though it encompasses both. Joy can be found in friendship, in hard work, in sport, in creative art, in purposeful action. There are many poor substitutes for it, but men and women will necessarily seek some approximation of joy. It is unrealistic, and also undesirable, to expect schools to provide the deepest fulfillments and joys, but it is possible for them to point to those deeper fulfillments and, in so doing, to engage the imagination and energies of young people to a far greater extent than they now do. Some suggestions for creating a more powerful aesthetic in schools will be offered in a later chapter. At this point, it is enough to say that however helpful Nietzsche may be in reminding us of the importance of aesthetics, schools should not allow themselves to be captured by a Nietzschean version of aesthetics: one that teaches students that their bodies will tell them what to do, that the content of their choices doesn't matter, and one that threatens to turn the classroom into a theater for radical politics. The aesthetic impulse is a basic and powerful instinct but it is not self-justifying. Unless it is bound by solid standards of right and wrong, it is capable of putting an appealing face on the most destructive personal desires or the most diabolical national schemes.

As it now stands, the question of the proper place of aesthetics in education remains an academic question. Insofar as the souls of the young are being shaped by any aesthetic, that shaping now takes place outside the schools. While educators have been scrupulously maintaining a wall of separation between aesthetics and education, others have had no such qualms. The importance of song, story, and image has not been lost on TV executives, advertisers, or the recording industry. They have been controlling the aesthetic environment for quite some time. By default the entertainment industry has become the real arena for moral education. To that subject we now turn.

MUSIC AND
MORALITY

No, this chapter is not about the latest dirty lyrics in the latest rap group's latest album (though some are included). Nor does it deal with rumors that the members of such and such a rock group are devil worshipers (though they might be). Rather, it attempts to get at an effect of music that is more basic than the lyrics or the singer's persona. We can start our discussion of this effect with the common observation that we tend to learn something more easily and indelibly if it's set to a rhyme or song. Advertisers know this and use it so effectively that we sometimes have difficulty getting their jingles out of our heads. But there are more positive educational uses. Most of us learned the alphabet this way and some of our history as well ("Paul Revere's Ride," "Concord Hymn"). Recently some foreign language courses have been developed which employ rhyme and song as the central teaching method. Similarly, one of the most successful new phonics programs teaches reading through singing.

This raises an interesting possibility. If Johnny can be taught to read through rhyme and song, might he also begin to learn right and wrong in the same way? It seems that something like this did happen in the distant past. As I noted earlier, the *Iliad* and the *Odyssey* played a vital role in the formation of Greek youth. But the ability of the Homeric bards to memorize these vast epics was due in large part to the rhythmic meter and repetitive structure of the poems. In turn, these epics were often sung to the audience to the accompaniment of a stringed instrument. In short, the foundational cultural messages of the Greeks were conveyed by sung stories. "Education in such cultures," writes Kieran Egan of Simon Fraser University, "is largely a matter of constantly immersing the young into the enchanting patterns of sound until they resound to the patterns, until they become 'musically' in tune with, harmonious with, the institutions of their culture."

Allan Bloom, in his controversial discussion of music in *The Closing of the American Mind*, says that music should be at the center of education. It does the best job of giving raw passions their due while forming them for something better. Bloom feels that music now plays the decisive role in the formation of a young person's character. In this respect, nothing has changed since the days of Homer, when, in Egan's phrase, the young were immersed "into the enchanting patterns of sound." Of course, Bloom is not happy with the results because what today's youth are "musically in tune with, harmonious with" are no longer the institutions of their culture or anything on which a culture could be built. They are vibrating to the beat of a different drum—usually the one in a rock band.

Bloom's comments are based on several passages from Plato, who was much concerned with the moral effects of music—so much so that in the ideal society he describes, many kinds of music would be censored. According to Bloom, these observations in *The Republic* stir up today's generation of students as nothing else in Plato can. They take music very seriously—as did Plato. Plato's argument is that certain kinds of music can foster a spirit of lawlessness which can creep in unnoticed, "since it's considered to be a kind of play," and therefore harmless. Despite the innocent appearance, however, some kinds of music are capable of subverting the social order.

To appreciate Plato's thesis, and to appreciate the mobilizing power of music, we might recall the role that the "Marseillaise" played in the French Revolution, or the role that "We Shall Overcome" played in the American civil rights movement. But this kind of large-scale revolution is not exactly what Plato had in mind. He was more concerned with music of a sensual or romantic type that would undermine discipline, moderation, and other civic virtues. The most obvious modern analogy—the one Bloom makes—is to the role rock music plays in prompting young people to throw off cultural and sexual restraints. The common adolescent practice of playing rock at a deafening volume in streets, buses, and public parks suggests how readily it lends itself to the violation of the simplest rules of civil behavior.

In Plato's view, music and character are intimately connected. Certain modes of music dispose the individual to "illiberality," "insolence," and other vices. By the same token, other modes suggest peacefulness, moderation, and self-control, and dispose one to an "orderly and courageous life." It's important to note that Plato is not talking about lyrics (although he was concerned about them) but about the music itself. A man raised on harmonious music, he says, has a better chance of developing a harmonious soul: he will be better able to see life as a whole, and thus "he would have the sharpest sense of what's been left out," of what is and isn't fitting.

Plato also addresses himself to stories, poetry, painting, and craft, and has much the same thing to say about them. Children ought to be brought up in an atmosphere that provides them examples of nobility and grace. This imaginative education is not a substitute for a reasoned morality, but it paves the way for it, making it more likely that the grown child will happily accept the dictates of reason. In this way, the child develops an "erotic attachment" to virtue, by which Plato meant not so much "sexual" as "passionate." Just as the senses can be enlisted on the side of vice, so (with a little more difficulty) can they be enlisted on the side of virtue. Through the senses the child can come to love justice and wisdom long before he can grasp these notions in their abstract form. As an example, Allan Bloom mentions the statues that graced the cities of Greece, and attracted young men and women to the idea of nobility by the beauty of the hero's body.

In our own society, however, we seem to have managed to create an erotic attachment to all the wrong things. Or more precisely, parents and teachers have, by default, allowed the entertainment industry ("a common highway passing through all the houses in America" is Bloom's description) to create these attachments. Rock music in particular, says Bloom, inclines children away from self-control and sublimation. It doesn't channel emotions, it pumps them up. Instead of a passionate attachment to what is good, noble, and just, youth develop passionate attachments to their own needs, wants, and feelings, and to people like Mick Jagger and Michael Jackson.

Bloom has been criticized for overdoing his attack on rock. And there is some truth in this. He fails to distinguish among various kinds of rock and he seems to believe that sex is rock's only appeal ("Rock has the beat of sexual intercourse"). Nevertheless, the hysterical tone of some of the reaction suggests that Bloom has hit close to home. William Greider, writing in *Rolling Stone,* says that Bloom is guilty of a "nasty, reactionary attack on the values of young people and everyone else under forty," and of compiling "a laundry list of cheap slanders." Another critic of Bloom gives an elaborate (and not very convincing) argument that the beat of rock is not the beat of sexual intercourse but "is, in fact, much closer to the regular motion of the heavenly bodies."

But the question is not whether Bloom has presented a nuanced portrait of rock and youth. The real question is whether music has the profound influence on character formation that he and Plato (along with Aristotle, Confucius, and Shakespeare) assert. That question alone deserves serious consideration and debate, but as Bloom writes, "That kind of critique has never taken place." Of the criticism that has surfaced since Bloom's book, most has focused on the lyrics rather than the music, and it has been hard enough to get a hearing for that. The music itself seems to be a taboo area.

Yet the basic proposition—that different kinds of music produce different effects on the soul—is not entirely radical. Would anyone assert that "(You Ain't Nothin' but a) Hound Dog" has the same "soul" as Gregorian chant? The one inspires to prayer and contemplation, the other to shouting and stamping. Not that there's anything wrong with shouting and stamping once in a while, but children these days tend to be raised almost exclusively on that sort of music. Besides, they don't need much incentive to shout, stamp, whine, and demand. They do these things naturally. Why should we want music that validates and confirms such juvenile states? Shouldn't children be exposed to other states of soul? Even if we were to succeed in creating schools that once again took virtue and character seriously, we would still have an uphill fight as long as rock music remains the dominant cultural idiom and as long as children's "erotic attachments" are formed by an industry that panders to juvenile emotions. What we currently have is a censorship by omission. Either parents don't know about or don't have a taste for alternative forms of music because they themselves were raised on rock; or they do know but are afraid to exercise their parental rights for fear that their children's allegiance has already been captured, and to stand up to the music would only widen the rift. What results, says Bloom, is a pattern of denial: "avoid noticing what the words say, assume the kid will get over it. If he has early sex, that won't get in the way of his having stable relationships later. His drug use will certainly stop at pot."

Bloom is actually more interested in the educational rather than the moral influence of rock: "The issue here is its effect on education, and I believe it ruins the imagination of young people and makes it very difficult for them to have a passionate relationship to the art and thought that are the substance of liberal education." This kind of education depends on sublimation. But if Bloom is not mainly concerned with moral effects, we can be. If rock can wreck the liberal imagination (in the nonpolitical sense of the word "liberal"), it can also wreck or stunt the moral imagination.

Am I shortchanging rock? After all, it's not all heavy metal and megawatt amplifiers. Many of rock's defenders say there is a deeper meaning to it than the hormonal one assigned by Bloom—namely, the feeling of spiritual oneness it can create: the feeling that there are no boundaries, that the whole world is one large community. Nietzsche understood the feeling. In *The Birth of Tragedy,* he writes, "It is only through the spirit of music that we can understand the joy involved in the annihilation of the individual." Once we can get beyond the barrier of individuation, we can break through to life itself, which is "indestructibly power-ful and pleasurable." The music at Woodstock (aided, no doubt, by considerable marijuana consumption) had this effect. So, ap-parently, did the Live Aid concert.

But the "soul" of rock music, even at its best and most brotherly, does not seem up to the task of creating a real community of purpose (as gospel music helped to do during the civil rights movement). The brotherhood rock yearns for is one that will come easily and not at the cost of self-discipline. Robert Pattison, in his book *The Triumph of Vulgarity: Rock Music in the Mirror of Romanticism,* argues that the spirit of rock music is really the spirit of nineteenth-century Romanticism, only with a heavier beat and a faster tempo. It is simply another version of Rousseau's belief that what is primitive is what is best, and that youthful passions, therefore, do not need to be educated or transformed. The rock myth, according to Pattison, is the same as the Romantic myth: a belief that it is possible to have a community innocent of civilizing restraints in which everything can be done on instinct, and in which everyone is free to express himself to the fullest. Moreover, as Stuart Goldman observes in commenting on Pattison's book, "the rocker feels that we are kept from this—our 'natural' state of oneness with the universe—by 'them': the government, teachers, politicians, our parents. All the usual suspects."

Pattison is a defender of both rock and Romanticism; however, as Irving Babbitt points out, the essence of Romanticism is that it is never in love with a particular object or person but only with the feelings which that person or object evokes. Consequently, the Romantic spirit is fickle; it is always changing its object of devotion, always in search of a new high. By necessity its interest is in novelty rather than stability. I don't doubt the sincerity of feeling in listeners who respond to "We Are the World" (the theme song of the Live Aid concert), but I question whether those are the sorts of feelings that can translate into committed and sustained action. The actual behavior of many young people who are hooked on rock suggests that their real agenda is "I am the world" and "The world owes me a living." Rock music allows us to indulge in *expressions* of strong emotion while freeing us from the obligation of *doing* anything.

When one looks more closely at rock, the notion that it is solidarity music falls apart. What it is, essentially, is performance music. It is not intended for participation but for dramatizing the ego of the performer. For the most part, it is too idiosyncratic and exaggerated for any amateur to sing. People do not stand around pianos and sing "Cum On Feel the Noize" or "Let's Put the X in Sex"; songs like these are basically unsingable. Even if audiences at rock concerts tried to sing along, they would be drowned out by the amplification. Although there are some forms of participation, they do not involve singing. At heavy metal concerts, for example, the audience can engage in "head banging," a rapid jerking of the head from side to side to the beat of the music. Or they can try "air guitar." Any individual in the crowd who is so moved may stand up and start playing riffs on an invisible guitar. If he is lucky, he manages to capture some attention, at least for a few brief moments. At the outset, then, rock music denies its audience one of the most powerful of all unifying experiences, the opportunity to join together in song. In a sense, it is the culmination of the Romantic shift of emphasis from the work of art to the artist himself. The song doesn't matter; what matters is the artist and his emotions. If one were to seek a fitting motto for rock, it would be difficult to find a more appropriate one than that memorable refrain from *The Cat in the Hat:* "Look at me! Look at me! Look at me now!"

What is the trade-off? What do young people get in exchange for giving up genuine participation? The answer is that like the performer on the stage, they get to feel and show their own emotions—if only through body language. Rock confirms their right to have and express strong, sensual emotions. The message is "Your feelings are sacred, and nothing is set above them." At the beginning of adolescence the discovery of one's emotional self seems like a profound discovery. This is the part of the self that adults "just don't understand." But rock music does understand, and what's more, it sanctions these feelings.

This, in its essence, is all that rock is about. And it is precisely because of this juvenile core that rock never delivers on its promise of creating community. Thus, in a recent *Newsweek* article, John Leland, a writer sympathetic to rock, laments, "The Live Aid

concert, and the lesser knockoffs that followed, was the last promise that there was something to pop music that held people of
different ages, classes and ideas together. This promise didn't
hold; even then it wasn't true . . ." Leland is more than a little
concerned about all the "adolescent rage" that runs through hard
rock and rap music. For example, he cites the following lyrics
from *Straight Outta Compton,* an album by the rap group N.W.A.:
"So what about the bitch that got shot / F— her. / You think I
give a damn about a bitch? / I ain't a sucker." In a similar vein,
Billboard in a November 1991 issue criticized rapper Ice Cube for
an album titled *Death Certificate* because its "unabashed espousal of violence against Koreans, Jews and other whites crosses
the line that divides art from the advocacy of crime."

This surprise and shock puts me in mind of C. S. Lewis's comment about people who "laugh at honor and are shocked to find
traitors in [their] midst." The kind of lyrics that *Newsweek* and
Billboard complain of were always implicit in the music itself. If
unrestrained emotion is to be king, there should be no complain-
ing about violent emotions. There was every reason to predict that
rock music would become increasingly violent. A music that proclaims that the gratification of one's immediate desires is para-
mount is bound to lead in the direction of frustration and then
anger, because the world never provides such gratification for
very long.

Of course, there are softer brands of contemporary music that
express kinder and gentler sentiments. But much of this is more
properly classified as pop music rather than as rock. It lacks the
heavy beat of rock, and it bears a strong resemblance to the pop
music and the popular ballad that predate rock. Some performers
alternate between the two modes. For example, when Elvis Pres-
ley sang "Love Me Tender," he dropped the heavy beat and
reverted to the ballad form. And a similar changing of tone has
been the pattern ever since. Whenever rock musicians try to
express sentiments that aren't merely self-centered, the distinctive
rock sound is either lost or muted.

This reversion to other forms of music says a lot about the
limitations of rock. Even more instructive, however, is the attitude
taken by rock aficionados toward pop music. For the most part

they despise it as being too soft and sentimental. By contrast, the kind of rock that is considered "real" and "powerful" by the critics is almost always laced with themes of anger, frustration, or self-indulgence. For instance, a recent review of the "best discs" of 1991 included such terms of approval as "raging guitars," "angry guitars," "brutal sonic assault," "piercing screams," "barbed wire lyrics," and "nerve-hitting." Anger is much closer to the center of rock than is kindness or caring, and it may even be edging out sex as the number-one preoccupation. Anger is, after all, a very common adolescent emotion, and it is easily exploited. "The anger is what helps you relate to the kids," said W.A.S.P. band member Blackie Lawless in a 1985 interview. "That's what makes rock 'n' roll what it is. You're pissed off. I'm still pissed off about a lot of things . . ."

One of the things that rock and the rock industry do best is to take normal adolescent frustration and rebellion and heat it up to the boiling point. A lot of this hatred is directed toward parents—the people who usually stand most directly across the path of self-gratification. Antiparent themes are quite common on MTV, and heavy metal has been described as "music to kill your parents by." When I once asked some recent college graduates to explain what they thought was the deeper meaning of rock, I was surprised at how frequently the word "alienation" came up over the course of several separate conversations. Robert Pittman, the inventor of MTV, confirmed this interpretation of the "meaning" of rock in a published interview with Ron Powers: "It's all attitude. The attitude is: nothing is sacred. We're all having a rilly good time. We're all in on something everybody else doesn't get. We're special 'cause we're keeping everybody else out." Thus much of the solidarity rock supplies its young audience is a negative solidarity, a bond achieved by excluding those who should be closest.

Parents are not the only focus of anger. Many types of rock have for a long time exhibited anger toward adults in general. What is fairly new, however, is the expression of contempt for age mates as well. Girlfriends—if that is the correct term—are not simply presented as sex objects but as objects of abuse. Most of the world only became aware of this trend with the flap that arose in 1990 over the rap group 2 Live Crew and their album *As Nasty as They Wanna Be*. The album, which sold several million copies, presents the sexual mutilation of women as the preferred way of obtaining sexual pleasure. But the trend was already pronounced by the mid-eighties. The popular Mötley Crüe, a heavy metal group, specialized in lyrics like the following: "I'll either break her face / Or take down her legs, / Get my ways at will. / Go for the throat / Never let loose, / Going in for the kill."

And in a 1984 song by Great White titled "On Your Knees," the following lyrics appear: "Gonna drive my love inside you / Gonna nail your ass to the floor."

Just to be sure the album-buying audience puts the correct interpretation on such lyrics, album covers often present graphic illustrations that leave little to the imagination. For example, the cover of the W.A.S.P. single "F**k Like a Beast" shows a close-up of a man with a bloody circular saw blade protruding from his genital area.

This attitude—that hostile sexual relationships are common and acceptable—is not new to rock music, but it is now much more widespread. Exactly what role rock plays in forming youthful ideas about sex is not something that can be quantified. But some children start to listen to the worst of rap and heavy metal at ages nine, ten, and eleven. And according to a report of the American Medical Association, the average teenager listens to 10,500 hours of rock between the seventh and twelfth grades—more time than he spends in school. To say that listening to rock music doesn't influence ideas and attitudes is tantamount to saying that we aren't influenced by our environment. Until recently, researchers debated whether or not heavy exposure to television violence and pornography creates greater acceptance of violence toward women. That debate has died down now that new and more definitive studies have shown that it does. Is there any reason to suppose that heavy exposure to violent audio messages will have a different effect? The evidence is that a great many youth are already seriously confused about the relationship between sex and violence. For example, two recent studies conducted in the Northeast revealed that one third of high school girls in a relationship are regularly abused by their boyfriends. That is disturbing in itself, but the reports went on to say that fully one half of the girls accepted the violence as a sign of love.

One question that logically arises here is whether rock can be reformed. Some seem to think it can be, that it's simply a matter of changing the lyrics, or attaching the music to a proper cause. Thus teachers use rock in classrooms, and educational films are made with rock sound tracks, and thus we have Christian rock and even Christian versions of rock magazines. The idea is that the energy of rock can somehow be channeled toward virtuous ends. This hope, it seems to me, arises from a basic misunderstanding about the nature of rock. I have already indicated that though the lyrics are important, they are secondary. The music is its own message. No matter what the words might say, the music speaks the language of self-gratification. Rock can't be made respectable. It doesn't want to be respectable. A respectable rock is a contradiction in terms. "Some dreamers have hoped to harness rock to propagate the values of transcendent ideologies . . . ," writes Robert Pattison. "But rock is useless to teach any transcendent values . . . Rock's electricity . . . gives the lie to whatever enlightened propaganda may be foisted on it." Pattison, who has written what is perhaps the definitive book on the rock myth, and who is himself a defender of rock, argues that rock in its essence is vulgar and narcissistic, based on a denial of any value outside the self. So, while it is possible to set a Christian hymn or a song about undying love to the beat of rock, it cannot be done convincingly. The music will simply subvert the words. The same holds true for rap, which, though it is different in significant ways from rock, has a similar beat. Some rappers preach positive anti-drug, antigang messages in their songs. But it's not a very good fit of words to music. The music is composed of explosive bursts of sound, somewhat like the sound of a semiautomatic weapon being fired. On an aesthetic level the positive lyrics don't work nearly as well as the violent ones. No matter how many reforms are attempted, rock and rap will always gravitate in the direction of violence and uncommitted sex. The beat says, "Do what you want to do."

A child's musical environment is a large part of his moral environment. Right now, most of that musical environment is supplicd by an industry that, as Allan Bloom says, "has all the moral dignity of drug trafficking." The first step in doing something about the situation is to wake up to its bizarre nature. For parents to give over a large part of their children's moral formation to people whose only interest in children is an exploitative one is a form of madness. But, as Bloom remarks, "It may well be that a society's greatest madness seems normal to itself."

In what direction does sanity lie? Parents need to realize that there is a *Kulturkampf*—a culture war—in progress. Rock and its representatives have known this for a long time; it's part of the reason they have been on the winning side. They have made no attempt to conceal their hostility toward parents and the values parents think are important. When Tipper Gore's group, Parents' Music Resource Center, asked the record industry to develop a labeling system similar to that employed by the movie industry, the rock world reacted with vicious personal abuse. And when Nikki Sixx, a member of Mötley Crüe, was asked by *Creem* (a teen magazine) how he felt about the concerns parents had with explicit lyrics, he replied, "You know what I say? I say fuck 'em. It's freedom of speech; First Amendment."

Parents need to reclaim some territory for their children. Of course, the odds are very much against them. But at least one factor is in their favor. When children are young, they are still open to all kinds of music; they haven't yet learned they are supposed to like only one kind. It's a good time to help them cultivate good taste in music against the day when the forces of pop culture will attempt to dictate bad taste to them.

What kind of musical environment can help to create a good moral environment? Here are some broad suggestions.

1. *Music that can be shared.* Rock drives a wedge between generations. Parents and children can't share songs like Prince's "Darling Nikki" (about a girl masturbating with a magazine) or Van Halen's "Hot for Teacher." This divisive effect was evident right from the time Elvis first appeared on television—a moment of nationwide embarrassment for families gathered in front of the set. Our society needs to return (or "move forward," if you like phrases with a progressive ring) to music that brings families together in song: children's songs, folk songs, ballads, show

tunes, parlor songs, carols, around-the-piano songs. Singable songs. Songs that don't need amplification, or stage sets, or a billion-dollar industry to keep them alive.

When the piano, not the television set, was the center of home entertainment, families enjoyed a common musical bond. The music belonged to everyone: not just to adults, not just to teenagers. But singing together is not merely an old-fashioned custom, it is a basic expression of family love. It is one of many rituals of participation that have been lost, and for which we have not found adequate substitutes.

2. *Music that channels emotions.* The basic appeal of music is an emotional one. Education is not a matter of denying emotions but of civilizing them—of attaching them to fitting objects. This process of sublimation does not weaken emotions; rather, it gives them more power by giving them focus. And serious moral endeavors, whether individual or communal, need such channeling. One such example is the civil rights revolution of the sixties. Churches played the key role, and the music that accompanied this revolution was, for the most part, church music: hymns, spirituals, and gospel songs. Folk songs also played a part. Rock music did not. The civil rights movement was a movement of great seriousness and dignity. It was propelled by powerful emotions, but it was essential to the success of the movement that those emotions be controlled and restrained. Consequently, there was no part for rock to play even though rock derives from black music (the revolution that rock accompanied was the sexual revolution).

The point is that in both public life and private, we need to be able on occasion to channel our feelings toward goals that go beyond immediate gratification. It's inevitable that children will be exposed to popular music. It's important that in addition to the pop sound, they sometimes hear a more profound sound.

3. *Music that shapes the soul.* Morality is not simply about learning the rules of right and wrong, it is about a total alignment of our selves. Because music moves our whole being, it plays a major role in setting that alignment. Certain types of music convey a sense of order, proportion, and harmony. There is an ancient belief that the stars, the moon, the planets, all of creation, move

to a heavenly music. The theme can be found in Plato, Plotinus, Shakespeare, Milton, and Dryden. According to some legends, God sang creation into existence. And this harmony extends to human nature.

Shakespeare wrote:

> Such harmony is in immortal souls;
> But whilst this muddy vesture of decay
> Doth grossly close it in, we cannot hear it.

Why not? Because, in Milton's words,

> . . . disproportion'd sin
> Jarr'd against nature's chime, and with harsh din
> Broke the fair musick that all creatures made
> To their great Lord, whose love their motion swayed.

Milton concludes:

> O may we soon again renew that song,
> And keep in tune with Heav'n, till God ere long
> To his celestial consort us unite,
> To live with him, and sing in endless morn of light.

One does not have to share Milton's Christian faith to appreciate the idea. Aristotle notes that "some philosophers say that the soul is a tuning." And he agrees that there exists in us an "affinity to musical modes and rhythms." In the ancient view the right kind of music helps to form character because it helps to tune the soul to the rhythms of a good life.

The trouble is, it is not at all easy to specify what that rhythm sounds like. Aristotle and Plato use words like "harmony," "melody," "grace," "order," and "proportion." But although it's difficult to say what arrangements of notes have the effect of bringing order to the soul, it's not as difficult to recognize them. We can hear this stately measure in Pachelbel, Handel, Mozart, Bach, and Beethoven. We can hear it in Gregorian chant, choral music, and the chanted Hanukkah blessings. We can hear it in ballads like

"Barbara Allen," in spirituals like "Go Down, Moses," and in lullabies like "All Through the Night." We can hear it in "Taps." Although we may know the actual composer, such music seems to originate from a higher source. It seems to transcend the composer's persona. Beethoven's personal life was rather a mess, but none of this is apparent in his music.

4. *Music that has stood the test of time.* The music mentioned above possesses another quality: timelessness. Thomas Day, in his short but instructive book *Why Catholics Can't Sing,* observes of certain chants, choral works, and hymns that "the melodies *sounded important,* as if they had existed forever." Many Christmas carols have the same quality. It is surprising to discover that some of them were written only a hundred years ago.

If I have been concentrating on sacred music, it is partly because rock invites the comparison. As Pattison writes,

> The rocker lives his music with an intensity few nominal Christians imitate in their devotion to the faith. He goes to concerts and listens to his music with the same fidelity with which the Christian of earlier generations attended church and read his Bible. One of the most frequently repeated mottos in rock lyrics is "Rock 'n' roll will never die!"—a cry of belief. The stars of rock undergo literal apotheosis: "Jim Morrison is God" is a graffito now perpetuated by a third generation of rockers.

The question of whether or not rock 'n' roll will ever die is not one that needs to be settled in these pages. But we do know that some other types of music have withstood the passage of time. The forty years that have passed since the introduction of rock is a short time when you consider that the music of Beethoven and Bach is still alive, or when you realize that in churches and cathedrals all over the world, you may hear hymns composed 500 years ago by Luther, or chants that were sung in monasteries 500 years before that. This timeless quality is not confined to church music or classical music. Some of the popular music of the thirties and forties seems to have this time-transcending quality: songs such as "Night and Day," "Stardust," "Deep Purple," and "As Time Goes

By." When the Beatles were in their heyday, they were hailed as
original geniuses. But would anyone today argue that songs like
"She Loves You," "I Saw Her Standing There," "I Want to Hold
Your Hand," or any of a dozen others are in the same league as
Cole Porter's "Night and Day"? Paul McCartney himself seems to
be aware of rock's limited scope. His recently completed *Liverpool*
Oratorio is in the tradition of Handel, not the Beatles. As McCartney said in an interview on the occasion of its Carnegie Hall
debut, "You can't be a teenager forever."

5. *Music that tells a story.* Music has traditionally been linked to
story. The Homeric poems recount long and detailed stories, the
traditional ballad tells brief and simple stories of love and tragedy,
country and western music tells everyday stories of marriage,
betrayal, and hard times. Even orchestral music is often composed
with a story in mind. "The 1812 Overture," *Swan Lake, Scheherazade,* and *Peter and the Wolf* are examples that come immediately
to mind. Opera, of course, is the supreme blending of song and
story. At another level the Broadway musical offers the same
potent combination.

Songs that tell a story have a natural attraction for us because
they suggest that the beauty and harmony of music is potentially
present in lives. Put another way, the events of life seem more
ordered and less chaotic when they can be given musical expression. Social and personal tragedy or joy, wars, revolutions, and
unrequited love take their place in a larger perspective. Life conceived as a comic opera or even a tragic opera is preferable to life
experienced as a random collision of random events. This sense
of meaning is also, as I argue elsewhere in the book, essential to
morality: morality does not thrive in a climate of nihilism.

One of the characteristics of pure rock—that is, rock that is not
combined with folk, blues, or ballad—is its absence of story.
Robert Pittman is instructive on this point. He describes how he
had to explain the concept of MTV to executives who wanted a
beginning, a middle and an end to their television. "I said, 'There
is no beginning, middle and end. It's all ebb and flow,'" boasts
Pittman. What these executives failed to realize is that "this is a
non-narrative generation." MTV, accordingly, does away with
narrative and replaces it with what filmmakers call montage: a

rapid sequence of loosely connected images. This is the perfect fit of medium to music because rock is about the flow of experience, not about making sense out of experience. This is also the reason rock delights in nonsense syllables such as "sha da da da." They are, according to Robert Pattison, "the most honest form of language . . . because they're meaningless."

Non-narrative is not exactly the same thing as nihilistic, but it's the next thing. Even the term "flow of experience" is misleading when applied to contemporary rock because the term suggests a connection or continuum. What rock presents, however, is not a flow but a series of disconnected episodes. This is typical of rap, also. And the chief episodic unit is sexual intercourse. A representative example is a "tune," which consists almost entirely of one repeated refrain, "it feels good," accompanied by background groans which leave us in no doubt about what "it" is. There is no development of the story line beyond that single sensation. Every night, big-city radio stations play hour after hour of music that varies only slightly in sound and theme from "Feels Good." If, as Plato says, "musical training is a more potent instrument than any other," it means that many youngsters are being trained to see life only as a series of sensual episodes which they are not obliged to connect.

In the world of MTV and rock radio, it is decidedly not "the same old story" of falling in love that song once celebrated and reinforced. For that matter, most of life's stories are missing from these formats. No connections are drawn to a life beyond the adolescent's fantasy life. No connections are drawn to past or future. Rock claims to be the most honest music, but this is not an honest picture of life. It does not help young people transmute immediate experience into something more. It does not teach them what happens when the limits are pushed too far, as, for example, country music—a much more honest form of music—does. It does not prepare them emotionally or cognitively for any sort of satisfactory adult life.

In summary, music has powers that go far beyond entertainment. It can play a positive role in moral development by creating sensual attractions to goodness, or it can play a destructive role by setting children on a temperamental path that leads away from

virtue. Other cultures have found ways of helping the temperamental self keep time with the social self—that is, with the self
that must live responsibly with others. That synchrony no longer
exists in our society. Until it is restored, the prospects for a moral
renewal are dim.

11.

LIFE IS A STORY

"Whether I shall turn out to be the hero of my own life, or whether that station will be held by anybody else, these pages must show."

So begins Dickens's *David Copperfield*. It's a wonderful passage, and immediately confirms Dickens's reputation for having captured the "feel" of childhood as few others have. The dream of being a hero or heroine is, perhaps, the child's most common fantasy. Children do, of course, also dream of wealth and ease, but they are more interested in the excitement and tension that heroism holds out. The hero makes demands upon himself, and that is what a child wants to do, must do in order to grow.

Thus when he daydreams, it is on a heroic scale. He wants to enlist in great causes, bring victory to the right side, keep vigil while others sleep, defend the innocent and rescue those in danger. Young David Copperfield is merely reflecting the hope of any normal boy or girl. Even Holden Caulfield, the cynical young narrator of *Catcher in the Rye,* dreams of being a hero. The story derives its title from his wish to spend his life catching children who might otherwise come too near a dangerous cliff.

Although they are less likely to admit it, adults also would like to be heroes of their own lives. Most parents want on some level to be heroes to their children, and most men would like to be heroes to wives or girlfriends. It's a familiar form of wishing. How many times have we imagined scenarios in which we come daringly to the rescue of lovers or spouses or children?

If the kind of stories we like are any indication, we have not lost the taste for heroism. Accounts of heroism figure prominently in popular newspapers and magazines. The policeman-as-hero and the doctor-as-hero are stock characters on television. Grown-ups as well as children flock to movies such as *Star Wars, Rocky,* and *Raiders of the Lost Ark.* We also make heroes of sports stars and often act as though something crucial were at stake when two teams clash. Professional wrestling, which is a cross between sport and entertainment, is deliberately cast in terms of heroes and villains, and is tremendously popular.

These hyped-up media events are easy to criticize; they are watered down or contrived versions of heroism. Nevertheless, they reflect a popular taste and instinct that goes back to Homer, for whom the best kind of life, the memorable life, was modeled on a heroic story.

Which leads to a second observation.

The desire to be a hero, so common to children and adults, is part of a larger wish: the hope that one's life can be like a story. It is such a basic wish that we hardly reflect on it. For the most part we simply assume that our lives will make sense. And the kind of "making sense" we intuitively have in mind is not the sense of a mathematical equation or of a scientific theorem but the kind of sense a story makes.

Even the kind of meaning philosophy offers does not quite do the trick. The Spanish writer Fernando Savater tells how his little brother picked up a philosophical essay from his desk and asked, "Does this have a plot?" When he found that it did not, he replied, "Then I can't imagine how it can be a book."

Like Savater's brother, most people want their stories to come with plots—just as they want their cars to come with wheels. It is the popular belief that stories ought to go somewhere. And most of them do. A surprising number of myths and adventure stories and even novels take the form of a journey. The *Odyssey, Treasure Island, Pilgrim's Progress, Moby-Dick,* and *Lord of the Rings* are but a few examples.

The same impulse that makes us want our books to have a plot makes us want our lives to have a plot. We need to feel that we are getting somewhere, making progress. There is something in us that is not satisfied with a merely psychological explanation of our lives. It doesn't do justice to our conviction that we are on some kind of journey or quest, that there must be some deeper meaning to our lives than whether we feel good about ourselves. Only people who have lost the sense of adventure, mystery, and romance worry about their self-esteem. And at that point what they need is not a good therapist but a good story. Or more precisely, the central question for us should not be, "What personality dynamics explain my behavior?" but rather, "What sort of story am I in?"

The reason why the rise of psychology has not ushered in the reign of happiness is that although it provides skills for life, psychology has never been able to say anything about the purpose of life. As Savater's brother might point out, the psychology books have no plot. Several prominent psychologists have been quite frank in admitting this. For example, Viktor Frankl has noted that the two major theories of motivation—tension reduction (Freud) and self-actualization (Maslow)—do not account for many of our actions. Our greatest need, says Frankl, is to find meaning in our lives; and the most effective therapy, he suggests, would help clients to see their lives as a meaningful story.

Bruno Bettelheim makes much the same point. His main task as a therapist of disturbed children was, he writes, "to restore meaning to their lives." What is the most important source of meaning? After his relationship with his parents, it is literature that best conveys meaning to the child. What type of literature? Fairy tales and hero stories, replies Bettelheim. Why? Because they teach that "a struggle against severe difficulties in life is unavoidable, is an intrinsic part of human existence—but that if one does not shy away, but steadfastly meets unexpected and often unjust hardships, one masters all obstacles and at the end emerges victorious." And what is true for children is true for adults. "To find deeper meaning," writes Bettelheim, "one must be able to transcend the narrow confines of a self-centered existence and believe that one will make a significant contribution to life—if not right now, then at some future time."

Nothing serves this purpose better than the ability to visualize life as a story. Chesterton wrote: "My first and last philosophy, that which I believe in with unbroken certainty, I learnt in the nursery . . . The things I believed most in then, the things I believe most now, are the things called fairy tales." This is all the more significant coming from Chesterton, who, among English writers, is perhaps unmatched in his sheer enthusiasm for life. The perspective he maintained as an adult was the same as in childhood. In *Orthodoxy,* one of his best books, he confesses: "I had always felt life first as a story."

Stories reinforce the sense that life makes sense—something we are prone to forget from time to time. And some stories do this better than others. Here is Michelle Landsberg describing how she stumbled onto the world of children's literature:

Like many another adult I became temporarily indifferent to contemporary adult fiction at a point in my life when I most needed reassurance about the purposefulness of life. My babies were young, I was busy and exhausted, and my emotions were unwontedly open and vulnerable . . . Contemporary fiction—a surrealistic blur of postnuclear nihilism, chic despair, fragmentation, incoherence, and sexual obsession—left me irritated and sickened. My daily concern was the nurturing of new life; an aesthetically fashionable alienation, or a flippant cynicism about human endeavor, was the last thing I needed or wanted . . . It was at this point that I rediscovered Charles Dickens. His tumultuous vitality, his relish for the human comedy, his robust affection, and his engrossing plots were just the infusion I needed. And rediscovering that primary pleasure of self-forgetfulness in an author's created world of plot and character led me back one step further. I found myself skulking off to the local library and returning laden with all my childhood favorites.

Landsberg emphasizes the self-forgetfulness that the story brings. She didn't pick up Dickens in order to discover the meaning of life. But it is only because Dickens's world is so rich with reassurance and meaning that we can enter so fully into it, leaving self-preoccupation behind.

Stories may occasionally play an even more important role. Paul Zweig, in commenting on the *Arabian Nights,* notes that "endless numbers of characters save their lives in the nick of time by coming up with a good story to tell." And of course, the frame tale for this collection of tales is the story of Scheherazade, who keeps alive by telling a story every night for a thousand and one nights. We all know that stories entertain, but as suggested by the Arabian storytellers, they can also serve a more basic function. Put simply, they save lives. The conviction that our life is a meaningful story can literally keep us alive. The stories we read or hear or see on film can reinforce and sustain that conviction. They help us to see that our lives are worth living.

This is a large claim, yet there is a strong case for it. For example, if we turn our attention to those who attempt suicide, we find that the problem is not so much that they have lost their self-esteem (although that is certainly part of it) but, more important, that they have lost the narrative thread of their lives. Life has become pointless, without plot or direction. We are willing to endure suffering when the suffering has meaning, but meaning is exactly what is absent in the case of a potential suicide. When suffering can be set within a narrative scheme, we manage to keep going; but if life itself is pointless, why put up with its thousand mockeries and cruelties?

In times of despair finding the right story can be lifesaving. There is, of course, no formula for predicting what will do the trick. What touches a chord in one person's life leaves another unmoved. Still, there are stories that allow those who have lost hope to place their plight within a meaningful pattern. It might be an inspirational book—something like the story of Jill Kinmont or Joni Eareckson. It might be a biography or a story remembered from childhood. It might be the story of Job, or the story of Viktor

Frankl's concentration camp ordeal recounted in *Man's Search for Meaning*. It need not be a story of clear-cut heroism or unequivocal triumph. Sometimes it is the unheroic hero who best meets our need, the kind one encounters, for instance, in the novels of Graham Greene: protagonists who themselves grope through darkness and despair, whose struggles go largely unrecognized and unrewarded, who nevertheless win through to some kind of victory.

I know a couple who get through a bad time by reading the Psalms to each other every night. The writer Lance Morrow describes a woman whose son died accidentally on the night of his high school graduation: "She told me she got through the weeks and months afterward by reading and rereading the works of Willa Cather. The calm and clarity of Cather's prose stabilized the woman and helped her through the time."

If a book can save one's soul (as many Christians believe), why shouldn't there be books that can save one's life? I believe there are. Those stories which help to explain our lives can sustain them as well. Like Scheherazade, it is always possible for us to cheat death by coming up with a good story at the darkest hour.

Still, it can be argued that other things are more important in sustaining us: love of friends or family, for example. No one would disagree with the centrality of love, of course; but a little reflection will show that we always tend to cast our love into the form of a story. Any love that lasts becomes a love story. A marriage, for example, is a shared story: the partners grow in love partly on the basis of shared memories, and partly on the conviction that they are on a journey together. In having children, they bring them into the story and introduce them to the characters— aunts, uncles, and grandparents—who are already a part of it. It is an expression of confidence that the story ought to be continued. Family life can be filled with unpredictable tragedies as well as unplanned joys, but the greater tragedy occurs when marriage and birth no longer fit within a story. It's not necessary to recount the sad statistics that tie singleness, divorce, separation, and illegitimacy to drug use, mental illness, and suicide. To lose one's story or never to have found one is a calamity of immense proportions.

Up to now I have suggested that stories can keep us going in the face of despair. Now I would like to suggest something further—the main point, really. Stories can also help to keep us on the path of virtue. They can give us not only a reason for living but also a reason for living well. This doesn't mean we should look for a simple connection such as, "People who read stories are better than people who don't." For one thing, it would depend on the kind of stories they read; for another, the link between stories and virtue is an indirect one. It has to do, once again, with this conviction that our lives are—or ought to be—stories. The sense that life makes sense is really the sine qua non for ethical behavior. If the larger thing—existence itself—means nothing, then individual acts performed within that meaningless scheme are themselves meaningless. "If stories weren't told or books weren't written," says a character in an Isaac Bashevis Singer tale, "man would live like the beasts, only for the day." "Only for the day" is not, of course, a time frame conducive to the development of character. Lynne Cheney, the chairman of the National Endowment for the Humanities, develops this theme in a recent article entitled "The Importance of Stories":

> But what about the other kind of story, the kind that opens our eyes, wakes us up to the fact that we are part of a continuity extending through time? What happens when these stories are neglected? Let me suggest there are grave consequences when we fail to awaken the time-binding capacity in the young. People who grow up without a sense of how yesterday has affected today are unlikely to have a strong sense of how today affects tomorrow. They are unlikely to understand in a bone-deep way how the decisions they make now will shape and affect their future. It is only when we become conscious of the flow of time that the consequences of action—whether it is taking drugs or dropping out of school—become a consideration. It is only when we have perspective on our lives that motives besides immediate gratification can come into play.

The point is this: The best motivation for acting well—and hence the surest foundation for morality—is the belief that we have a role to play in life. When Alexander Pope wrote, "Act well your part: there all the honour lies," he cut through to a basic truth about morality. Morality is not merely a matter of rule keeping but of role-playing.

This, of course, sounds wrong to the modern ear. We have been taught that role-playing is bad, that we should simply be ourselves. But there is another way to look at the matter. The early Greeks, for example, viewed life as a unique drama in which each man had the chance to become a hero—even if only a tragic hero. And in this context, acting your part well was understood not in the sense of pretending to be someone you were not but in the sense of rising above yourself. Acting truly, acting nobly, acting rightly were not behaviors that came easily or naturally to men but behaviors that required high purpose, a sense of mission, good examples to follow, and—above all—an audience who would appreciate the words and deeds. This was the dramatic sense of life, and because life turns partly on fate, it was never far removed from the tragic sense of life. This outlook was reflected and nourished in epic, poetry, and drama.

The ancients did not make the divisions and categories we make today. For the Greeks drama, religion, and morals were intimately bound together. As far as we can tell, plays first made their appearance in the context of religious festivals. And although not every play was a morality play, the theater was always understood to serve a crucial function in keeping passions within bounds.

And this brings me back to the original point. Morality needs to be set within a storied vision if it is to remain morality. Conceived of as rule keeping or as refraining from wrongdoing, it never works for long. Instead, it withers into something cold and cautious and, all too often, into self-righteousness. It is, of course, important to keep the rules, but the spirit in which they are kept is equally important.

Virtue must be first of all a positive quality. It avoids what is wrong because it is powerfully attracted to what is right. We admit as much in our instinctive dislike of all that is pharisaical or prudish. A virtue is a strength, not a timidity or incapacity. It has to do with a frame of mind that is confident, is willing to risk all, wants to do the right thing because it is seen as the noble and loving thing to do. It does not refuse the adventure even if that may mean making mistakes.

What I am getting at here is captured in the Spanish expression *tener la moral alta, tener mucha moral* ("to have high morale, lots of morale"). The word "morale" denotes spirit, hope, enthusiasm, readiness for action. Significantly, it derives from the word "moral." The study of word origins helps us to see how people originally felt about concepts, and originally they saw a connection between high spirits and morality. There is a similar connection in Latin between the words "virtue" and "virility." Both come from the Latin word *vir* or "man." "Virility" means "manly vigor or force"; and "virtue" also was understood as a force or strength. The point intended here is not, of course, to suggest that men are the more virtuous sex but to call attention to the role that vitality plays in morality.

The connection between morale and morality is an important one, and one that our present society seems to have lost sight of. Virtue, understood in its original sense, requires a certain passion for life. And stories can supply some of that passion. Even stories that do not conform in every respect to our code of right and wrong may still supply the passion for keeping that code in the right spirit. Achilles and Ulysses, for example, are heroes, but not all of their actions are admirable. What they do exhibit in abundance, though, are qualities of endurance, resourcefulness, and willpower. And these things, although they are not virtues in themselves, are prerequisites of virtue. To do the virtuous thing may in some situations require great tenacity and boldness. Reading the *Iliad* and the *Odyssey* is not the same as reading the Bible, but reading the former can have the effect of restoring our morale and calling us back to the lists. The problem of the sometimes amoral hero is only a problem if we are looking for a direct modeling effect, and we needn't always do this. Some credit must be given to the reader. A young reader may thrill to Ulysses' revenge on the suitors, but he still knows he is not supposed to loose arrows at his own enemies. That is not the sort of lesson the *Odyssey* teaches him.

Even so, a problem remains. By now it will have occurred to

most readers that the term "heroism" needs some qualification. Part of the difficulty can be removed if we make a distinction between hero and adventurer. The adventurer, though he has many admirable traits, is to some extent amoral. He doesn't always care about the distinctions between right and wrong. He lives primarily for adventure—that is, for himself. The hero, on the other hand, is selfless. His energies have been channeled to serve the good of society. Indiana Jones is sometimes a hero, sometimes a reckless adventurer. Galahad, Saint George, and the Lone Ranger are, more strictly, heroes: their skills are always at the service of society.

But there is a deeper problem. An adult can never be satisfied with such heroes in the way a child can. For the child heroism means daring deeds, high adventure, much praise, and plenty of free time between episodes. Children—particularly boys—seem to prefer the type of hero who isn't tied down to commitment (other than the general commitment of doing the right thing at the right time). Jim Hawkins, Luke Skywalker, Bilbo Baggins, Wonder Woman, and Indiana Jones are different kinds of heroes and heroines, but they all have this in common: they are not burdened by commitments to spouse and children, and although they do have mothers, fathers, or siblings, this never presents an obstacle to having adventures. They are selfless, true, but certain types of selflessness are never required of them.

In addition, for the child, half the adventure consists in telling the adventure. What good is an adventure if it can't be related? Heroism that is unrecorded, unsung, and unacknowledged is not what the child has in mind. This is also the way adults looked at things when the human race was in its childhood. Heroism and storytelling went hand in hand. The adventurer was not only a man of action, he was a talker, too. After each adventure, he finds an audience and tells his story. Indeed, part of the reason for having an adventure is to tell about it. And for this there have to be periods of leisure—troughs in the wave. In the *Odyssey,* for instance, there are long interludes between adventures which serve not only to give Ulysses a rest but to let him tell his story. The same holds true for Sindbad the Sailor, whose seven voyages are interspersed with six tranquil interludes of feasting and tale telling. And in the Arthurian legends, the knights regroup from time to time at the Round Table to exchange stories of adventure.

Another element that ties in here and is, perhaps, a psychological necessity for the child is that the adventurer or hero is often trying to get home. Ulysses' adventure ends at home. So does Jim Hawkins's. So does Bilbo Baggins's. *The Hobbit* is a good illustration of this point and the previous one. For Bilbo much of the appeal of his adventure lies in his dream of returning home to the Shire, having cakes and ale again, and telling his story to an admiring crowd of friends and neighbors. The child is like Bilbo. He wants to have his adventure but he wants to be able to go back home when it is over. Having had the adventure is as good as the adventure itself.

All of this stands in contrast to the life story of the average adult, and we are forced to come out and ask what our own lives can possibly have to do with heroism of this kind. The opportunity for scaling castle walls or struggling hand to hand with monstrous villains is not afforded to most of us. As we grow up, we inevitably find that occasions for glorious exploits rarely, if ever, present themselves. Moreover, the stories we seem to be in are not nearly as clear and conclusive as the ones we daydreamed as children. We find that the outline is blurred, the plot murky, our choices far from clear.

At the point that we realize this (if we are normal and still want to be the heroes of our own lives), we will find ourselves developing a more mature understanding of what heroism may require. We will have to exchange one notion of heroism for another: one that is not only less glorious but is, in a sense, more demanding.

In other words, we come to realize that there are more ordinary kinds of heroism, from which daring deeds and high adventure are absent, which are for the most part unsung and unrecorded, but which nevertheless require great endurance and ingenuity. This adventure will take the form of a journey, but it will most likely be an interior journey. There will be a desire to tell the story, but the audience for it will be small: perhaps only one or two others will know, perhaps only God. The most common form this adventure takes is marrying and raising a family—although there are certainly other forms.

The difference between the hero of legend and the hero of everyday life may be put this way: For the traditional hero such as Ulysses or Jim Hawkins the adventure takes place away from home. Home is where you go after the adventure; it is essentially the end of the adventure. For the average adult, on the other hand, home *is* the adventure, the place where he lays himself on the line. The adventure consists precisely in those commitments with which the classical hero or child hero rarely allows himself to be entangled. The temptation for the traditional hero is to avoid the adventure and settle down; the temptation for the ordinary hero is to avoid commitment and have an adventure. For the ordinary hero it is staying home that is the hard thing, the thing that requires courage and energy. He must put aside the child's fantasy of escaping. Once having accepted the main adventure, he cannot allow himself to be distracted.

Now, it might be objected here that if this is so, then children ought not to read or hear traditional fairy tales or adventure stories. Since they focus on escape, journeys, and the like, they would seem to offer poor preparation for the kind of life most children will grow up to lead. But this is not the case. To see why, let us refer back to the discussion of morale and morality. The argument there was that hope and high spirits can sustain us in the face of hardship or temptation. But everyday heroism is, in some senses, a more demanding and rigorous journey than adventure heroism. There is one main reason why this is so. The story of our everyday life is continuous, not episodic. We are not afforded the luxury of "time out" in between adventures. The heroic thing required of ordinary people is sustained commitment. There are very few if any breaks in the story where one is allowed, like Ulysses, to have weeks of feasting and storytelling on the island of the Phaeacians or seven years of ease on Calypso's island. In short, the kind of lifelong commitment required in marriage or parenthood or devotion to some important life task is beyond the comprehension of the child, and outside his time frame. He can grasp the glory of putting oneself to the test in ten or twenty tremendous exploits interrupted by rest and recreation, but he is not ready to grasp the notion of extended heroism: putting oneself to the test day after day for ten or twenty years—

and having most of it remain unsung. This would be intolerable for the child. He needs to think heroically, but he also needs lots of time off for play. Hence his preference for the episodic type of hero story.

What I have been calling ordinary heroism is not the stuff adventure stories are made of. Because of this, the adult, if he retains his interest in reading, will often shift his attention from adventure stories to novels. The novel seems to offer a more realistic account of everyday problems. But this may amount to a miscalculation of even an adult's real needs, especially if he turns his back on the stories of his youth as though they were so many illusions. To lead the kind of life the ordinary adult must lead, and to live it well, requires (to go back to our Spanish phrase) "high morale, lots of morale." For this kind of life one has to be willing to do the right thing whatever it may be and whatever it might require, to give one's all, to have one's loyalty tested over and over again, and above all, one must be able to cast events in the mythic mold, to see things from the hero's point of view, to transmute both success and suffering into a story with vigorous meaning.

But where does one get these sorts of skills? For a child the best imaginative preparation for ordinary heroism is given by traditional fairy tales and adventure stories: they predispose him to accept whatever challenges ordinary heroism will require of him as an adult. The complicating parts of the story, the fine shadings and ambiguities, can come later. But this is what ought to come first. This is why Chesterton could say that the fairy stories he learned as a child were the stories that served him best in his adult life. Along with stories of heroism, they form a deep and inexhaustible well to which we can return again and again for fresh drafts of morale.

One of Chesterton's essays is entitled "Fiction as Food"; and it seems appropriate to conclude this analysis with an illustrative story—a morsel of fiction to chew on. Happily there exists a story, well known to most Americans, that draws together many of the strands I have discussed. Frank Capra's film *It's a Wonderful Life* is one of the finest pieces of storytelling to have come out of Hollywood; it is also a superb example of the story of everyday heroism. As one of the most popular films ever made, it proves the point that our instincts tend toward viewing life as a story.

The hero of the story, as you will remember, is George Bailey, an Everyman who has lived his whole life in one small town, Bedford Falls, and whose dreams of escape and adventure have never been realized. Boyhood and adolescent dreams of travel and excitement are yielded up one by one as George's sense of duty compels him to take up civic and family obligations. His reward for all this is a growing sense of burden and frustration. And when he is threatened with scandal and the possibility of jail because of another's mistake, his frustration slides into despair.

The thing that saves him from despair and suicide is a visit from his guardian angel on Christmas Eve. This may sound contrived to anyone who has not seen the film, but in fact, the angel's appearance (as a lovable old man) is so skillfully rendered that it seems the next thing to normal. The angel's task is to help George rediscover the meaning of his life. And he does this by allowing him to see what the world— particularly the world of Bedford Falls—would be like if he had never been born. So the angel— Clarence is his name—escorts George on a tour of the town minus the life of George Bailey. What Bailey (and we) discover is the enormous hole left by his absence. We see many of the characters—his mother, his uncle, his wife, the druggist, a young woman whom he has helped—as they would have been had they never felt his influence. His mother is embittered and suspicious, his uncle gone insane, his wife a timid old maid, the druggist a ruined man, the young woman a prostitute.

What the angel allows George to see is what the viewer of the film has been witness to all along: that the life of George Bailey is a hero's story. He is, moreover, a hero we can readily identify with. His heroism is the heroism of sustained commitment in the face of unlooked-for burdens and unforeseen turns of fate. His heroism, like that of most adults, consists in refusing the temptation to be free and uncommitted. His despair is the despair of a man who no longer understands the story he is in. His life makes no sense. What restores his morale and thus prevents him from doing a very immoral thing is the restoration of the narrative thread: the ability to see his life whole.

What Clarence reminds George—that his life is a meaningful story—is what the film reminds its audience about their own lives. And this no doubt accounts for its immense popularity.

There are few stories that can match this one in its ability to replenish morale.

One final point. In the traditional hero story, the hero ventures forth and then returns from his adventure to bestow a boon on his fellowman. In this film, it is the hero's renunciation of adventure—his quiet commitment to home and neighbor—that bestows a blessing on the people of Bedford Falls. But he is able to do this not because he has given up on the heroic dreams of boyhood but because he has remained true to the best part of them. They have remained all along a source from which he draws renewed commitment for his own very different kind of adventure. There are three possibilities in regard to the heroic and romantic dreams of youth. We can turn our backs on them, become "realistic" about life, and attempt to feed only on fact, never on fiction (this is a constant temptation for George, who is as prone to cynicism and compromise as any man). Or we can wallow in our romantic dreams, always wishing for a life that cannot be, never satisfied with the one we have (this is what happens to Emma Bovary in Flaubert's novel). Or—best of all—we can transmute them, realizing, in Savater's words, that "the best part of an adventure tale is to sense it as prologue and initiation of our own adventure."

George Bailey has chosen the best part (although he requires an angelic revelation to fully realize it), and that is how he turns out to be the hero of his own life—and of other lives as well.

American schools were once able to convey this sense of life as a story. History books bore titles such as *America's Story, Our Country's Story,* or *The Story of Western Civilization.* And the manner in which subjects such as history and literature were taught left no doubt that teachers had a sense of mission that went beyond the goal of bringing knowledge to students. They also understood their job as one of bringing students into a tradition, an ongoing story. Although some textbook titles may still convey that message, many teachers have abandoned the goal of conveying a larger point or purpose to which students might connect their lives. In the psychological version of life to which many educators now subscribe, the self is not bound to any story, only to its own development.

But this is not a truthful vision. Alasdair MacIntyre observes that we necessarily find ourselves part of a story that has already begun, playing "roles into which we have been drafted." The narrative thread of our lives is woven in part out of strands that preexist us, and we can never hope to understand ourselves without knowing about the stories we belong to; nor can we ever fully understand why we must sometimes act against our own self-interest for the sake of something larger.

When the narrative sense is absent from individual lives, society also suffers an impoverishment. Saul Bellow has said that Jewish culture could not have survived without the stories that gave point and meaning to the Jewish moral tradition. Both for society and the individual the loss of story and history amounts to a loss of memory. We become like amnesiacs, not knowing where we are going, because we don't know where we have come from, and—for the same reason—susceptible to the most superficial attractions.

12.

MYTH WARS

Despite all that I have said about the neglect of stories in the recent past, I think the nineties and the decade that follows will see a resurgence of interest in stories among educators. In the years following Bill Moyers's televised interviews with mythologist Joseph Campbell, storytelling and mythology have begun to experience a renaissance. A number of books aimed at showing the links between myth and life (such as Jean Shinoda Bolen's *Goddesses in Everywoman* and Krippner and Feinstein's *Personal Mythology*) have sold briskly in recent years. The attempt to match one's own life pattern to those of Persephone, Demeter, Artemis, and Perseus has apparently become a serious preoccupation for many Americans. The idea has caught on in therapy, too: therapists now regularly encourage clients to find their stories. Of course, in one group—Alcoholics Anonymous—the practice of telling one's story as a means to recovery has long been a staple. And as more and more recovery groups adopt the AA model, more and more people are getting in the habit of discerning and telling their life stories.

Meanwhile, in the field of education itself, increasing numbers of elementary schools are switching to reading curriculums that are touted as "literature-based." At the same time, the National Endowment for the Humanities has established summer institutes for the purpose of teaching teachers how to teach the classics. As a result, in some elementary schools children are hearing the *Odyssey* told and sung, and in some cases they stand up before younger groups and tell the tale themselves. Another result of this renewed interest is that school assemblies these days are as likely to be given over to a professional storyteller as to an AIDS activist.

Will educators shift to the new myth/story paradigm? It seems likely. The field of education is due for a change. Almost everyone agrees that something new and imaginative needs to be done. Stories are becoming "hot," and educators, as I have suggested, have a weakness for the latest trend.

The question, to my mind, is not whether educators will shift to a renewed emphasis on stories. The question is, what kind of stories? Different kinds of stories can inspire different kinds of imagination, and the imagination, in turn, shapes our will and our character. It makes a difference, morally speaking, whether a youngster reads *To Kill a Mockingbird* or the latest book in the *Baby-Sitters Club* series. A regular diet of the latter makes it more difficult to acquire a taste for the former. Because when we talk about imagination, we're not talking just about books but about a whole cast of mind. In this sense, an entire era can be colored by a certain cast of imagination. That's what we mean when we refer to the Romantic period or the Victorian imagination or the Postmodern imagination. What is considered interesting and important to a society depends to a large extent on the imaginative vision that governs it. Likewise with education. Behind the choice of books, courses, and curriculums lies some imaginative picture of how children should develop.

Now that imagination is back on the agenda, what sort of imaginative path will educators take? Let me suggest that when it comes to moral development, there is an easy path and a difficult path; and educators, being human, will be strongly tempted to take the easy path—in fact, nearly the same one they've trodden in the recent past. Let's call the easy path "the idyllic imagination," and the difficult one "the moral imagination." The first term is discussed at length in Irving Babbitt's *Rousseau and Romanticism,* though it may have older origins; the second term originates with the English statesman and philosopher Edmund Burke. The terms "idyllic" and "moral" refer not only to types of literature but to states of mind. A simple way to describe the difference is to say that the moral imagination is concerned with things as they ought to be, while the idyllic imagination is concerned with things as they can never be—that is, the moral imagination works within the limits of reality and the idyllic imagination does not. The moral imagination holds up an ideal that is attainable, although only through hard work; the idyllic imagination holds up an ideal that can never be attained in reality, but can easily be attained in fantasy or in feeling.

The idyllic imagination wants to escape from the harsh realities of ordinary life, either to a dream world, or to nature, or to a more primitive life. It follows mood rather than conscience, and rejects conventional morality in favor of a natural morality that will, it believes, emerge spontaneously in the absence of cultural restraints. When the idyllic imagination takes a spiritual turn, as it often does, it prefers a spirituality without morality or dogma.

The idyllic imagination, in short, is not unlike a child's imagination. It likes to daydream. If all goes well, however, a child gradually adjusts his imaginary dream world to his real situation. In the process, he develops an imagination that is more realistic, one that serves him better in making sense of the world of hard facts. But not everyone wants to grow up. Babbitt points to Rousseau as the supreme example of the urge to stay forever young and innocent. A letter Rousseau wrote at age fifty-five to the bailli de Mirabeau is a good illustration of the idyllic imagination at work:

> I love to dream, but freely allowing my mind to wander without enslaving myself to any subject . . . this idle and contemplative life . . . becomes to me daily more delicious; to wander alone endlessly and ceaselessly among the trees and rocks about my dwelling, to muse or rather to be as irresponsible as I please . . . finally to give myself up uncon-

strainedly to my fantasies . . . that, sir, is for me the supreme enjoyment . . .

At its best the idyllic imagination provides a respite from the serious business of living, but for the serious business itself—the call of duty, the necessity of hard work, the taming of selfish and violent emotions, facing sickness and death—the idyllic imagination is inadequate. The serious business of life requires a more serious imagination: the moral imagination. The latter term, first used by Edmund Burke, was used much later by Russell Kirk to describe the frame of mind of Burke, Johnson, Babbitt, Eliot, and other traditionalist men of letters.

The moral imagination may be described as a disposition to grasp reality and conform to it, as opposed to the idyllic desire to ignore reality and please one's self. The moral imagination takes guidance from external reference points which are considered binding: either God, natural law, or tradition. In Sophocles' play, Antigone recognizes a law that is set above both her city's law and her own self-interest. In addition, the moral imagination recognizes that appetites need to be restrained, and that this does not come easily but has to be worked at. Finally, the moral imagination recognizes that reality does not conform itself to our wishes but often thwarts them. Far from being omnipotent, the self is often at the mercy of forces beyond its control. The moral imagination recognizes the sometimes tragic nature of life.

The dramas of Sophocles and Aeschylus would come under the category of the moral imagination. So would the work of Dante, Shakespeare, Tolstoy, Austen, Melville, Conrad, Hawthorne, and Eliot. The moral imagination is also shaped by history and biography. Some less serious forms of literature, such as the detective story, would also qualify, since they assume the existence of a morally ordered universe and the importance of restoring that order when it is violated. Finally, it should be noted that some writers manage to blend the two imaginations with some success. C. S. Lewis and Charles Williams, for example, have been described as "Christian romantics"; and many of Shakespeare's plays are built on a masterful counterpointing of the idyllic and the serious.

What is the proper place of the idyllic imagination in our lives?

In simple terms, it is recreative, just as a daydream is recreative. Babbitt observes: "Apollo cannot always be bending the bow. Man needs at times to relax, and one way of relaxing is to take refuge for a time in some land of chimeras, to follow the Arcadian gleam. He may then come back to the real world, the world of active effort, solaced and refreshed." The problem comes, says Babbitt, when the idyllic sets itself up not as a respite from the serious business of life but as a substitute for it—that is, as a serious explanation of life, as a philosophy and a religion. This is always bad news for society because, as Babbitt says in a chapter ironically titled "Romantic Morality," "there is no such thing as romantic morality." But it is bad news for the individual, too, because the idyllic imagination is not up to coping with reality. Since the idyllic imagination misconstrues the nature of things, it usually, as Russell Kirk observes, "terminates in disillusion and boredom." Babbitt notes that the Romantic movement, which is an expression of the idyllic imagination, "began by asserting the goodness of man and the loveliness of nature," and "ended by producing the greatest literature of despair the world has ever seen."

The idyllic imagination lacks a tragic sense, and as a result, is more easily defeated by tragedy. Last year's Romantic idealist turns out to be this year's suicide. And because the Romantic is essentially naive about evil, he is less resistant to it. As a result, the idyllic imagination, upon encountering boredom, frustration, or temptation, sometimes evolves into a third kind of imagination. T. S. Eliot and Russell Kirk suggest that the idyllic imagination, if not tempered by the moral imagination, often becomes "the diabolic imagination." This seems to be true to some extent of Byron and Shelley, who were both enamored of the occult and fascinated by the idea of incest. Byron was even proud of the fact that he was rumored to have murdered a man. Baudelaire, a later Romanticist, considered himself to be of "the Satanic School."

Why is this discussion of the idyllic and moral imaginations important for us? Because in the late sixties and the subsequent decade the popular imagination was captured by an idyllic vision. During that time, millions of young people turned away from the work ethic and immersed themselves in a world of idyllic dreams.

If the transformation couldn't always be accomplished spontaneously and naturally, it could be assisted by a cornucopia of drugs which provided easy escape to never-never land. Music also helped to establish the mood. Popular songs promised that Arcadian simplicity was just around the corner ("If you're going to San Francisco, you're gonna meet some gentle people there"), or that daydreaming could solve the world's problems ("Imagine there's no countries . . . nothing to kill or die for").

As with previous idyllic flings, however, this one quickly developed a dark side. What began as a vision of Edenic innocence soon evolved into something else. If youngsters of the sixties were wearing flowers in their hair, many youngsters of the next generation were wearing spikes instead of flowers, and listening to a music preoccupied with themes of hopelessness, destruction, suicide, Satanism, and sexual mutilation. In the sixties the balance between the idyllic imagination and the moral imagination was tilted very much in favor of the idyllic. For a great many people it proved to be an inadequate preparation both for coping with their own lives and for raising children who could cope.

The effects of that idyllic interlude are still with us. In addition, we are currently experiencing a nostalgia for the sixties that overlooks its negative side. Some look back to that period as a mellower time. Many see no necessary connection between the troubles we have now and the experimentation we had then. A large number of people, including a significant number of educators, think those idyllic ideas are still valid.

The persistence of this strain of imagination is perhaps best illustrated by the revival of interest in the thought of Joseph Campbell, who first achieved a mild degree of fame in the sixties when his book *The Hero with a Thousand Faces* became popular on college campuses. His star rose again in the mid-eighties with the broadcast of the PBS series *The Power of Myth with Bill Moyers.* The series was a great success for PBS, and the companion volume, *The Power of Myth,* was on the best-seller lists for seventy-four weeks.

The keys to Campbell's success are several: first, he is knowledgeable and charming; second, people really do, as he asserts, hunger for myth; and third, he offers an undemanding version of myth—that is, Campbell's vision is governed by an idyllic imagination. Ethics are, as he told Bill Moyers, "out of date." The key to happiness is to "follow your bliss." The reason why ethics are out of date is that good and evil, like yin and yang, are relative terms. Since it's impossible to have one without the other, good and evil are useless categories that we need not worry about. Any divisions of reality—whether into "good and bad," "us and them," "me and you"—are illusions because, in fact, there is only Oneness.

As a result, Campbell tends to ignore myths and stories that are products of the moral imagination, and when he does have to deal with them, especially with the stories and scriptures of Islam, Judaism, and Christianity, he claims that these "myths" have been misinterpreted. Sometimes he proceeds to reinterpret them as Eastern myths. Otherwise he simply ridicules them. Because the Western religions draw sharp distinctions between God and His creation, and between good and evil, they don't fit well into Campbell's scheme. Moreover, the Western religions claim to be based on historical (rather than mythical) events—an idea that does not comport with Campbell's belief that all myth, and indeed all of life, is a dream. And of course, these religions make moral claims on the believer that jar with Campbell's views: "Follow your bliss" is not one of the Ten Commandments.

The best myths from Campbell's perspective are Eastern and primitive ones, especially those that tell us nature is divine and we are a part of it. The beauty of pantheistic philosophies and myths is that they leave us free to follow our own agendas. Since we are all one—since the whole is contained in each person—then each person, by following his own bliss, is doing what is best for everyone. There is some debate among scholars about Campbell's reliability as an interpreter of myth, but these debates seem secondary to the Campbell phenomenon itself. *The Power of Myth* appeared at a time when many were experiencing dissatisfaction with materialism and technocracy. Campbell tapped a yearning for something more spiritual, more poetic. But what he offered was a fairly easy form of spirituality: one that required not self-discipline but self-awareness—a recognition that we are already perfected. Although the root meaning of "religion" is "to bind," here was a religion that wasn't binding at all.

For those who didn't read *The Power of Myth* or see the series on television, a still more popular version of Campbell's mythology was available at the local cinema. George Lucas, the creator of *Star Wars* and its sequels, drew his inspiration for Luke Skywalker and Obi-Wan Kenobi from his reading of Campbell. Lucas, of course, had to create a sharper distinction between good and evil than Campbell did, because an adventure story doesn't work well without that distinction. Nevertheless, at the end of the series Darth Vader and Obi-Wan Kenobi are revealed to be moral equivalents, both just playing their respective roles as yin and yang. Campbell, in turn, seems to have been influenced by Lucas. The PBS interviews were filmed at the Lucas ranch in California, and when Campbell was asked by Moyers to name a myth suitable for our own culture, he singled out *Star Wars*, and commenced to expound on it at length.

Although *Star Wars* sparkles with gadgetry, one of its premises is that you don't really need technology as long as you have inner wisdom. Even here inner wisdom seems somehow connected to nature. After all, Luke Skywalker learns some of his most important lessons in self-knowledge from a swamp creature. These twin themes of wisdom within and the wisdom of nature have now become a Hollywood staple. In *Poltergeist II*, for example, the source of evil is a Christian sect (antinature), while release from evil is effected by a practitioner of a nature religion, an Indian medicine man. Likewise in *Dances with Wolves*, one of the most popular of recent films, the Indians, because they revere nature, are portrayed as superior to the white men, who do not.

If the rest of the country is undergoing a nostalgia for the sixties and, by extension, for the primitivism that the sixties represent, many educators have never really left that decade. One of the unstated premises underlying the move toward multiculturalism in schools is the assumption that cultures which are less advanced technically are more natural, and hence have something to teach Western culture (which, again, is supposed to have cut itself off from nature). Although multiculturalism is portrayed as a yet-to-be-accomplished goal, it has, in fact, been around for a while. Paul Vitz's content analysis of ninety of the most widely used school textbooks in 1983 showed that an elementary school child would receive a more thorough grounding in American Indian

spirituality than in the religions of the West. My daughter's experience in public schools seems to confirm this. The bulk of her
social studies courses for grades four, five, and six were taken up
with the study of Native Americans and Eskimos (although it must
be admitted that a change from one school system to another may
have created an overlap).

The idyllic imagination is not, ironically, a product of primitive
societies but of Western societies. It flourishes particularly among
the educated classes. It might, at first glance, seem strange that
teachers, who have so much responsibility for disciplining and
socializing the young, are so susceptible to it. Yet those who are
most likely to want to work with the young are most likely to be
predisposed to believe in the natural goodness of children. Moreover, the Romantic admonition "Up! up! my friend, and quit your
books" has a particular appeal to those who have to spend hours
every day with textbooks and workbooks.

The idyllic imagination is taken very seriously by one group of
educators who, though their number is relatively small, nevertheless have a sizable influence. When Marilyn Ferguson wrote *The
Aquarian Conspiracy* in 1980, she noted that "of the Aquarian
Conspirators surveyed, more were involved in education than in
any other single category of work. They were teachers, administrators, policymakers, educational psychologists." What is the
Aquarian Conspiracy? According to Ferguson, "its members have
broken with certain key elements of Western thought." Nevertheless, it is a benign conspiracy of individuals "who seek power
only to disperse it." These people explore "extraordinary reaches
of conscious experience," "revolt against imposed patterns," are
aware of the brain's "awesome capacities to transform and inno-
vate," seek "the mystical experience of wholeness," and embark
on journeys of "self-transcendence" in order to find the "God-
within." "Together," says Ferguson of her fellow conspirators,
"we can do anything. We have it within our power to make peace
within our torn selves and with each other, to heal our homeland,
the Whole Earth . . . We can be our own children."

The label that came to stick to this loose band of conspirators
was not, however, "Aquarians" but the "New Age" movement.
Once again, the number of educators who consciously subscribe

to New Age thinking is probably not large. But since most teachers don't have a well-thought-out philosophy of education, and since New Agers do, their influence is out of proportion to their number. That influence will probably continue to grow because many of the goals of the New Age movement coincide with the goals of multiculturalists and also with the goals of environmentalists ("to heal our homeland, the Whole Earth"), and with the goals of some feminists (to find a nonpatriarchal form of spirituality).

Because the New Age movement in education has staked out the imagination as its special province, it is likely to have a particularly strong influence on the kinds of stories that are emphasized in schools. And indeed, this already appears to be the case. Ferguson says that the "new paradigm of learning" will use "imagery, storytelling, [and] dream journals." One of the most influential of the New Age educators is Jack Canfield, the author of "The Inner Classroom: Teaching with Guided Imagery" and other articles. In an article entitled "Education in the New Age," Canfield and coauthor Paula Klimek recommend "Sufi dances," "warm fuzzy stories," "chanting," "music and imagery" (they recommend "Stairway to Heaven" by Led Zeppelin), "psychodrama," "dreamwork," "fantasy literature," and "meditation/centering" ("What's this thing called the Force in *Star Wars*? How does Luke communicate with it? . . . Would you like to have this kind of experience?").

Canfield's most notable contribution is the technique of "guided fantasy" or "guided imagery." One exercise described in "The Inner Classroom" asks children to close their eyes and visualize "a wise old teacher inside our minds." They first imagine themselves "walking in a friendly foreign land" and ascending a mountain ("It is an easy path with no obstacles or difficult places . . .").

When you get to the top you notice a temple—a very special building. As you approach it, you can feel the solemnity and sacredness of this place. You decide to go inside, but before you do, you carefully remove your shoes and place them beside the doorway . . . Once inside, you notice thousands of candles burning, creating a great light inside. At the far end of the room you see a very kind and wise old person. As you approach this person, you see a very loving smile and bright, happy eyes. As you get closer, you realize that there is a question about life—your life in particular or life in general—that you want to ask this wise old person. When you are ready to ask, ask your question and let him or her respond. If at first you don't understand the answer, ask for more clarity. Have as long a conversation as you need to understand the answer. (Long pause—about one minute) Okay, now realizing that you can always come back to this wise friend, say goodby for now and begin to leave the temple.

I wouldn't want to issue a blanket condemnation of visualization techniques. Visualization is an important way of rehearsing for or shaping a performance, whether it be imagining a football play, a painting, or the design of a house. But this is a little different. Anyone who has come to the point of actually executing a play on the playing field or an architectural design on the drawing board has already learned a great deal about how these things are traditionally done. But guided imagery is meant to guide the child back to himself, not to any traditional body of wisdom. Canfield describes one girl in his class who asked her wise old woman, "What is the meaning of life?" The wise old woman "didn't say anything but held up a mirror to her"—an answer that Canfield calls an "amazingly sophisticated insight." "To me," writes Canfield, "the most interesting use of guided imagery is the evocation of the wisdom that lies deep within each of us."

This and similar exercises recommended by Canfield and various other educators seem to be designed to exercise the idyllic imagination: they provide a daydreamlike escape to an exotic place, and they suggest that the self is sufficient unto itself. In another guided exercise, students are invited to "Experience the good that is you . . . (pause) Now see yourself as absolutely perfect . . . capable of achieving anything you want . . . Repeat to yourself: I am a perfect person . . . (pause) I am a perfect student . . ."

Canfield does seem to think that children are well-nigh perfect: "These children of the New Age are incredibly conscious and will teach us an incredible amount—if we truly open to them. The only requirement is to provide a space and an environment where these beautiful young spirits can open up and allow their wisdom to be seen." But embedded in that New Age sentiment is an idea that really isn't new at all; it is a modern version of the "Noble Savage" view that children, like primitive peoples, are innocent and free, and hence, blissful. It says, in effect, "Your culture has nothing to offer; we adults have nothing to offer but facilitation: there is no code to be learned; all answers are locked inside you." If this sounds more than vaguely familiar, it's because what Canfield offers is a back-to-the-future model of education. It is Values Clarification with a mystical twist. Any answer is as good as any other as long as it feels right and as long as you first check it out with your inner spirit guide. In fact, the Canfield/Klimek article devotes several paragraphs to recommending four books by Sidney Simon, including *Values Clarification* and "his now famous children's story, *I Am Loveable and Capable.*"

It is significant that Simon himself has also taken the inner journey (which always seems to be in an Eastern direction) and now offers summer workshops at the Omega Institute for Holistic Studies in upstate New York. Almost all of the major figures in the human potential movement have undergone a similar metamorphosis. Before he had his second thoughts about the movement, Abraham Maslow had developed a keen interest in mystical "peak experiences" and had formulated the idea of a "Eupsychean Network" somewhat similar to Marilyn Ferguson's Aquarian Conspirators. In fact, when Ferguson asked her sample of 185 Aquarian Conspirators to name the individuals whose ideas influenced them, the four most frequently mentioned were Pierre Teilhard de Chardin, C. G. Jung, Abraham Maslow, and Carl Rogers. Rogers himself had, in his later writings, come to see his work as "a bridge between Eastern and Western thought." Jack Canfield now seems to serve a similar bridging function: in addition to his New Age activities, he is the spearhead of self-esteem legislation in California public education.

"I now consider it possible," wrote Carl Rogers in 1980, "that each of us is a continuing spiritual essence lasting over time, and occasionally incarnated in a human body." Whether or not this is true of individuals, it does appear to be true of the human potential movement itself. It now seems to have reincarnated itself as a quasi-mystical movement.

Is this cause for concern? I think so. It is more than a little disquieting to find that the party that introduced Values Clarification and affective education into schools now wants to take on the task of introducing youthful imaginations to Eastern spirituality. The myth that is being enacted here is what Joseph Campbell calls "the myth of eternal return." In our case, it seems to be the continual recycling of the sixties myth—as though there were no deeper source of wisdom in our history. It is, of course, supposed to be a return to ancient wisdom. But that is hard to credit. While there is much to be said for Eastern spirituality, it seems legitimate to ask whether American-bred human potentialists are the best ones to interpret and apply it. Rather, the New Age movement in education appears to be one more instance of idyllic dreamers trying to evade the demands and responsibilities of their own culture.

New Age educators stress their affinity with the East, but in regard to many crucial aspects, they misinterpret and misrepresent the Eastern tradition. In this respect, it is worth dwelling for a moment on two points. First, Irving Babbitt, who was a serious scholar of Buddhism, observed that it is essentially at an opposite pole from Romanticism. Buddha put his greatest emphasis on self-restraint and the curbing of desires—concepts that are alien to Romanticists and human potentialists alike. New Age believers are, in fact, mainly attracted to Taoism and Zen Buddhism—the more bohemian forms of Eastern spirituality. Second, the daily conduct of the Chinese and other Asian peoples over the centuries has been governed as much by the teachings of Confucius as by those of Buddha. The former place great emphasis on ethical duties, on justice, on family devotion, on personal virtue, and on education. Put simply, Confucius was an advocate of character education. He is rarely mentioned in New Age literature.

The New Age movement has made considerable headway in schools, particularly in the Pacific states. But although New Age themes are beginning to show up in reading series, and although several drug and lifestyle curriculums employ guided imagery, most teachers are not committed devotees of the movement. If they are using guided fantasy or "fuzzy stories," they tend to see these as relaxation techniques or as a means to help students feel good, not as pathways to a new age. But teachers ought to keep in mind that these techniques only exercise the idyllic imagination. And to the extent that we emphasize the idyllic imagination, we tend to forget the moral imagination.

A child who consults with his wise and kindly inner person is not likely to get the slap of self-recognition that a powerful story delivers, even though he may sorely need it. The exercises in Canfield's books seem to be set up to elicit only reassuring messages of self-esteem. A teacher who invites the child to "see yourself as absolutely perfect . . . capable of achieving anything you want" might consider balancing this by inviting him to read a biography of Frederick Douglass to see how much work is required in order to achieve. But the more the teacher is imbued with the idyllic view, the less he is likely to do that. Furthermore, extolling children's great inner wisdom and beauty seems just another rationale for absolving teachers of the hard work of teaching them, and of providing good example. It gives the adults license to stand around and shake their heads in wonderment and say things like "Far out! I wish I could find that in me." (This, according to Canfield, is the way teachers respond when they see his students' art work).

I don't see any conspiracy here; all I see is the persistent attempt to find alternatives to growing up and raising the next generation. Presumably, the goal of inner-child education in the classroom is to encourage children to be their own mothers and fathers and spiritual guides so that they can emerge into adult life as self-sufficient entities. It is a familiar form of wishing, but we should recognize that it deprives children of the guidance they really need. In the sixties, values clarifiers told children that whatever they chose was right for them—advice that if taken seriously could lead to a drug overdose or a jail cell. Once again, educators seem to be setting up expectations about reality that can't be fulfilled, expectations that will likely lead to another round of frustration and anger.

In another context, I have heard it argued that children, particularly urban children, need the dreamlike escape that idyllic stories and exercises offer. Of course, some balance between the idyllic and the serious is desirable. It's important, however, to keep a few things in mind. First, the best retreat for a child who lives in a threatening world is a secure and well-ordered school where discipline is maintained. Many inner-city children like school for that very reason. They appreciate the relative peace, orderliness, and predictability of a well-run school. Second, no teacher can succeed in creating, even for a short time, an idyllic classroom climate unless someone else, usually someone possessed of a moral imagination, has created another kind of climate surrounding and protecting that classroom. Third, children are most in need of the kind of reassurance that is built on a realistic view of life—one that acknowledges both tragedy and evil.

Children of the ghetto are surrounded by tragedy and sudden death, and they are daily subjected to temptations from those who have already succumbed to the diabolical imagination. The idyllic imagination is no match for that environment. Either it will be crushed by it or it will yield to its temptations. William Bennett, in an article entitled "Drugs and the Face of Evil," makes some illuminating observations on the subject:

> I continue to be amazed at how often people I speak to in treatment centers refer to drugs as the great lie, the great deception, indeed as a product of the Great Deceiver. An astonishing number of people in treatment have described crack cocaine to me simply as "the Devil." This has come up too often and too spontaneously in conversation to be ignored.
>
> You will know what I mean, then, when I say that in visiting treatment centers, prisons, inner-city communities, and public housing projects across the country over the past twenty-one months I've seen what I can only describe as the face of evil.

Bennett goes on to offer some concrete examples of this evil—a mother who hands over her daughter to a dealer to pay a drug debt, parents who kill their baby by blowing crack smoke into his mouth. His conclusion is that a moral and spiritual response is required: "If one doesn't believe in the struggle of the *psychomachia*—what I was taught to recognize as the struggle between good and evil for the possession of the human soul— then one might never get to the heart of this drug problem." The point is that inner-city children, more than most, need to be introduced to an imaginative world that makes sharp distinctions between right and wrong rather than dreamworlds that fuzz over that distinction. They need to learn what needs to be loved and what needs to be resisted. And they need heroes. Equally important, they need disciplined teachers who can help them acquire good habits of character.

The persistence of the idyllic imagination among educators prevents them from seeing what is really needed in schools. And there is another form of imagination— the utopian imagination— which acts in the same way. The utopian imagination is actually a close relative of the idyllic imagination. In fact, idyllic thinkers often have utopian dreams about an ideal society or ideal social structures that will "take care" of everything. Rousseau is a good example. When he didn't want to deal with the reality of his own children, he gave them to the State. He later described his actions as those of a good citizen. If there is a major difference between the two types of imagination, it is that the utopian imagination locates Eden in the technological future rather than in nature or in preindustrial societies. Otherwise, the similarities go deep.

Therefore, it is not surprising that educators, who succumb so readily to the idyllic imagination, are also attracted to the utopian vision. Because of his idyllic assumptions, the utopian underestimates the degree to which human problems are the result of human nature. Accordingly, he overestimates the ease of solving them through institutional initiatives. As a result, when individuals are struck with the utopian temptation, they typically take on more than they can handle. In recent decades we have seen the schools go into the sex education business, the drug education business, the death education business, the psychotherapy business, the Values Clarification business, the sensitivity group business, the self-esteem business, the day-care business, the health care business, the social work business, and the multicultural business.

One result is that none of these things are done well. Another result is that the main business of the school—teaching history, literature, and science—suffers. A third result is that those institutions that are better equipped to perform nonacademic functions—such as the family, the churches, and voluntary organizations—begin to yield to the schools, and in the process lose their ability to function effectively. As Neil Postman points out, "If the school . . . assumes the prerogatives normally exercised by the family, the family loses some of its motivation, authority and competence to provide what it is designed to do." In blurring the lines of authority between itself and other institutions, says Postman, the school not only weakens these other institutions, it weakens its own capabilities as well. The word "utopia" means "no place," and that is exactly what schools become when they attempt to do everyone's job—no place in particular. Instead, they become generalized multiservice institutions, and in the process they lose the distinctive identity that is necessary to challenge and lead young people.

But the worst utopian temptation is the desire to shift the focus of responsibility from the individual to the institution. Like the idyllic imagination, the utopian imagination denies that tragedy and suffering are inherent in the human condition, and like the former, it hopes to relieve individuals of the burden of personal morality. It is the habit described by T. S. Eliot of "dreaming of systems so perfect that no one will need to be good." An individual governed by the utopian imagination doesn't see moral problems, he sees technical problems, and as a result, his solutions are technical: clean needles, safe-sex kits, and improved communications skills. Bennett makes reference to this frame of mind in citing the recommendations of a commission made up of members of the American Medical Association and the National Association of State Boards of Education. The commission had concluded that "unlike the problems of earlier generations, those of today's teenagers are rooted in behavior rather than physical illness"—behavior such as excessive drinking, drug use, promiscuity, and violence. Having diagnosed the problem as a crisis of character, the commission then went on to recommend its solution—more health clinics. Bennett comments:

> The approach of the commission indicates the intellectual poverty of modernity, with its reliance on technological, psychological, and governmental solutions for moral and spiritual problems. The evidence in this case is clear. Never has our scientific, technological, or governmental know-how been greater, and never has the condition of our young been worse.

Throughout this book I have been emphasizing the connection between vision and virtue. I hope I have made it clear that not just any vision will do. Some ways of envisioning the world are more realistic about human nature than others. The idyllic and utopian visions mistakenly imagine that virtue and character can be safely left out of the picture. But when that happens, vice only looms larger. Moreover, when we ignore or minimize the tragic limitations of life, tragedy is only multiplied. Contemporary sex education, which tends to be governed either by the idyllic imagination, or by the utopian, or a combination of both, illustrates how inadequate they are. What sex educators have in the backs of their minds, I believe, is a picture of some imaginary Scandinavian town where, by the miracle of social engineering, life is lived with as much rationality and as little suffering as possible, and where healthy, honest, and guilt-free boys and girls sample the joys of sex while enlightened adults beam proud approval. That is the idyllic/utopian vision, but the actual result of their programs looks more like a vision from Kafka.

Now that we are beginning to realize again the power of imagination, educators have an opportunity to take back some of the territory that has been lost to the entertainment industry. The question is whether they can resist the lure of more faddishness. One temptation is to simply ape the entertainment media in the hope that, with more audio-visuals and fun activities, schools can be made into places of entertainment. Or education can elect to take the yellow brick road: the path of New Age mythology, guided fantasy, and therapeutic stories—a path that, to my mind, only circles back to education's most naive and soft-headed era. Still again, educators can push farther along the utopian path in the hope that improved technology and better social science will prove a substitute for character.

The other option—the most difficult, yet the most realistic—is to reestablish schools as places of serious moral purpose. In such schools, students would, through the curriculum, be introduced to works of the moral imagination. But the reform that is needed goes beyond changing the curriculum to changing the ethos of the schools themselves. They can no longer afford to be neutral bureaucracies or shopping malls or service providers. They need to embody the kind of character they hope to instill.

The next chapter looks at some ways of accomplishing this task.

13.

WHAT SCHOOLS
CAN DO

The core problem facing our schools is a moral one. All the other problems derive from it. Hence, all the various attempts at school reform are unlikely to succeed unless character education is put at the top of the agenda.

If students don't learn self-discipline and respect for others, they will continue to exploit each other sexually no matter how many health clinics and condom distribution plans are created.

If they don't learn habits of courage and justice, curriculums designed to improve their self-esteem won't stop the epidemic of extortion, bullying, and violence; neither will courses designed to make them more sensitive to diversity.

Even academic reform depends on putting character first. Children need courage to tackle difficult assignments. They need self-discipline if they are going to devote their time to homework rather than television. They need the diligence and perseverance required to do this day after day. If they don't acquire intellectual virtues such as commitment to learning, objectivity, respect for the truth, and humility in the face of facts, then critical-thinking strategies will only amount to one more gimmick in the curriculum.

If, on the other hand, the schools were to make the formation of good character a primary goal, many other things would fall into place. Hitherto unsolvable problems such as violence, vandalism, drug use, teen pregnancies, unruly classrooms, and academic deterioration would prove to be less intractable than presently imagined. Moreover, the moral reform of schools is not something that has to wait until other conditions are met. It doesn't depend on the rest of society reforming itself. Schools are, or can be, one of the main engines of social change. They can set the tone of society in ways no other institution can match.

How difficult will it be to make these reforms? Very difficult. Much ground has been lost.

Some of the problems we now have are the result of stupid and naive experiments in the curriculum: the adopting of programs that let children choose their own values, and that left them morally confused. Many of these children grew up unable to make commitments, and had children of their own who, in turn, became morally confused. These programs must be discarded, and new character education and sex education curriculums must be developed in their place. But the situation has deteriorated far past the point where curriculum changes alone will reverse the slide. Courses on ethics are desirable but, at this point, hardly sufficient.

The primary way to bring ethics and character back into schools is to create a positive moral environment in schools. The ethos of a school, not its course offerings, is the decisive factor in forming character. The first thing we must change is the moral climate of the schools themselves. What we seem to have forgotten in all our concern with individual development is that schools are social institutions. Their first function is to socialize. Quite frankly, many of them have forgotten how to do that.

In the wake of the swift and decisive victory over Iraq in the Desert Storm campaign, many have asked why, if we can soundly defeat the fourth-largest army in the world in a matter of weeks, we can't turn our schools around just as decisively. The argument usually advanced is that the sort of money that went into the war could do wonders if it went into schools. I'm not so sure. Part of that victory was quite obviously due to the factor of more money and better technology. But there were other factors at work. The military had other things going for it besides money. In fact, the annual defense budget is far less than the amount of money spent annually on schools. Moreover, since the mid-fifties school budgets have, on the whole, grown every year as a proportion of total tax revenues despite the fact of a smaller school age population in recent years. Finally, even some of the wealthiest school districts have serious problems with drugs, discipline, and teen pregnancy. Money is important, if you know how to use it, but it's not the only thing.

What the military has that so many schools do not is an ethos of pride, loyalty, and discipline. It is called esprit de corps. The dictionary defines it as "a spirit of devotion and enthusiasm among members of a group for one another, their group, and its purposes." That spirit has not always been high, but after the Vietnam War, a concerted effort was made to reshape the military ethos—apparently with great success. So much so that the armed forces actually outshine the schools in doing things the schools are supposed to do best, such as teaching math, science, technological skills, history, languages, geography, and map reading. Even in the matter of racial equality—something about which educators talk incessantly—the military has shown far more success. In fact, the armed services are the most thoroughly integrated institutions in our society: promotions are on the basis of merit, black officers can dress down white soldiers, there is a spirit of camaraderie and mutual respect among the races that extends well beyond tolerance. Schools, by contrast, are rife with racial tension, hostility, and self-segregation. Not only high schools but colleges as well. According to Dinesh D'Souza's *Illiberal Education* and other reports, universities are far more segregated than they were twenty years ago, and the level of racial hostility is much higher.

How does the military manage to create such a strong ethos? First, by conveying a vision of high purpose: not only the defense of one's own or other nations against unjust aggression, but also the provision of humanitarian relief and reconstruction in the wake of war or natural disaster (the classic case being the role played by the American military in rebuilding war-torn Europe and Japan). Second, by creating a sense of pride and specialness (the Marines want only "a few good men")—pride reinforced by a knowledge of unit tradition, by high expectations, and by rituals, dress codes, and behavior codes. Third, by providing the kind of rigorous training—physical, mental, and technical—that results in real achievement and thus in real self-esteem. Fourth, by being a hierarchial, authoritarian, and undemocratic institution which believes in its mission and is unapologetic about its training programs.

Schools can learn a lot from the Army. That doesn't mean they need to become military schools—although, of course, there are many successful military schools. But there are enough important similarities between the two institutions to suggest that there are lessons to be learned. Both, after all, work with the same "raw material"—young men and women—and both seek to give their recruits knowledge, skills, and habits they previously lacked.

In the past, schools *were* run on similar lines. They had a vision of high purpose: not just preparing students for jobs and consumership, and AIDS avoidance, but preparing them for citizenship and lives of personal integrity. There was also a sense of pride in one's school—a school spirit that was reinforced at frequent assemblies, through school traditions, and by dress codes, behavior codes, and high academic standards. Schools were serious about their academic mission, and students were challenged to respond accordingly. Finally, schools were unapologetically authoritarian. They weren't interested in being democratic institutions themselves but in encouraging the virtues students would need for eventual participation in democratic institutions. Schools also had more autonomy from state and federal bureaucracies and from the courts. They could punish, suspend, and expel unruly students when and how they wished—something that is not easily accomplished these days, now that students have the right to counsel, hearings, and appeals. Some private and parochial schools still retain this climate of authority and autonomy. It may be a large part of the reason for their success. A well-known study conducted by sociologist James Coleman in the early eighties showed that parochial schools in inner cities, despite a lower level of funding, far outperformed their public counterparts. Children not only do better academically in these schools, they behave better. And they are happier. The almost absolute investment of moral authority one finds in Catholic schools creates in students not more hostility but less.

What became of the moral climate that was once so prevalent in schools? One of the most perceptive comments on its disappearance comes in a new book by Professors Edward Wynne and Kevin Ryan titled *Reclaiming Our Schools: A Handbook on Teaching Character, Academics and Discipline.* The authors acknowledge the destructive influence of Rousseauian philosophy in the sixties, but they also suggest that part of the explanation for the deterioration of the moral climate simply lies in the demanding nature of character education. To make rules and enforce them consistently, to give challenging assignments and correct them diligently, to keep in contact with parents and with other teachers, to police bathrooms, playgrounds, corridors, and lunchrooms, to demand respect from students and mutual respect for one another—all this requires considerable time and energy. And because it is all such hard work, there is a persistent temptation to find alternatives to it.

The authors note that in a great many schools, a strong pattern of work avoidance prevails—avoidance by both pupils and teachers. "Students and teachers essentially carry out mutual 'pacts' to avoid creating trouble for each other. The pupils avoid conspicuous breaches of discipline . . . and the teachers do not 'hassle' pupils with demanding assignments." As time passes, though, breaches of discipline do tend to become more conspicuous. And more and more, teachers are tempted to look the other way. The upshot of this tacit agreement is that school is not taken seriously by either: both student and teacher come to look on it as a form of time serving. For the teacher teaching becomes less like a vocation and more like a job. The idea is to leave as soon as you've put in your hours, and to take home as little work as possible.

That description does not do justice, of course, to the many teachers for whom teaching is still a vocation. But the more other teachers slack off, the greater the burden placed on those who don't, and the greater the temptation for them to follow suit. Not all of these problems are created within the schools. The authors point to a number of court decisions that have helped to create an air of confusion among teachers, leaving them uncertain of their right to discipline. The result is that schools become more depersonalized, less familial. Teachers become more indifferent, retreating from the kind of engagement and concern that was possible under the older order of authority. In addition to losing the power to discipline, they lose the power to care. Their attitude becomes that of the bureaucrat toward the client he must serve.

"Much of this book," write Professors Wynne and Ryan, "is about establishing a stronger, more wholesome ethos, one which contrasts with the loose, low standards and self-oriented tone currently permeating many of our classrooms." What do they propose? The key phrase is "profound learning"—learning that is absorbed by participation in the activities and pursuits of a serious community. This "serious, non-sentimental conception of education" is opposed to the doctrines of "learning is fun" and "happy think" which have reduced education to a game of trivial pursuits. "It is impossible," they contend, "to form 'strong personalities' without a profound molding system." Although such a system is subject to abuse, there is really no substitute for it. Why pretend that schools can be democracies when they so clearly cannot?

Wynne and Ryan agree with Aristotle that learning character is largely a matter of habituation. Consequently, one of the main ways to develop character is to provide planned activities which invite students to practice good habits. The authors suggest a number of such activities, among them tutoring younger pupils and school service projects to the community. Equally important are behavior and discipline codes which serve as guides to behavior, and which need to be clearly identified and enforced. School-wide policies need to be specified about such matters as cheating, overt acts of affection, fighting, dress codes, disobedience and disrespect, vulgar language, and so on. The list would depend upon the particular school and upon past experience.

The same holds true for individual classrooms. The authors point to research showing that "effective teachers spend a significant amount of time during the first two weeks of school establishing rules and procedures . . . such veterans seemingly sacrifice a great deal of time on drilling or 'grooving' students on classroom procedures in the early weeks." It's hard work but it pays off, say the authors:

> We know a first year teacher who patiently explained to his fifth grade students that they were not to talk in the hall on their way to gym. He soon discovered that the message did not get through. Instead of letting it go on or displaying aimless anger, he had them come back. He explained again and gave them another chance. They talked. He called them back again. Having missed twenty minutes of precious gym time, his fifth graders made it on the fifth try. There was no more talking in the halls and many other messages got through with greater speed and accuracy.

Naturally, rules need punishments to back them up. Strangely, when one considers how much of a teacher's time is taken up with unruly student behaviors, textbooks for teachers devote very little space to the subject—and much of that "surrounded with warnings about the dangers of punishment." Professors Wynne and Ryan are less reticent. They have a lot to say about punishment, about how and when to apply it, and what it should consist of.

Isn't it better that people behave themselves without compulsion? Yes, eventually, but sometimes compulsion is what is needed to get a good habit started. We don't wait for a child to decide for himself that tooth brushing is a good habit. The same applies to weightier moral matters. "You can't legislate morality" is a terribly simplistic formula. In fact, many laws *are* aimed at legislating morality, and—if morality is understood as proper conduct—many of them are quite effective at doing so. Rules and laws can even work to change habits of the heart. I think there can be little doubt that the civil rights legislation of the sixties had that effect. Laws granting equality of access to blacks in the South may have been hated and obeyed grudgingly at first. Nevertheless, obeying the law over a long period of time induces certain habits which alter attitudes. Many southerners have had a change of heart about issues of basic fairness.

Schools, like society at large, need to insist on proper habits of conduct. "At this moment in our history," observe Wynne and Ryan, "too many public schools are overly permissive. Thus, they fail to instill in our young the self-discipline needed for citizenship and full adult development. We believe strict schools (certainly by today's standards) are happy schools and, more important, schools that serve children and society well."

The ethos that the authors suggest, however, could hardly be called a legalistic one. Their concern is to show how educators can create a sense of pride and specialness—of classroom spirit and school spirit. In the best schools, they suggest, there is a strong sense of family and community. The attitude teachers communicate is one of "You belong to me" and "I belong to you." This sense of spirit and specialness can be reinforced by mottoes, posters, pictures, pledges, symbols, and song. For example, they recommend that schools might consider developing a list of songs "of relatively persisting value which all students . . . and faculty should learn and sing together." For emphasis, they quote a nineteenth-century description of students at Harrow singing at mealtime: "When you hear the great volume of fresh voices leap up as larks from the ground, and swell and rise, till the rafters seem to crack and shiver, then you seem to have discovered all the sources of emotion." (It's worth noting, by the way, that some of our most successful drug rehabilitation programs use group singing—sometimes involving more than a hundred youngsters and staff—as a method of creating a new sense of identity and purpose.)

The final chapters of *Reclaiming Our Schools* are devoted to the importance of ceremonies in transmitting moral values. This is another area that is almost entirely neglected in educational research. Although they are often considered extraneous to the real business of school, rituals and ceremonies are among the most effective ways of impressing students with the significance of values held in common. As Wynne and Ryan put it, "Public, collective activities have teaching power because we are properly impressed with values to which large numbers of persons display dramatic, conspicuous allegiance or respect." Graduation ceremonies are a prime example. Among other things, they signify the importance of learning, and the value placed on it by the community. The authors suggest that educators need to deliberately design more such school ceremonies as a means of transmitting vital messages.

It should be apparent at this point that what is being suggested here is radical in the context of today's schools. It is quite different from the two current models of schooling—the laissez-faire model, on the one hand, and the rationally based managerial model, on the other. It is a much more comprehensive view because it takes account of all the elements that go into good schooling: not just academics but character, pride, symbol, and ritual. As opposed to the superficial fun culture children encounter outside of school, it is a counterculture in the true sense.

To some ears, the measures proposed in *Reclaiming Our Schools* will sound excessive. However, in some cases, even stronger measures are needed. In the last few years, for example, a number of black educators have been calling for all-male, all-black schools run by black, male teachers. The argument is that boys need appropriate discipline as well as role models. But male role models are in short supply. Schools are staffed mainly by women, not men. (Last year, for example, Boston College's School of Education graduated over 200 students; only five of them were males.) The situation is intensified in the inner city. Not only are there few male role models in the school, there are few at home. Because of many factors, homes are dominated by females. The main source of male models, then, is to be found in the streets. And, as has always been the case with boys, the tendency is to identify with those who have power. Sometimes, fortunately, this means following in the steps of an older athlete, youth worker, or policeman. But often it means that drug dealers and gang members set the tone and temper of youthful aspirations.

I'm not convinced that such schools should be for blacks only or that they need Afrocentric curriculums, as is sometimes proposed. Both ideas are ill advised. But the idea of all-male schools makes sense. The lives of inner-city youth are so much at risk (the leading cause of death for black males up to age forty-four is homicide) that radical measures are in order. And the principle behind this particular measure is a sound one. In fact, it is not especially radical. The idea that boys should be taught by men is an ancient and honorable one, practiced for centuries across a wide variety of cultures and settings, ranging from primitive tribes to English boarding schools. This idea also has a substantial basis in psychology, sociology, cultural anthropology, and criminology. It has long been known in these fields that boys have a more difficult time than girls in the formation of sex identity. The fewer strong male models in a boy's life, the more trouble he has. In the absence of an involved and committed male, boys tend to form simplified and stereotyped notions of maleness. Surrounded by women, desperately anxious to establish their maleness, they often compensate for their insecure sense of identity by adopting a hypermasculine aggressive pose. As is now well known, boys without fathers are substantially more involved in delinquency and violence than boys with fathers at home. When they go to school, they bring this aggressiveness with them.

The answer to masculine overcompensation is not to surround boys with more women at school and expect them to adopt a "let's-be-nice-to-each-other" attitude. As even the most ardent of feminist psychologists now admit, boys *are* inherently—biologically—more aggressive than girls. They need to do something with that aggressiveness. Either it has to be channeled by adults who are strong enough to channel it, or it erupts in ways that are destructive both to the individual and to society.

Other societies have found ways to do this. Initiation rites, for example, are elaborately constructed educational devices for teaching both boys and girls how to grow up. In most societies, the preparation period for these rituals (many months, in some cases) involves the segregation of boys and girls. Boys are prepared by the men, and girls are prepared by the women. Although some of the final rituals may involve boys and girls together, certain parts of the initiation process are distinct—the rituals for boys involving more active displays of initiative and physical courage. The upshot is that young males are provided an opportunity to affirm their manhood under the tutelage of adult males. They prove themselves within a social framework, rather than at the expense of society.

The same system holds in the Army, which for very good reasons was until recently a sex-segregated institution. In boot camp, the drill instructor functions in a way similar to the male supervisors of initiation rites. He expects the recruits to act like men, he offers himself as a model, he puts them through arduous initiation exercises. As a result, he is simultaneously hated and admired. The recruits resent his demands, yet they respect his abilities. Secretly they want to be like him—at least in some crucial respects. Secretly, also, they know he has their best interests at heart. It is a process of maturation through identification and through ritual challenge. The film *An Officer and a Gentleman* is a good—if somewhat overdramatized—depiction of the process.

All of this is sometimes difficult for women to comprehend. Indeed, it must seem slightly absurd. Because women possess a stronger sense of sexual identity, they don't as a rule feel a corresponding compulsion to prove their womanhood. This difference between men and women is reflected in the practices of primitive societies. Initiation rites for women are usually in the nature of an acknowledgment of what is already present rather than—as in the case of male rituals—an attempt to create something that does not yet exist. As Margaret Mead observed of the societies she studied: "The worry that boys will not grow up to be men is much more widespread than the worry that the girls will not grow up to be women . . ." The latter fear, she noted, is almost nonexistent.

"Why can't a woman be more like a man?" asks Professor Henry Higgins in *My Fair Lady*. But for many women the question is just the reverse. The answer seems to be as follows: Growing up into the socialized world of adults is a more natural process for a woman. For a man it requires more of a transformation. His natural inclinations are short-term, aggressive, irresponsible. Boys have little natural interest in babies, or in eventually growing up to raise their own. For the average boy masculinity does not mean the steady, responsible life of a husband and father but rather masculine exploits centered around strength and bravery. Attempts to teach the right type of masculinity directly—for example, classes in homemaking or child care—are like attempts to teach self-esteem directly: they don't have much impact unless other things are in place. A young man needs to develop some assurance about his basic masculinity before he can learn the more responsible kind of masculinity. Thus the importance of transformative institutions for boys: rites of passage, boarding schools, military service. These are the kinds of institutions that can provide a "profound molding" experience. Those who have seen a male friend or relative go off to the Army or to military school or merely to Boy Scout camp can attest to these transformative powers. I recall a classmate in high school, a gawky, aimless, passive boy, the butt of countless jokes, who nevertheless somehow managed to enlist in the Marine Corps. When I met him again five years later, he had become a thoroughly adult, thoroughly calm and confident man. He told me that he was about to open his own construction business. After talking with him, I had no doubt he would succeed—and he did.

There is a risk to such all-male groups: If not handled properly, the training process can result in misogyny, insensitivity, and a collectivist mind set. Instead of moving on to a greater maturity, young men can get fixated on the initiation process itself—forever in the process of proving themselves. But these dangers could be easily avoided at the grade school and high school level, especially since the institutional aim would not be preparation for war but education in character and academics.

In communities with strong fathers at home and positive male role models in the neighborhood, coed schools staffed mostly by females can do a decent job in educating and socializing boys. But where those other conditions have broken down, the idea of all-male schools run by men makes sense. These might or might not be boarding schools. That would depend on the local situation. They don't have to be military schools, but—in this age of commitment to diversity—that option ought certainly to be entertained. As writer Leon Podles puts it:

> Why can't some schools be run for boys by men? A dozen
> military schools in each inner city, complete with uniforms,

drill, and supervised study, staffed by retired black and white officers (*without* education degrees) would go far to making our cities livable, and giving black boys a shot at a decent life.

Such schools, as I have indicated, would serve as a counterculture. They would provide a code and aesthetic counter to, and more attractive than, gang life. They could establish an ethos of pride and purposefulness, and in doing so, they could transform the lives of a generation that might otherwise become yet another lost generation.

Is this draconian? Let me suggest that the status quo is far more draconian. As it is, more young black males in our society go on to prison than go on to college. Meanwhile inner-city dwellers live in constant fear of crime and random violence. And if we are worried about public schools that might resemble military schools, we should keep in mind that many inner-city schools have already begun to resemble prisons in their attempts to seal themselves off from outside dangers.

Unfortunately, the few attempts to institute all-male public schools have run afoul of feminist ideology and sex discrimination statutes. For example, last year in Detroit, a federal judge ruled that an all-male inner-city school could not open unless it admitted girls. Thus the chances of both boys and girls were sacrificed for an abstract notion about gender equality. Although the ruling reflects current sensibilities among upper-class whites, it is at variance with the real psychological and social needs of inner-city children. It tends to confirm the judgment of one of Dickens's characters, who declares, "The law is a ass." (In the same vein, the civil rights division of the Justice Department has tried to force the Virginia Military Institute to admit women. In this case, however, the law was not an "ass." Judge Jackson Kiser, following the advice of scholars like Harvard's David Riesman, ruled that—in the name of diversity—VMI ought to be allowed to march "to the beat of a different drummer.")

One could, of course, argue that though forceful measures may be necessary in inner-city schools, this is not the case in suburbs. Does Elmwood High really need the steps outlined earlier—increased attention to rules and conduct, stronger discipline and punishment? Does it need increased attention to ritual, symbol, and ceremony? And aren't these forms of mind manipulation? My answer is essentially the same. Would you rather a youngster learn discipline in school, or later on from a probation officer, a drug rehabilitation center, a divorce court judge, or the boss who fires him? Should males learn habits of the heart when they are young, or should they learn them belatedly from a harassment officer on the job or at college? When a society fails to develop character in its young people, it is forced to adopt all sorts of poor substitutes for it when they grow up. In colleges and workplaces across the country, we are now seeing the creation of draconian harassment codes which spell out in minute detail exactly how men and women are to behave toward one another (codes that in many cases are unconstitutional)—all because they failed to learn certain codes and habits by heart at an earlier age. Thomas Jefferson said, "That government is best which governs least," but the rest of the quote—the part that is usually left out—continues, "because its people discipline themselves." Without such self-discipline, learned at an early age, we are only inviting *more* control of our adult lives by governments, courts, and bureaucracies.

But besides these indirect methods, which work at changing the school environment, there are more direct methods of teaching character. Over the course of the last six or seven years, a small but growing number of schools have been devising explicit ways to teach the virtues. One such system is the North Clackamas School District in Oregon. Teachers there have developed a four-year cycle designed to emphasize a particular set of character traits each year. Year one concentrates on patriotism, integrity and honesty, and courtesy; year two focuses on respect for authority, respect for others, for property, and for environment, and self-esteem; year three, on compassion, self-discipline and responsibility, work ethic, and appreciation for education; year four, on patience, courage, and cooperation. After the first four years of school, the cycle begins again with the difference that students are now expected to understand these traits on a deeper level. The curriculum includes definitions, the study of people from the past and present who have demonstrated a particular virtue, concrete ways of putting the virtue into practice, and activities such as poster, essay, or photo contests. Here are examples of definitions:

Patience is a calm endurance of a trying or difficult situation.
Patience reflects a proper appreciation and understanding of
  other people's beliefs, perceptions or conditions. Patience
  helps one to wait for certain responsibilities, privileges or
  events until a future maturity level or scheduled time.
Patience is:
  waiting one's turn.
—appreciating people's differences.
—enduring the skill levels of younger children when playing
  a game.

Courage is upholding convictions and what is right or just.
  Courage is being assertive, tenacious, steadfast and reso-
  lute in facing challenges and social pressures.
Courage is:
—resisting negative peer pressure and providing positive
  peer pressure.
—being loyal to someone even though social popularity
  may dictate otherwise.
—defending the rights of self and others.

After learning these definitions, students are encouraged to discuss the concepts. Although the character trait itself is never called
into question, there is room for exploring its proper application.
For instance, the unit on respect for authority asks students to
research examples of legitimate resistance to authority—examples
such as Thomas Jefferson, Rosa Parks, and Martin Luther King, Jr.
   One problem with such lists is that it's difficult to agree on what
should be put in and what left out. For example, I'm not convinced that self-esteem is a virtue. Nevertheless, these are character traits that most parents in most communities would endorse.
In the last analysis, each school district would have to make its
own determination. However, there is at least one important reference point. Most scholars who advocate a character education
approach are agreed that, as a bare minimum, every list ought to
contain the four cardinal virtues that have come down to us from
the Greeks: prudence, justice, courage, and temperance. They are
called cardinal because they are the axis (cardo) on which the
moral life turns. They are, of course, sometimes known by other

names. Prudence is "wisdom" or "practical wisdom," courage is "fortitude," temperance is "self-discipline" or "self-control."

It is difficult to improve on what the classical writers said on the subject of the virtues, and a teacher who takes the time to read up on the subject will find that, presented in the right way, the classic conception of the virtues is capable of generating many rewarding discussions. Among other things, such discussions could examine the notion that the virtues form a unity: that in order to be a person of character, you must have all four working together. What good is it, for example, to believe in justice if you lack the courage to stand up for someone unjustly accused? And what good is courage if you lack justice and wisdom? (The Vikings were courageous in battle, but exceedingly cruel to their victims. It is brave to administer first aid to a wounded man on a battle-field, but not very helpful unless you know what you're doing.) Aristotle's notion that each virtue is a mean between two extremes should also come in for discussion. Courage, for example, is opposed not only to cowardice but also to foolhardiness. A man who lacks sufficient respect for the dangers involved is not a courageous man but a foolish man. In fact, Aristotle said that only the man who feels fear yet overcomes it for the sake of a good deed should be called courageous.

A number of other things could be said on the virtue of courage. Students ought to learn the difference between physical courage, moral courage, and intellectual courage, and that people who have physical courage do not necessarily possess the other two. And they need to know that courage is not confined to spectacular acts of bravery. In a letter to his children, Edwin Delattre talks about another kind of heroism:

> Still heroism is more than this. It doesn't mean just doing particular actions that are brave. It means being the kind of person who does not run away when physical, moral, or intellectual bravery is called for. So, for example, you might have a woman whose husband dies and leaves her to raise several young children by herself. The person who does not run away, who does her best to be a good parent in these difficult circumstances exhibits deep and continuing bravery and so is especially heroic, even though there may be no

single events like rescuing a drowning person to catch our attention. It is a quiet, durable heroism that consists of facing up to whatever the world puts before us and refusing to give up. This is the heroism that deserves respect above all, and the place to look for it is in the people you know and love.

Before teachers can teach about the virtues, however, they may need to brush up on the classical sources. One school that has provided such preparation for its teachers is the Thomas Jefferson High School of Science and Technology in Alexandria, Virginia. During the summer of 1990, thirty-five members of the school's faculty attended a three-week institute to study the foundations of ethics in Western society. The program centered on Plato's *Republic* and five of his other dialogues, Aristotle's *Nicomachean Ethics,* and selections from four books of the Bible: Genesis, Exodus, Samuel, and Matthew. These texts, according to the institute's descriptive summary, raise fundamental questions: "What is a good life? What constitutes good character? What is virtue? What is a good society? . . . In essence, what kind of human beings should we be?" During the summer institute and in seven follow-up sessions during the school year, teachers also discussed concrete ways these ideas could be incorporated into the social studies and English curriculums. By the middle of the school year teachers reported a changed atmosphere: students had become excited about virtue, and many of them had taken to wearing the institute's special T-shirts, which depict Plato and Aristotle walking together, engrossed in conversation.

Professor Christina Hoff Sommers describes a similar response on the part of college students. Sommers originally employed a dilemma format in her ethics course at Clark University, but she became disturbed by student comments on the course evaluation forms, such as one student's remark "I learned there was no such thing as right or wrong, just good or bad arguments." As a result, Sommers decided to teach a course on the philosophy of virtue, with an emphasis on Aristotle:

Students find a great deal of plausibility in Aristotle's theory of moral education, as well as personal relevance in what he says about courage, generosity, temperance and other virtues. I have found that an exposure to Aristotle makes an immediate inroad on dogmatic relativism; indeed the tendency to dismiss morality as relative to taste or social fashion rapidly diminishes and may vanish altogether. Most students find the idea of developing virtuous character traits naturally appealing.

Sommers continues:

Once the student becomes engaged with the problem of what kind of person to be, and how to *become* that kind of person, the problems of ethics become concrete and practical and, for many a student, morality itself is thereafter looked on as a natural and even inescapable personal undertaking.

One of the best ways to teach the virtues is in conjunction with history and literature. In that way, students can see that they are more than abstract concepts. In Robert Bolt's play *A Man for All Seasons,* we see a remarkable combination of all four virtues in one man, Sir Thomas More. The plot of *High Noon* revolves around a tension among justice, courage, and prudence. *To Kill a Mockingbird* shows one kind of courage, *The Old Man and the Sea* another. *Measure for Measure* and *The Merchant of Venice* teach us about justice. *Moby-Dick* depicts a man who has lost all sense of prudence and proportion. In the character of Falstaff, we are treated to a comic depiction of intemperance; in the story of David and Bathsheba, we are shown a much harsher view of a man who yields to his desires.

History and biography offer innumerable examples of virtue in action. A very short list for this century would include Jane Addams, Marie Curie, Winston Churchill, Douglas MacArthur, Anne Frank, Raoul Wallenberg, Rosa Parks, Ruby Bridges, Lech Walesa, and Benigno Aquino. It is true that great persons sometimes also have great faults. But for a student who has learned something of the virtues, and of the difficulty of possessing them, such revelations, when they come, are less likely to be occasions of cynicism. He can understand that people are not measured by occasional failings but by their whole lives.

A study of the cardinal virtues in conjunction with history and literature can lead to worthwhile classroom discussions. Notice, however, that such discussions are a far cry from Values Clarification exercises based on nothing but a student's feelings or uninformed opinions. In one case, students carry out their discussions within a framework of moral wisdom. In the other, there is no framework, and morality becomes a matter of "what I say" versus "what you say." A knowledge of the virtues provides a standard by which opinions and feelings can be measured. A student who has begun to understand them can more accurately weigh moral arguments. He can begin to discriminate between values that change and values that don't. He can learn the difference between values that are subjective (a preference for frozen yogurt over ice cream) and values that are objective (the obligation under justice to share food with someone who is hungry, the obligation under temperance not to gorge yourself to the point of throwing up).

Knowledge of the virtues also gives students a gauge for choosing their models. Many young people confuse fame with heroism. They can begin to ask not only what the difference is between a hero and a celebrity but also what the difference is between someone who has physical courage (a sports hero) and someone who has both physical and moral courage (an Aleksandr Solzhenitsyn, a Martin Luther King, Jr.). They will then be in a better position to decide which qualities of famous people are worth emulating, and which are not. I am not suggesting that discussion be aimed at picking apart a student's favorite hero. Such a discussion of qualities doesn't require a naming of names. However, in the case of some famous people whose personal lives and indiscretions have become a matter of public record, that may be unavoidable. Students will bring them up anyway. For example, since the case of Earvin "Magic" Johnson has been thrust onto the public scene, it provides an opportunity for making some distinctions. Johnson is certainly courageous in both the physical and moral sense. It takes physical courage to play professional basketball; it takes physical courage to face the pain of disease. It took moral courage to make his announcement when he did instead of waiting. Johnson does not, however, seem to have made much effort to practice the virtue of temperance. A *Los Angeles Times* reporter who knows Johnson well was quoted in *Newsweek* as suggesting that Johnson slept with more than a thousand women. How about prudence? Certainly his sexual activities were not prudent. But beyond that lies the question of the wisdom of his anti-AIDS campaign tactics. Johnson originally took a stand in favor of safe sex, not abstinence. Is that prudent advice, or does it, by legitimizing teen sex, simply increase sexual activity and lead to more, not fewer, cases of AIDS? A similar question could be asked about Johnson's more recent advocacy of both safe sex and abstinence. Is that a clear message or merely a confusing one? (A further question, of course, is why we should look to basketball players for wisdom. Does the fact that we do so suggest that something is out of order in our priorities?) The virtue of justice? Johnson seems to be a just man in many respects. He has not been stingy with either his time or his money in helping the less fortunate. On the other hand, the women he put at risk might question whether Johnson acted justly in relation to them.

The purpose of such a discussion would not be to make classroom capital out of a tragic situation, or to either condemn or exonerate Magic Johnson. The virtues are not clubs to hit other people over the head with but strengths that we should try to acquire in our own lives. But just as Magic Johnson's sickness has been made an opportunity for AIDS awareness, it could also serve as an opportunity for increased virtue awareness—in the final analysis, a much better weapon against AIDS.

The United States has an AIDS problem and a drug problem and a violence problem. None of this will go away until schools once again make it their job to teach character both directly, through the curriculum, and indirectly, by creating a moral environment in the school. Schools courageous enough to reinstate and reinforce the concept and practice of the virtues will accomplish more toward building a healthy society than an army of doctors, counselors, and social workers.

14.

WHAT PARENTS CAN DO

An acquaintance of mine, a well-educated man from another country, told me that the most shocking aspect of the culture shock involved in moving to America was to discover how badly behaved American children are. He said that this was also the reaction of the other transplanted parents he knows. Since this man had moved not to some gang-ridden region of the inner city but to a wealthy suburb with a reputation for having one of the nation's best public school systems, his observation merits some consideration. Moreover, since he happens to be a practicing psychiatrist with a thorough knowledge of child development, his judgment can hardly be dismissed as an example of outdated, Old World thinking.

His is not an uncommon experience. Even A. S. Neill, the founder of the English school Summerhill, and one of the world's foremost proponents of "natural education," was appalled at the behavior countenanced by his American disciples. He particularly didn't like the fact that children were allowed to continually interrupt adult conversations. Neill concluded that Americans didn't really understand what he meant by freedom.

One would expect that unpleasant behavior on the part of children might eventually provoke a hostile reaction on the part of adults. And indeed, this seems to be the case. There are mounting indications that Americans don't like children—at least, not nearly as much as they once did. One leading indication was the response to an Ann Landers column in the mid-seventies. She asked readers: If you had to do it over again, would you have children? Seventy percent of the 10,000 respondents wrote that they would not. This revelation was followed by a number of books and articles devoted to the same theme. I remember one article with the title "Do Americans Like Kids?" The gist of these books and articles was that parents were too stressed to pay much attention to their children; either that, or they were too absorbed in the pursuit of their own individual fulfillment. According to these accounts, children were increasingly seen as an inconvenience. Some authors suggested that this antipathy was symbolically represented by a spate of Hollywood films that depicted children as demonic.

The situation seems no better now. The April 6, 1990, issue of the *Wall Street Journal* reported that on the average, American parents spend less than fifteen minutes a week in serious discussion with their children. For fathers the amount of intimate contact with their children is an average of seventeen seconds per day. And whereas strangers would once make favorable comments about children in the company of their parents, nowadays they are just as likely to glare unapprovingly or make disparaging remarks—at least, that is the testimony I have heard from a number of parents.

The simple explanation for this aversion is that children and adolescents are increasingly disrespectful and disobedient to adults. One reaction, especially toward older children, is the "to-hell-with-them" attitude expressed in the bumper sticker slogan "I'm spending my children's inheritance." The other reaction is to shun the company of children. The increasing number of children in day care may be one manifestation of this shunning. For many, of course, day care is an economic necessity, but for many others there is another motivation. As Mary Pride, the author of a book on child rearing, points out, "One of the biggest reasons that mothers today are so anxious to get a job is simply in order to get away from the children. If I had a dime for every mother with a child in day-care who went to work 'to get out of the house,' I could buy Wyoming." "Why are grown women incapable of bearing the society of their own children for more than a few hours a day?" asks Pride:

> The reason, of course, is that *the children are no fun to be around*. Misbehaving, bothersome children would wear anyone down. The prospect of facing all that hooting and hullaballooing alone for eighteen years is frightening.

What's the point of making these observations? I mention them because I think they help to bring perspective not only to our discussion of moral education but also to the discussion of child rearing in general. Child-rearing experts never cease to remind us that love is the central ingredient in raising children. And of course, they are right. But what also needs to be acknowledged by the experts is something they rarely say: it's easier to love children who are lovable. And all things considered, better-behaved children are more lovable than badly behaved children. Of course, we still love our children when they are nasty, whiny, disobedient, disrespectful, and selfish. But if that becomes their habitual behavior, the love of even the best parents begins to wear thin. By contrast, children who are obedient, respectful, and considerate have our love not only because it is our duty to love them but because it is a delight.

If parents are really serious about loving their children (and having others love them), the sensible course of action is to bring up lovable children. One of the most important things parents can do in this regard is to help their children acquire character. To do so has mutual benefits: it makes life easier for parents, but it also makes life easier for children. Well-behaved children are happier children, and they grow into a happier adulthood. Aristotle, who had a very practical cast of mind, recommended virtue not because it was a duty but because it was the surest route to happiness (which he considered the chief good and purpose of life). Many of the arguments in his *Nicomachean Ethics* (named after his son, Nicomachus) and *Politics* build the case that happiness and virtue are inextricable, and that true happiness cannot exist without virtue. For Aristotle a happiness based on virtue can never be taken away, whereas happiness based on other things (money, health, love) is always subject to the whim of fate.

Most parents want their children to be honest, reliable, fair, self-controlled, and respectful. They know these virtues are good in themselves, and also good for their children. What prevents them from taking strong action to encourage the development of such traits?

Part of the answer lies in the influence of powerful myths, some old and some new, which dominate our thinking about child raising:

- The myth of the "good bad boy." American literature and film loves to portray "bad" boys as essentially lovable and happy. Tom Sawyer and Buster Brown are examples from the past; the various lovable brats featured in film and television are contemporary examples. This strand in the American tradition has such a powerful hold on the imagination that the word "obedience" is very nearly a dirty word in the American vocabulary. The myth of the good bad boy is connected to . . .
- The myth of natural goodness. This is the Rousseauian idea that virtue will take care of itself if children are just allowed to grow in their own way. All that parents need to do is "love" their children—love, in this case, meaning noninterference.
- The myth of expert knowledge. In recent decades parents have deferred to professional authority in the matter of raising their children. Unfortunately, the vast majority of child-rearing experts subscribe to the myth of natural goodness mentioned above. So much emphasis has been placed on the unique, creative, and spontaneous nature of children that parents have come to feel that child rearing

means adjusting themselves to their children, rather than having children learn to adjust to the requirements of family life.

- The myth that moral problems are psychological problems. This myth is connected to all of the above. In this view, behavior problems are seen as problems in self-esteem or as the result of unmet psychological needs. The old-fashioned idea that most behavior problems are the result of sheer "willfulness" on the part of children doesn't occur to the average child expert. If you look in the index of a typical child-rearing book, you will find that a great many pages are devoted to "self-esteem," but you are not likely to find the word "character" anywhere. It is not part of the vocabulary of most child professionals. For some historical perspective, it's worth noting that a study of child-rearing articles in *Ladies' Home Journal, Women's Home Companion,* and *Good Housekeeping* for the years 1890, 1900, and 1910 found that one third of them were about character development.

- The myth that parents don't have the right to instill their values in their children. Once again, the standard dogma here is that children must create their own values. But of course, children have precious little chance to do that, since the rest of the culture has no qualms about imposing values. Does it make sense for parents to remain neutral bystanders when everyone else—from scriptwriters, to entertainers, to advertisers, to sex educators—insists on selling their values to children?

This is not to suggest that the problem is simply one of sweeping away myths and illusions. Character formation is a difficult task even when we have a clear picture of what it entails. In addition, our society has a special structural problem that makes the job even more difficult. The problem is divorce—up 700 percent in this century, with most of the rise occurring in recent decades. Obviously, the advice that parents should stay together comes too late for many, but it needs to be stated anyway: the best setting for raising good children is in a two-parent family. We now have an unmistakably clear picture of the effects on children of parental absence. Raising children out of wedlock is a formula for disaster. So, very often, is divorce. There now exists a vast body of research on divorce and parental absence, and it all points in the same direction: children from single-parent homes are more at risk than other children for drug use, delinquency, emotional problems, and unwanted pregnancies.

They also appear to be more confused about right and wrong. Dr. Judith Wallerstein, a California psychologist who has been studying children of divorce since 1971, notes: "Children felt that their conscience had been weakened by their disenchantment with the parents' behavior, and with the departure of the very parent who had more often than not acted as their moral authority." Moreover, "the shaky family structure of the newly divorced family and the loosened discipline of the transition period combined with parental self-absorption or distress to diminish the available controls." On a more profound level divorce seems to shake the child's confidence in the existence of a morally ordered, meaningful world. Some psychologists have even concluded that the pain of parental divorce is more difficult for a child to overcome than the death of a parent.

One of the surest routes for bringing morality back to this society is to bring back marriage. As Mae West said, in a somewhat different context, "A man in the home is worth two in the street." He's worth a lot more than that in terms of raising disciplined and well-behaved children. His influence on his sons will be particularly marked. Boys whose fathers are present in the home are significantly less involved with drugs and delinquency, more self-controlled, more successful academically. Daughters too benefit when a father is present in the home. They have fewer emotional problems, are more immune to self-destructive behaviors, and are more likely to postpone sex. All this is widely documented. Also well documented is the fact that single mothers have extreme difficulty in controlling adolescent sons. This is not to detract from all that a mother does but to suggest how difficult it is to do the job alone.

However, just as the available research on the adverse effects of

smoking was ignored for years, so was the large body of knowledge about the effects of single parenting. As Harvard psychiatrist
Armand Nicholi, Jr., observes, "We refuse to accept findings that
demand a radical change in our lifestyle." Even today one hears
arguments that single-parent homes work as well as two-parent
families. In a 1989 *Time* interview, Toni Morrison, the Pulitzer
Prize—winning author, stated, "I don't think a female running a
house is a problem, a broken family. . . . Two parents can't raise
a child any more than one. . . . The little nuclear family is a
paradigm that just doesn't work. It doesn't work for white people
or for black people. Why we are hanging on to it, I don't know."

It is possible, as Morrison says, for a woman to raise a family on
her own and to do a good job of it. Many women do—although
most do it out of necessity rather than conviction. But it is one
thing to recognize that something can be done, and another thing
to recommend it. Many people are capable of working two eight-
hour shifts each day, but it doesn't follow that this is a preferable
alternative to holding one job. Women who are thinking of having children should think twice about Morrison's belief that "two
parents can't raise a child any more than one." A better course of
action for our society, one suggested by James Dobson and Gary
Bauer in their book *Children at Risk,* is to restore the idea of the
"good family man," the man who puts his family first and takes
a hand in their moral education: "Fathers must be there to tame
adolescent boys, to give a young son a sense of what it means to
be a man, and to explain why honor and loyalty and fidelity are
important. For daughters, a father is a source of love and comfort
that can help her avoid surrendering her virtue in a fruitless search
for love through premarital sex." What Dobson and Bauer recommend does not have the fashionable ring of Morrison's statement.
Even so, it is their assessment, not Morrison's, that most closely
fits the hard data about homes without fathers. One startling
statistic which gives the lie to the notion that any family formation
is as good as any other is the repeated finding that children are
five to six times more likely to be sexually abused by a stepparent
or boyfriend of the mother than by the natural father. A Canadian
study published in the *Journal of Ethology and Sociobiology* reports that a preschool child living with a stepparent is *forty* times

more likely to be abused than a child living with his or her biological father.

No matter what their marital situation, however, parents need to be working toward the creation of what Louis Sullivan, the secretary of health and human services, calls a "culture of character." As Sullivan says, "A new culture of character in America, nurtured by strengthened families and communities, would do much to alleviate the alienation, isolation and despair that fuel teen pregnancy, violence, drug and alcohol abuse and other social problems afflicting us." Sullivan points out that "study after study has shown that children who are raised in an environment of strong values tend to thrive in every sense."

But while working toward that goal, parents have to be realistic about the present situation. Parents cannot, as they once did, rely on the culture to reinforce home values. In fact, they can expect that many of the cultural forces influencing their children will be actively undermining those values. Sometimes, unfortunately, this even applies to the schools.

It doesn't make sense for parents to work at creating one type of moral environment at home, and then send their children to a school that teaches a different set of values. Families concerned to instruct their children in virtue and character cannot rely on schools to do likewise. As we have seen, many schools have adopted theories and methods that are inimical to family values. Indeed, some educational theorists seem to proceed on the assumption that parents and families hardly matter. John Dewey, still considered America's chief philosopher of education, conspicuously omitted any mention of home or family in his otherwise exhaustive *Democracy and Education*. Dewey's omission is now reflected in the classroom. Paul Vitz's 1983 study of elementary school textbooks concluded that "traditional family values have been systematically excluded from children's textbooks." Philosopher Michael Levin of New York University goes further by describing current public school textbooks as having "a decided animus against motherhood and the family." The attitude of many educators is that parents are hopelessly out of date. Thus Princeton sociologist Norman Ryder approvingly observes that "education of the junior generation is a subversive influence," and identifies the public school as "the chief instrument for teaching citizenship, in a direct appeal to the children over the heads of their parents."

Enough has been said in previous chapters about public school sex education programs, "lifestyle" curriculums, and Values Clarification courses to suggest that they reflect a commitment to moral relativism and a rejection of traditional values. Some public schools have rid themselves of such programs, and others are now beginning to institute programs in character education. Nevertheless, parents who are not interested in having their children learn the lifestyle-of-the-month cannot assume that their concerns are shared by the average public school. They will need to make some inquiries.

Often a visit to the school will be sufficiently instructive. The behavior of students in the classrooms and corridors is a good indication of a school's basic philosophy. When a school values order, discipline, and learning and expects students to value these qualities, the results are tangible. One does not have to be a trained sociologist to get an accurate impression of the school ethos.

But clean corridors, smiling students, and enthusiastic teachers do not always tell the whole story. It is wise to check further. For example, it is legitimate for parents to ask about curriculums in values, in sex education, in social studies, in home economics (not what it used to be), and in health science (units of which may turn out to be neither scientific nor healthy for your child). It is legitimate to ask to see classroom materials. As a parent you should realize that teachers and administrators are busy people, and you should be willing to work around their schedules. However, if you do that and still meet nothing but resistance and evasion, it's a sign that something is amiss. Parents should also be prepared to translate educational jargon. Educational language is designed to give comfort and reassurance, and is almost always upbeat. But parents need to understand what the terms actually mean. The repeated use of such code words as "values," "value-neutral," "holistic," "humanistic," "decision making," "awareness of their sexuality," and "responsible sex" is a good indication that the school has no real commitment to character formation. (Parents can also observe how teachers and principals react to words such as "character," "virtue," and "abstinence.")

Parents who aren't satisfied with what they find have one of two options. They can combine with other parents in an attempt to influence the school in the direction of character education, or they can look for another school. The first option is feasible in some situations: very often school personnel have the same reservations as parents about certain programs, and they will welcome information about better approaches. Parents should familiarize themselves with successful programs and be ready to provide sample materials as well as data on program effectiveness. Statistics can be persuasive. For example, a survey of schools using materials developed by the American Institute for Character Education found that 77 percent reported a decline in discipline problems, 64 percent a decrease in vandalism, and 68 percent an increase in school attendance.

In the case of a school or school system with a strong ideological commitment to "humanistic" or rational utopian education, however, the first option entails a long, difficult struggle. The second option is one that an increasing number of parents are pursuing. An article in the December 9, 1991, *U.S. News & World Report* entitled "The Flight from Public Schools" claims that "the nation's faith in its public schools is fading fast." Some families are abandoning public schools because they view them as educationally ineffective, some because they consider them dangerous, and some because they are seeking more traditional forms of moral or religious education.

What are the alternatives to public education?

- Private schools. The existence of private preparatory schools makes it possible for parents to choose a school with a philosophy and tradition in keeping with their own. In addition, some private schools offer another alternative which some parents may consider to be in the best interest of their children—the opportunity to attend a single-sex school. The private school option is, however, an expensive one and beyond the reach of most families.
- Religious schools. The number of private schools in-

creased by nearly 30 percent during the 1980s, with most of the increase accounted for by Christian schools and academies. While many of these new schools are as yet untested, the results of Catholic religious education are well known. According to the *U.S. News* article, Catholic schools boast a rate of graduation of 95 percent versus 85 percent for public schools, and they send 83 percent of their graduates to college as opposed to 52 percent of public school graduates. What accounts for the success of Catholic schools? Paul Hill of the Rand Corporation explains it this way: "If a school says, 'Here's what we are, what we stand for,' kids almost always respond to it by working hard. Catholic schools stand for something; public schools don't."

- School choice. The idea of parental choice and voucher plans that would allow parents to pick among public schools or receive public funds for private or parochial schools has been gaining steam in recent years. Such plans are already being put into effect in some states. For parents in search of schools with a commitment to character education, the school choice movement offers cause for optimism.

- Home school. The number of students schooled at home jumped from 10,000 in 1970 to 300,000 in 1990. Home schoolers take seriously the adage that "parents are their children's first and most important teachers." The advantage claimed by home schoolers is that parents can provide an education in keeping with their own religious and moral values, and at the same time supply more personal attention to their children's educational needs. Many good home school curriculums are currently on the market, but before getting started, parents should check with a local home school organization, since there are legal requirements for home schooling which vary from state to state.

Up until recent decades, schools were considered to be acting *in loco parentis*—in the place of the parent (this principle even prevailed in many colleges in the recent past). The idea that the parent is the first and foremost teacher was taken seriously: teachers acted for the parents as trustees of children's education. The culture of the school and the culture of the home reinforced each other; both had similar goals and values. It was, in short, a very sensible arrangement. It meant that children were not exposed to sharply conflicting moralities before they learned basic morality. Instead, moral lessons were doubly reinforced. It is still possible to find or create this kind of moral continuity between home and school. It simply requires a great deal of work and determination.

What else can parents do? Perhaps the most important thing is to realize that families, even more than schools, need to create a moral ethos. "A family is a group of people," according to the definition in one second-grade textbook cited in Professor Vitz's study of textbooks. But a family ought to be more than that. A family is part of the larger culture, but ideally, it is also a culture in itself. As the Puritan preacher William Gouge observed, "A family is a little church and a little commonwealth." We might add that it is also a little school and, hopefully, a school of goodness. There are practical methods for promoting character formation, but the most practical is to create a culture of the home.

The word "culture" comes from the word "cultivation." Both plants and people grow best when a good environment has been prepared for them. For the youngest and most tender plants the best environment is a greenhouse. It gives them a head start: upon being transplanted, such plants are larger, stronger, and more resilient to disease than other plants. Children need similar protection and nurturing for healthy moral development. "Then," as it says in the Psalms, "our sons in their youth will be like well-nurtured plants" (Psalms 144:12). The child brought up in a good home environment will be stronger, healthier, and more resistant to the various moral diseases circulating in the larger culture. This analogy, so plain to agricultural societies, is less obvious in industrial societies, where most people have little experience in growing things. We do, however, seem to retain some instinctive nostalgia for this "simpler" approach to child rearing. Perhaps this is the reason so many of our stories about wholesome family life are set on farms.

At a certain point, of course, the analogy between the gardener and the parent breaks down. The plant is passive; the child is active, a bundle of energy, intellect, and will. He needs to take an active role in his own development, and he needs to learn to set limits to his own behavior. Even so, children still need a lot of assistance; and the chief way for a parent to help is to encourage the development of good habits—habits that will someday turn into virtues.

The first way to develop good habits is through good discipline. When Jeane Westin, the author of *The Coming Parent Revolution*, asked parents of grown or nearly grown children what they would do differently, the most frequent response was "increased discipline." These parents felt themselves victims of parenting advice that put a premium on "understanding" children and "relating" to them. As a result of such advice, many of these mothers and fathers had "understood" themselves into immobility. Unable to set limits, they found themselves accepting their children's most outrageous demands and behaviors. They were acting on the assumption that discipline must come from within the child. The problem, as Westin points out, is that children never learn to discipline themselves unless parents start them on that road.

As uncomfortable as it is for our psychologized generation, parents who wish to raise well-behaved children must say no to actions that are harmful to their children. And getting his way when he shouldn't is considerably more harmful for a child than occasional frustrations of his desires. Christopher Lasch, author of *Haven in a Heartless World*, writes: "Without struggling with the ambivalent emotions aroused by the union of love and discipline in his parents, the child never masters his inner rage or his fear of authority. It is for that reason that children need parents, not professional nurses and counselors." This view is corroborated by research into family patterns conducted by Dr. Diana Baumrind of the University of California at Berkeley. She found that the best-adjusted and most self-possessed children had parents who were loving, but also demanding, authoritative, and consistent in their discipline. By contrast, permissive parents, no matter how loving, produced children who lacked self-control, initiative, and resilience.

Setting limits and enforcing habits of good behavior is not easy in the short run, but it is the best policy for the long run. One paradoxical benefit for the child is more freedom when he grows older. Psychologist William Coulson observes of several friends, accomplished musicians who were made to practice their instruments as youngsters, that they "are able to do what they want today because they weren't free to do what they wanted when they were young." Some of this increased freedom will, of course, show up long before adulthood. A child who has learned discipline (the Latin root means "teaching") will, among other things, be much freer of the tyranny of the teenage peer group. Another paradoxical benefit is that good discipline improves the quality of the parent-child relationship. When authority is exercised with the proper combination of firmness and love, the effect is increased love and respect for the parent. Parents, in turn, find it easier to love well-behaved children. Finally, it should be noted that families are not the only beneficiaries of order and discipline. According to psychologist William Damon, respect for the parent who exercises proper authority leads to respect for legitimate social institutions, and to respect for law. In his book *The Moral Child,* Damon writes, "The child's respect for parental authority sets the direction for civilized participation in the social order when the child later begins assuming the rights and responsibilities of full citizenship." Damon calls this respect "the single most important moral legacy that comes out of the child's relations with the parent."

Another good habit for children to acquire is helping with household chores. According to a Harvard study, which followed the lives of 465 boys into middle age, boys who were given jobs or household chores grew up to become happier adults, had higher-paying jobs and greater job satisfaction, had better marriages and better relationships with their children and friends, and were physically healthier than adults who had not assumed similar responsibilities as children. Psychiatrist George E. Vaillant, who directed the study, has a simple explanation: "Boys who worked in the home or community gained competence and came to feel they were worthwhile members of society. And because they felt good about themselves, others felt good about them."

The point of chores is to give children a sense of contributing to the family. And this sense of contributing increases the sense of belonging. Moreover, by encouraging a child to help with the work of the household, parents develop the child's natural desire to imitate into a habit that will serve him or her well for a lifetime. This is not to say that the chores are entirely for the sake of the child. At a certain age a child can begin to make solid contributions to the work of the family. In addition to regular chores, family members can undertake common projects such as cleaning out a cellar, remodeling a room, or building a deck. Working together on difficult projects is an activity that goes a long way toward solidifying family bonds.

Parents should also encourage habits of helping outside the home. The fact that "charity begins at home" does not mean it should end there. Children can help with community drives, with environmental cleanups, with collecting money for worthy causes, with church work. However, the most important experiences are person to person: visiting a sick relative, helping elderly neighbors with chores, delivering groceries to a shut-in, babysitting without charge for a family experiencing an emergency. An article by Beverly Beckham in the *Boston Herald* suggests that the habit of caring for others has fallen into neglect. She tells of visiting an elderly acquaintance after many years and finding his house in a state of deterioration: "The grass was too high . . . the porch was shabby . . . the window box was empty." Beckham continues: "Leaving, I drove by children—11, 12, 13 years old—riding their bikes along the sidewalk and I thought: wouldn't it be nice if they rang this man's doorbell and offered to cut the grass for him, for free? Or volunteered to take care of his garden?" Her conclusion is not that the children were selfish, simply that they didn't know how: "Years ago, neighbors would have rallied around this man. Years ago, children would have automatically reached out. They would have learned *how* from their parents."

Habits, however, are not the whole story. Something else is necessary, something more basic. Parents need an organizing principle of family life if they hope to enforce good habits; and without such a principle, they will be hard-pressed to decide what constitutes a good habit in the first place. Earlier I indicated that

260   WHY JOHNNY CAN'T TELL RIGHT FROM WRONG

a family is best thought of as a small culture, and that this cultural aspect is the key to character formation. Let me explain more fully by referring once again to Diana Baumrind's study of family discipline patterns. In addition to the three patterns—authoritarian, authoritative, and permissive—revealed by her research, there existed a small subset of "harmonious" families. William Damon, in commenting on Baumrind's work, notes: "In these families, the parent rarely needs to assert control, because the children anticipate the parent's directives and obey without command or discipline. Like children of authoritative parents, these children from 'harmonious' families turned out competent and socially responsible." Continues Damon, "Such family patterns may be far more common in Eastern cultures . . . indeed a sizable proportion of the few 'harmonious' families in Baumrind's own data base were Japanese-Americans."

I think Damon is correct in assuming that such patterns are more common in Eastern cultures. Eastern cultures have a strong sense of family and also of family ritual. In some senses family life itself is an object of religious devotion. Not much of this sense of tradition and ritual is left in American families. The only daily ritual practiced regularly in American households is the ritual of watching television. And family bonds have been weakened by the emergence of what social analyst Francis Fukuyama describes as a "social contract" model of the family: a model in which rational self-interest replaces absolute obligation. But as Fukuyama says, "families don't really work if they are based on liberal principles, that is, if their members regard them as they would a joint stock company, formed for their utility rather than being based on ties of duty and love. Raising children or making a marriage work through a lifetime requires personal sacrifices that are irrational, if looked at from a cost-benefit calculus."

Clearly, as Fukuyama implies, the family needs a stronger unifying principle than that of a voluntary association of self-interested individuals. Otherwise it cannot call forth the acts of self-denial on which its existence depends. To the extent American families are based on these individualistic principles, to that same extent family harmony will remain an elusive goal.

When I think of the American families I know that would fit

under the category "harmonious," it strikes me that they all have a very strong sense of family and of ritual. I once asked the father of one such family what sort of rules he used to keep order among his eight well-behaved children. "We don't have any rules," he replied. I think that may have been a slight exaggeration, but I understood his point. The thing that seemed to make the rules quite secondary was a strong sense of family purpose and direction. What gave this particular family direction was a firm religious faith—Catholic, in this case. It was a family with a commitment, and the commitment was reflected in grace before meals, in nightly devotions, and in regular family liturgies which followed the Church's liturgical calendar. The other binding agent was what might loosely be called "the family business." The parents ran a small private school in their very large house, and as their own children grew older, they would lend a hand either with the teaching or with other attendant responsibilities. There existed a third commitment in this family—what can simply be described as a commitment to culture. Painting, music, sculpture, and drama were studied along with philosophy, history, and literature. One of the boys was an accomplished pianist, other family members painted or sculpted, all either played an instrument or sang; plays were staged twice a year; dances, sing-alongs, and concerts involving family friends (themselves members of large families) were a common occurrence.

Yes, it's beginning to sound like an American version of the Trapp family, and in this case the comparison would be apt. Obviously, this is an exceptional family—too exceptional to be offered as a model. Still, when we look at other successful families, we find similar elements at work. Probably the most important of these is the sense of family purpose or mission. Paul Hill's explanation of the success of parochial schools—"If a school says, 'Here's what we are, what we stand for,' kids almost always respond to it by working hard"—applies to families as well.

One group that has succeeded in raising loving and stable families is the Lubavitcher Hasidim. Although the Lubavitchers live in densely populated urban areas, their children are remarkably free of the plague of drugs, violence, and irresponsible sex from which other urban children suffer. For the Lubavitchers and other Orthodox Jews the center of religious life is the home. They regard the home as a sacred place, and their major priority is their children's moral and spiritual development. Lubavitchers place great emphasis on respect for parents and other elder relatives, such as grandparents. Close contact is maintained with relatives, and major Jewish holidays are occasions for convivial get-togethers.

Edward Hoffman, a clinical psychologist who has studied and written about the Lubavitchers, provides some revealing details of Lubavitcher life:

> Religious rituals like the weekly lighting of Sabbath candles on Friday evening are a focal point for the entire family; everyone is expected to be present and attentive. Similarly, all family members participate in singing the traditional thanksgiving prayers to God after each meal. In this way, youngsters are trained to develop the emotions of gratitude and reverence for something greater than their own ego's desires.

In addition,

> Far more than in mainstream America today, Lubavitcher children are taught to be compassionate and altruistic. Because charity is venerated as an act of piety, youngsters are expected to make a small contribution every Friday (before Sabbath) to the "charity box" that is prominently displayed in their home. In accordance with biblical precepts Lubavitcher parents are expected to tithe their income to charitable causes. In this way, too, family members learn to think in terms of mutual sharing rather than egoistic gratification.

If life among the Lubavitchers is more harmonious than in most families, part of the reason seems to lie in their orientation to a higher plan and purpose than the merely secular. Hoffman writes, "Lubavitchers partly attribute their vibrant family life to the fact that children do not 'take orders' from parents. Rather, as one Hassidic rabbi explained to me, 'All family members "take orders" from God, as we understand His commands in the Bible and other sacred books.' In the Hassidic view, the presence of clear religious dicta delineating right versus wrong behavior makes the parental role far easier—and less conflicted—than that faced by nonreligious parents in America."

The Lubavitchers seem like a curiosity to most Americans. Yet we find a similar orientation to family and religion—among other groups who maintain thriving and cohesive families: other observant Jews, Greek Orthodox, Black Muslims, Mormons, Amish, and Asian-Americans. From a historical perspective, the greater curiosity is the current assumption that the family can thrive as a purely secular entity. In Hebrew, Roman, and European civilizations of the past, and even in this country during the eighteenth and nineteenth centuries, the idea of the sanctity of the home was the rule, not the exception. And as with the Lubavitchers, many religious rituals or scripture readings took place in the home. Thus home life was linked to something larger than itself, to a larger vision and purpose. This twin vision of the family as being sacred in itself and as set within a larger sacred framework gave added authority to parents, and added strength to family bonds

Is it possible to establish a secular equivalent of this sense of family sanctity? Many families that are not religious do seem able to create a strong sense of family mission and purpose. But as with religious families, this seems to work best when there is a commitment to some larger goal or tradition or cause. Family life requires considerable sacrifice of individual wants, and it helps if a child can be given a vision of something big enough and good enough to make those sacrifices for. Families that have the loyalty of their children manage to convey a sense that they are engaged in important work: in carrying on a faith, a tradition, a craft, a philosophy, a vision of the way things ought to be.

Unfortunately, many families today don't stand for anything. Neither "little churches" nor "little commonwealths," they are more like "little hotels"—places where one stays temporarily but with no particular sense of commitment. This is true not only of those children who regard the home merely as a way station on the road to autonomy but also of those parents who do not feel unconditionally bound to their offspring. What changed the family from a community to a collection of individuals each pursuing his or her own individual fulfillment? Certainly, modern psychology is one of the culprits. Its emphasis has never been on family or marriage but rather on separation and individuation. It is significant that Alfred Adler, who is considered the father of the optimistic American strand of psychology, called his theory "individual psychology." A second factor in the atomizing of family life is our Rousseau-like reliance on the strength of natural affections: we have forgotten that natural affections need to be cultivated if they are to grow. A third cause is the easy availability of divorce and the resulting view of marriage as an experiment rather than a sacrament or lifetime commitment.

But these destructive forces are not nearly as immediate and tangible as the fourth—the one that sits in nearly every living room. If there is a cultural vacuum in many homes, a large part of the reason is that television has become the organizing principle of family life. Television, as critic Kenneth Myers has observed, can no longer be considered simply a part of the culture; rather, as Myers puts it, "it *is* our culture." "Television," he goes on to say, "is . . . not simply the dominant medium of *popular* culture, it is the single most significant shared reality in our entire society. . . . In television we live and move and have our being."

More than any other medium or institution, television defines what is and is not important. It shapes our sense of reality. It confers significance on events by paying attention to them, or, by withholding attention, it denies them significance. It does not, for example, confer much significance on religion. Although religious faith still plays a significant part in the lives of real families, it is close to nonexistent in the lives of television families. As critic Ben Stein observes in the *Wall Street Journal,* almost never does a TV character go to church or temple, seek religious counsel, or pray for moral guidance. Another impression left by television is that sex underlies everything: that it is constantly on everyone's mind—or should be. At the same time, as content-analysis studies have shown, television sex rarely takes place within the context of marriage but almost exclusively outside it. If schools are sometimes working at cross-purposes to parental values, the dichotomy between television and traditional family values is even sharper. As one Lubavitcher father observes, "It opens up the home to become the receptacle for whatever somebody in Los Angeles, or wherever, wants to dump onto your living room floor and into your kids' minds." "Those who think that *their* children will remain immune are just kidding themselves," says another Lubavitcher father.

Perhaps the most profound effect of television watching, however, is its effect on family relationships. Regular television viewing deprives families of opportunities to interact with one another. There are just so many hours in the day, and, right now, for many families television takes up a disproportionate number of them. Watching TV is much easier than conversation, and it is certainly easier than confrontation—although confrontation is sometimes what is called for in family life. Because TV tends to pacify children, thus providing temporary harmony, many parents use it as a substitute for the hard work of establishing real discipline. As Marie Winn observes in *Children Without Childhood,* "Instead of having to establish rules and limits . . . instead of having to work at socializing children in order to make them more agreeable to live with, parents could solve all these problems by resorting to the television set. 'Go watch TV' were the magic words." Kenneth Myers makes a similar observation: "I do believe that addiction to television (as opposed to deliberate, measured viewing) makes sincere and deep relations with people and with reality more difficult to sustain."

One important step that any parent can take to restore family culture, to improve family relationships, and to take moral education out of the hands of "somebody in Los Angeles" is to revive the practice of family reading, once so common. There are many benefits. The close personal contact of sitting together as a family group, or just two, creates a bond of unity and a bond of mutual enthusiasm. And it is not an activity that needs to stop once children are old enough to read for themselves. At one time it was common practice for adults and children of all ages to take turns reading aloud from the works of Dickens, Twain, and Stevenson. Of course, the practice is not entirely extinct. One family I know describes "long evenings of absolute suspense" reading aloud from *The Lord of the Rings.* As with other pleasurable activities, part of the pleasure of reading good books is the pleasure of sharing them.

An added benefit is that reading together acts as a stimulus to conversation. And unlike the forced "therapeutic" discussions that take place in some modern households, it is a type of conversation that flows naturally. It often goes much deeper as well, allowing parents and children to share thoughts about questions that are at the center of human concern. In reading or listening to stories, moreover, children are learning to think and imagine more freely. Their emotional and intellectual response is their own, not the cued response generated by a television laugh track.

In addition, good stories can provide pictures of family life that act as an antidote to current shallow notions about the family. A good example is the *Odyssey,* several fine versions of which can be read by or to children. As Thomas Fleming, a writer and classics scholar, points out, "Even the plot is a paradigm of domestic fidelity":

> Odysseus, who had fought for ten years at Troy, is held captive by a beautiful goddess who wants to make him her immortal companion. Instead, the poor man pines for a sight of home—a rugged and worthless scrap of rock—and longs for his middle-aged wife and a son he hasn't seen for twenty years. Back at home, his wife has been resorting to every sort of stratagem to keep a flock of noble suitors at arm's length, while her son spends his days brooding over his absent father. Odysseus' homecoming is for many readers the most dramatic and joyful moment in literature. After he slaughters his rivals and persuades his wife of his identity, the couple, after their joyous reunion, spends the night exactly as a modern couple would: they talk till the sun comes up.

On a cost-benefit calculus, the actions of Odysseus, Penelope, and Telemachus don't make any sense. But Homer paints on a larger canvas. He presents us with a conception of family life that far transcends such a limited calculus.

The most important benefit of reading is the positive effect on character. In reading to a child, you—not some distant script-writer—get to choose the models and morals that come into the home. Reading and listening to the right sort of stories creates a primitive emotional attachment to behavior that is good and worthy; it implants a love and desire for virtue in the child's heart and imagination; it helps to prevent moral blindness.

Finally, reading together puts you and your children in touch with one of the great civilizing traditions of the human race. All the great cultures of the past preferred to express their most serious thought through stories. The wonder of it is that we can share in many of those same stories today. They have survived because the truths they tell are timeless. Jim Trelease, author of *The Read-Aloud Handbook,* puts the matter well in explaining why he read to his children:

> I read because *my* father read to *me.* And because he'd read to me, when my time came I knew intuitively there is a torch that is supposed to be passed from one generation to the next. And through countless nights of reading I began to realize that when enough of the torchbearers—parents and teachers—stop passing the torches, a culture begins to die.

15.

GUIDE TO GREAT
BOOKS FOR
CHILDREN AND
TEENS

One of the difficulties in compiling a list of good books is that there are so many good ones to choose from. What follows is only a representative list. It is far from being comprehensive.

The books on the list have been chosen because they are the kinds of books that help youngsters to grow in courage, charity, justice, and other virtues. But they would not be included if they were not also good stories. Since good books do their own work in their own way, it is not necessary or wise for adults to explain the "moral" in each story. Shared reading may prompt youngsters to ask questions about moral issues, but adults should be careful not to treat books like doses of moral medicine.

The three reading levels are only a rough guide. Children do not seem to have much respect for such age gradings, and tend to tramp back and forth across them. Some middle readers (roughly eight to twelve years old) can read and enjoy Tolkien. Some children in the same age group may just be getting started on *Little House in the Big Woods*. And the youngster who can read novels may still delight in hearing fairy tales read to younger siblings. Likewise, beginning readers or nonreaders will often enjoy listening to read-alouds selected from a middle reading level.

A word of explanation is in order about the term "older readers." I have used it instead of the more common classification "young adult." Many of the young adult books aimed at teenagers tend to reflect back to them their own limited adolescent world, thus leaving the young reader with the impression that there is nothing more profound in life than the teenage view of things as seen through the lens of popular culture. If teenagers really are to be treated as young adults, then they deserve acquaintance with books that offer a broader and deeper vision of life.

Like singing, reading draws families together. Shared reading provides mutual delight and establishes intimacy in a way that few other activities can match. And the gift of good books is a better gift than clothes or toys. The clothes and toys won't last and won't make a lasting difference. But what a child reads becomes a permanent part of his life, giving direction to his imagination and his actions.

PICTURE BOOKS, STORY BOOKS, BEGINNING READERS

Aesop's Fables. Illus. by Fritz Kredel. Grosset, 1947, 1983. 234 pp.
"The Fox and the Crow," "The Hare and the Tortoise," "The Wolf in Sheep's Clothing," "The Boy Who Cried Wolf": these little stories-with-a-moral go back at least 2,300 years, but their shrewd observations about human foibles are still timely. We still need to be reminded that we can't trust flatterers, that we can't please everyone, and that we shouldn't pretend to be what we're not. Listeners and readers of all ages will take pleasure in these pithy and entertaining lessons in living.

Beauty and the Beast. Retold and illus. by Jan Brett. Clarion, 1989, 1991. 31 pp.
Beauty and the Beast is just the right antidote to our modern

obsession with looks, surface charm, and casual sex. It speaks volumes about the meaning of true love and true beauty, and about the importance of restraining our animal nature until love has had time to grow. Children will appreciate the mystery and romance of this story; adults will appreciate its depth and wisdom. Jan Brett's illustrations are elegant and enchanting, but older readers should be directed to Madame Leprince de Beaumont's longer version—especially for Beauty's observation that "handsome looks [may] hide a false and wicked heart."

Betsy-Tacy. Maud Hart Lovelace. Illus. by Lois Lenski. Harper, 1940, 1979. 112 pp.

Betsy and Tacy are firm friends—such firm friends that their names are always mentioned in the same breath: Betsy-Tacy. This book is the first in a series that describes Betsy's lighthearted childhood in a small midwestern town, shortly after the turn of the century. The innocent amusements and loving family relationships present a happy portrayal of family life and of childhood full of mirth, unsullied by false sophistication. The sequels (which gradually become more advanced in reading level) all maintain a refreshingly wholesome attitude.

Book of Greek Myths. Ingri and Edgar Parin d'Aulaire. Illus. by the authors. Doubleday, 1962, 1980. 192 pp.

A splendid collection of Greek myths adapted for children, and graced with imaginative drawings. These easy-to-read stories recount the exploits of Zeus and the other immortals, who, despite their divine status, had the full complement of human vices and virtues. A good read-aloud.

Another good choice is *A Child's Book of Myths and Enchantment Tales* written and illustrated by Margaret Evans Price (Checkerboard Press, 1954, 1989. 160 pp.). The striking illustrations are done in Art Nouveau style, and the stories include such morally instructive myths as "Pandora's Box" and "Midas and the Golden Touch."

The Children's Bible in 365 Stories. Mary Batchelor. Illus. by John Haysom. Lion Pub. USA, 1985, 1987. 416 pp.

Short, well-written, and accurate stories from the Old and New Testaments. Good for parents who wish to establish family Bible readings. Other good choices are *The Zondervan Bible Storybook* (Jenny Robertson. Illus. by Alan Parry. Zondervan, 1983, 1988. 377 pp.), with concise and colorfully illustrated stories; *Catherine Marshall's Story Bible* (Catherine Marshall. Avon, 1985. 200 pp.), a compilation of thirty-seven Bible stories told by one of America's most popular Christian writers; and *The Tall Book of Bible Stories* (Katherine Gibson. Illus. by Ted Chaiko. Harper, 1957. 128 pp.).

The Children's Homer: The Adventures of Odysseus and the Tale of Troy. Padraic Colum. Illus. by Willy Pogany. Macmillan, 1918. Collier, 1982. 248 pp.

It's all here: the Trojan horse, the travels of Odysseus, the encounter with the Cyclops, Circe's enchanted isle, the ingenuity of Penelope, the revenge on the suitors—and it's retold by a master of the English language in prose that captures the power and simplicity of the original. These stories are one of the primary mythic sources of Western culture, and they have exercised a power over the imagination for more than 2,500 years. But of course, Homer is far more than a lesson in cultural literacy: Padraic Colum's splendid retelling shows us why the *Iliad* and the *Odyssey* rank among the best adventure stories ever told. For ages ten and up, these stories can also be read aloud to somewhat younger children.

Two other fine retellings of Homer are *The Adventures of Ulysses* (Gerald Gottlieb. Illus. by Steele Savage. Random House, 1959. 170 pp.) and *Tales of Troy and Greece* (Andrew Lang. Illus. by Edward Bawden. Originally published in 1907. Faber & Faber, 1978. 300 pp.).

Clancy's Coat. Eve Bunting. Illus. by Lorinda Bryan Cauley. Warne, 1984. 48 pp.

The mending of a coat becomes the means by which two Irish neighbors learn to make amends. Ever since Tippitt's cow, Bridget, got into Clancy's garden, the two friends haven't spoken a word to each other. But Clancy's coat needs turning, and he won't trust anyone but Tippitt the tailor to do the job. So he grudgingly brings it over. The mending of the coat seems to take forever, thereby providing an excuse for more visits to check on its progress. The coat never does get mended, but the friendship is renewed. In the meantime each man learns to temper his temper with self-restraint, and the reader is treated to a flow of witty and inventive dialogue.

The Clown of God. Tomie dePaola. Illus. by the author. Harcourt, 1978.

A retelling of an ancient legend, this superbly illustrated book tells the story of Giovanni, a beggar boy who becomes a famous juggler. Giovanni travels up and down Italy, playing before dukes and princes, but when he grows old, people tire of his act. Giovanni washes off his clown face, puts away his juggling tools, and returns to begging. One day, however, his travels take him to a monastery church where he finds himself called upon to perform one last time. The story's theme of self-giving is capped by a poignant and perfectly realized conclusion.

Dogger. Shirley Hughes. Illus. by the author. Bodley Head, 1977. 32 pp. (First American edition published in 1978 by Prentice-Hall under the title *David and Dog*.)

This is a story about one of those small everyday sacrifices family members make for one another. David takes his worn, stuffed dog, "Dogger," everywhere; but one day on a walk with his mother, David manages to lose Dogger. The whole family joins in the search, but to no avail. The next day at the school fair, Dogger is found in the possession of a little girl who has just purchased him from a toy stall. In order to get Dogger back from the reluctant girl, Bella, David's older sister trades a large and beautiful stuffed bear she has just won.

The Door in the Wall. Marguerite De Angeli. Illus. by the author. Doubleday, 1949. 111 pp. Dell, 1990. 120 pp.

A heartwarming and inspiring tale of a young boy left crippled by illness, and of his victory over his seemingly hopeless situation. With the help of the monks who heal his broken spirit as well as his body, Robin learns that when the way to the future is blocked, there is always a "door in the wall" for those willing to look for it. Set in late-medieval England, this beautifully written tale brings alive the texture and richness of life in castles, monasteries, and market towns.

The Emperor and the Kite. Jane Yolen. Illus. by Ed Young. World, 1967. 31 pp. Philomel, 1988. 28 pp.

Set in ancient China, this simple yet powerful story tells of courage and loyalty. Djeou Seow's brothers are like "four rising suns" and her sisters like "midnight moons" in the eyes of her father, the emperor. But Djeou Seow is the youngest, and so insignificant the emperor often forgets he has a fourth daughter. When the emperor is kidnapped, his children flee and do nothing. All except Djeou Seow. She keeps him alive by using her kite to bring him food. And eventually, with the help of her kite, she effects his escape. Like King Lear, the emperor learns that a daughter's loyalty is shown by deeds, not words. The elegant illustrations are a perfect marriage to the text.

How Many Days to America?: A Thanksgiving Story. Eve Bunting. Illus. by Beth Peck. Clarion, 1982, 1988. 32 pp.

"Because we do not think the way they think, my son." In these words, a father explains to his son why they must leave everything behind and flee their country. Together with other families, they make a perilous journey in a small boat in search of America. After encountering storms, pirates, sickness, and near starvation, they finally arrive in America. Unbeknownst to the refugees, it is Thanksgiving Day, and they find a welcoming dinner waiting for them. This powerful, nonpolitical story of modern-day pilgrims conveys courage, hope, and determination.

If You Give a Mouse a Cookie. Laura Joffe Numeroff. Illus. by Felicia Bond. Harper, 1985, 1992. 32 pp.

A boy offers a mouse a cookie, and soon finds that one kind act is often followed by a request for more. The energetic mouse next asks for a straw, a napkin, and so on, until the boy's whole day is consumed. Preschoolers might catch on to the intended parallel here—a child's never-ending demands, and a parent's inexhausti- ble patience—but don't count on it. Your reward for reading this delightful book may well be a request for an encore.

John Henry, An American Legend. Ezra Jack Keats. Illus. by the author. Knopf, 1965, 1987. 29 pp.

This is a lively retelling of the legend of the steel-driving man, "born with a hammer in his hand." Bigger than life, John Henry works his way across the land, risking his life for others as he goes. Ezra Keats's bold drawings capture the action of the work as well as John Henry's exuberance for life.

Just Enough Is Plenty: A Hanukkah Tale. Barbara Diamond Gol- din. Illus. by Seymour Chwast. Viking Kestrel, 1988. 27 pp. Puffin, 1990.

Before sitting down to eat, Papa whispers to Mama, "Is there enough?" "Just enough," says Mama. It is the first night of Hanuk- kah. In other years Malka's family would fill the whole house with guests. But because of a bad year in Papa's tailor shop, they can invite only two—and even that requires stretching. The family's hospitality is stretched even farther when a knock is heard. "I saw the Hanukkah lights in your window," says the old peddler at the door. Despite Papa's worried look, Mama invites the man in, saying, "We always have something for the stranger who knocks on our door." Mama gives the old man a latke from her plate, and each family member does likewise. But the old man has some- thing to share as well. He is full of surprises, and the biggest surprise comes when, after his mysterious departure, his true identity is learned.

Keep the Lights Burning, Abbie. Peter and Connie Roop. Illus. by Peter E. Hanson. Carolrhoda, 1985. 40 pp. Houghton Mifflin, 1989. 40 pp.

Abbie's mother is sick, so her father, the lighthouse keeper, must take their small boat to get medicine and other supplies. "Keep the lights burning, Abbie!" is the last thing he says to his eldest daughter, who has never done so by herself. When her father's return is delayed for weeks by a mighty storm, Abbie takes charge of her sisters and keeps the light burning despite many obstacles. The lights give not only safety to ships but comfort to her father. "I was afraid for you," he says on his return. "Every night I watched for the lights. Every night I saw them. Then I knew you were all right." This true story, based in part on Abbie Burgess's own account, is accompanied by marvelous watercolor illustrations.

The Little Engine That Could. Watty Piper. Illus. by George and Doris Hauman. Platt & Munk, 1930, 1990. 39 pp.

This classic has been putting children on the right track for generations. A train carrying toys and food to children in a distant city needs an engine. Several big engines refuse, but the little blue engine offers to pull it over the mountainous route. What the little engine lacks in size, he makes up for with determination. More than a lesson in positive thinking, the story is also about charity and the lack thereof. In their refusal to get involved, the big engines remind us of the priest and the Levite in the parable of the Good Samaritan. This is an especially effective read-aloud: the catchy refrain—"I think I can"—resembles the sound of a locomotive picking up speed.

Little House in the Big Woods. Laura Ingalls Wilder. Illus. by Garth Williams. Harper, 1932. 237 pp. Cornerstone, 1989. 300 pp.

In a small log cabin in the deep woods of Wisconsin, little Laura Ingalls lived with her ma and pa and her sisters, far from other folk. In a style simple yet elegant, the story of Laura's life is told through the course of a year: harvesting and putting by for the winter, hunting and fishing for food, long winter evenings, warm shelter and family times. The description of the hard work involved in maintaining the home, the sense of a family all working together in harmony for a mutual goal, the shared play when work is done: all affirm traditional family roles and values. The most admirable quality of this book and its sequels—except for the last, *The First Four Years*—is its atmosphere of gentle affection among the family. (The last book does not share the harmonious flavor of the earlier volumes; published posthumously from a manuscript found among the author's papers, the story of the first four years of Laura's marriage, when every sort of disaster occurs, has a passive and resentful tone.) Note: boys enjoy the *Little House* series as much as girls do.

The Little Match Girl. Hans Christian Andersen. Illus. by Rachel Isadora. Grosset, 1944. 24 pp. Putnam, 1990. 32 pp.

If you want your children to feel compassion for the plight of the poor, you could belabor them with facts about poverty rates and homelessness, or—better—you could read *The Little Match Girl* to them. The spurt of the matches against the cold brick casts more light on the tragedy of poverty than any number of statistics or news reports. Moreover, the compassion the story evokes is based not on a sense of duty but on a sense of identity. We are brought too far inside the girl's rich imaginative life for it to be otherwise. Rachel Isadora's illustrations nicely capture the mystical quality of Andersen's vision.

Magical Hands. Marjorie Barker. Illus. by Yoshi. Picture Book Studio, 1989. 26 pp.

Four men—a cooper, a baker, a fruit seller, and a dry goods merchant—meet every day for lunch. Vincent's birthday is near, and Philip remarks that a man shouldn't have to work on his birthday. "Imagine," he laughs, "if we had a magical hand to do all our work." As each merchant's birthday comes around, however, he discovers that most of the day's work has already been done by "magical hands." Both illustrations and text glow with warmth in this story of craftsmanship, friendship, and doing for others.

Marta and the Nazis. Frances Cavanah. Illus. by Wayne Blickenstaff. Scholastic, 1972, 1974. 104 pp. (Originally published by Western Publishing for Grosset in 1941 under the title *Marta Finds the Golden Door.*)

Will nine-year-old Marta and her father be able to escape Austria after it is taken over by the Nazis? Will Marta have the courage to go on alone after her father is arrested? Marta and her father have been living happily in Vienna until the Nazis invade; then, suddenly, familiar people and kind Viennese begin to behave like swine. A trusted servant encourages Nazi thugs to loot and vandalize Marta's lovely home; later a jeering crowd forces Marta's gentle father to scrub anti-Nazi slogans off the streets while Marta, horrified, stands helplessly by. When Marta is left to fend for herself after her father's arrest, she remembers the Golden Door that her American cousin told her about—the Statue of Liberty and its inscription "I lift my lamp beside the Golden Door"—and she finds the courage to continue alone. Marta's bravery, quick thinking, and devotion to her father underlie this swift-moving story, which includes smuggled treasure, the Statue of Liberty (and what it symbolizes), and a Viennese Christmas. Young readers particularly enjoy one humorous moment, when young Marta cons a gullible German into believing that "Baloney!" is English for "Heil Hitler!" Later Marta learns that not all Germans support Hitler, and some suffer greatly from Nazi crimes. This story is written in a simple, direct style, and makes an excellent choice to read aloud; however, parents should exercise discretion, since the subject matter may be distressing to some young children.

A Tale of Three Wishes. Isaac Bashevis Singer. Illus. by Irene Lieblich. Farrar, Straus, 1975, 1976. 27 pp.

Nobel Prize–winner Isaac Bashevis Singer's tales for children are full of wisdom and wonderment, and this one is no exception. Three Jewish children who seek a miraculous shortcut to wisdom, learning, and love discover, by way of a mysterious encounter, that wishes must be earned by effort. When we next meet them, as grown-ups, we find that they have learned the lesson well, and that a much slower but still miraculous transformation has, indeed, taken place in each.

Thy Friend, Obadiah. Brinton Turkle. Illus. by the author. Viking, 1969. 37 pp. Puffin, 1987.

This story is set in nineteenth-century Nantucket Island in a Quaker community rich in tradition and virtue. The drawings are so fresh you can almost smell the salt air and hear the sea gulls crying to one another. One such sea gull takes a liking to young Obadiah and follows him everywhere, even to the meetinghouse.

Obadiah is annoyed with all this attention and refuses to befriend the bird. But when winter arrives and the sea gull no longer comes around, Obadiah wonders why. When he discovers the bird's plight, he has a change of heart, and learns a lesson in friendship. In *Obadiah the Bold* (Viking, 1965. 36 pp. Viking Kestrel, 1988), Obadiah learns from his father of the bravery of his sea captain grandfather after whom Obadiah is named. He is promised his grandfather's chronometer when he grows up. The *Obadiah* series (four books in all) has been a favorite with young children ever since its inception.

Waiting for Hannah. Marisabina Russo. Illus. by the author. Greenwillow, 1989. 32 pp.

This warm, simply told story is similar to *Yonder* (below), except that the setting is urban and modern, and the time frame much shorter. To be exact, the time frame is the summer during which Hannah's mother and father await her arrival. The mother recounts for her daughter the preparations they made, including the planting of a morning glory vine which blossoms on the same day Hannah is born. Engaging illustrations.

When I Was Young in the Mountains. Cynthia Rylant. Illus. by Diane Goode. Dutton, 1982, 1985. 32 pp.

Grandparents and grandchildren share the pleasures of rustic life in this remembrance of childhood. Scenes of family worship, family meals, and quiet evenings on the porch combine to create an atmosphere of wholeness and stability. A Caldecott Honor book.

Yonder. Tony Johnston. Illus. by Lloyd Bloom. Dial, 1988, 1991. 32 pp.

There's no particular moral in this story, just a loving evocation of one family's history. A nineteenth-century farmer marries. The two have children. The seasons march by. The children grow up and marry and start their own families. Trees are planted, and prayers are said to mark each new arrival and each death. The vibrant illustrations and simple text combine to present a reverent tribute to family life.

MIDDLE READERS

All-of-a-Kind Family. Sydney Taylor. Illus. by Helen John. Follett, 1951. 188 pp. Dell, 1989. 188 pp.

In this spirited, lighthearted family are five daughters (hence "all-of-a-kind"), whose mother and father are fond and firm parents. The story takes place in the early 1900s on Manhattan's Lower East Side. The girls are gently guided by their wise parents, who share with them and pass along to them their rich Jewish traditions and heritage. This book (and its sequels) gives the reader a glimpse into Jewish life in that time and place, while also providing a happy model of family life and a strong moral code firmly but lovingly maintained.

Black Beauty. Anna Sewell. F. M. Lupton, 1877. 245 pp. Worthington Press, 1990. 224 pp.

Anna Sewell's famous novel is a brilliant exposé of cruelty to animals, but it is also much more: it is a first-rate story. The story is narrated by the horse, Black Beauty, who tells the story of his life from his days as a carefree colt, through his later mistreatment by foolish, drunken, or greedy humans, to his pitiful collapse as an abused London cab horse. The story and the virtues and vices portrayed come alive from the first page of the book. Although outward circumstances have changed in the century since this book was written, the human heart has not. We still need to be warned against ignorance, drunkenness, greed, recklessness, cruelty; we need to be told of the cost of these vices to ourselves and to others; and we need to be encouraged in the direction of kindness and generosity. Of course, if *Black Beauty* were only a sermon, not many people would continue to read it; but it is also a rich description of Victorian life, filled with unforgettable characters—human and animal—and told in clear and captivating prose.

Blue Willow. Doris Gates. Illus. by Paul Lantz. Viking, 1940. 172 pp. Puffin, 1976.

Ten-year-old Janey Larkin, daughter of migrant workers, has one precious possession: a blue willow plate, her sole link to a happier past, the time before her father lost his ranch in Texas and was forced to turn to migrant work. For Janey this pretty plate, symbol of the settled life, "had the power to make drab things beautiful, and to a life of dreary emptiness bring a sense of wonder and delight." Janey's longing for a real home increases as the family moves into an abandoned shack in the San Joaquin Valley, but when her stepmother becomes ill and her father can find no more work, Janey's dream of settling down appears to be even farther from reality. Janey then learns what moral courage is: she gives up her beloved willow plate as substitute for the rent they cannot pay in cash. But is anything sacrificed for love ever really lost? The story's resolution is simple and satisfying, and its underlying themes of unselfish love and moral courage in the face of adversity are timeless.

Caddie Woodlawn. Carol Ryrie Brink. Illus. by Trina S. Hyman. Macmillan, 1935. 192 pp. Aladdin, 1990. 275 pp.

The appeal of the frontier is endless, and this is one of the stories that make it so—the story of a year in the life of Caddie Woodlawn, an eleven-year-old tomboy running wild on her folks' farm in Wisconsin in 1864. Caddie's adventures demonstrate her impetuous, honest, fearless character. When her Indian friends are threatened by panicky white settlers, Caddie travels secretly to warn her friends to flee from danger. In the course of the story, Caddie learns, sometimes painfully, about courage and kindness, love and loyalty to friends, family, and country. Her elegant mother longs to make her into "a lady," and tomboy Caddie dreads becoming "a silly affected person with fine clothes and manners"; but her strong, kind father teaches her that she can grow up to be "a woman with a wise and understanding heart, healthy in body and honest in mind," whose work is "something fine and noble to grow up to, and . . . just as important as a man's." The story never slows down, but is exciting to the end: Will Caddie's father return to England to take his rightful place in the House of Lords? Or will he stay in Wisconsin, where he has made a place for himself and his family through his own efforts?

More stories of Caddie Woodlawn are collected in *Magical Melons* (Carol Brink. Illus. by Marguerite Davis. Macmillan, 1939, 1990.

193 pp.); each story in this volume emphasizes a different moral virtue, such as not eating melons that do not belong to you, or saving another's life even at the risk of your own; and the stories are so engaging that the moral is never difficult to swallow.

The Chronicles of Narnia. C. S. Lewis. Illus. by Pauline Baynes. Macmillan, 1950–56, 1988.

Four children enter a wardrobe in an empty room, and come out into a strange kingdom of never-ending winter populated by fauns, giants, dwarfs, talking animals, a singularly evil witch, and an extraordinary lion. Thus begins *The Lion, the Witch and the Wardrobe,* the first in the seven-book series that has commanded the loyalty of millions of children worldwide. It is difficult to pinpoint the source of Lewis's success, since he does so many things so well: he has created a thoroughly convincing secondary world, his plots are marvelously constructed, his characters (both human and nonhuman) are closely observed, and his stories are deeply moving. In addition, the *Chronicles* are packed with suspense, surprises, and adventure. As engrossing as the action is, the interior struggles of the several characters are just as compelling. The children battle recurring temptations to cowardice, meanness, pride, and even treachery. Although they don't win all the battles, they do grow in goodness and nobility. Reading the *Chronicles* is, among other things, an education in virtue. It is also satisfying reading for adults. Readers who first chance upon the series at age twenty or thirty are as likely to become loyal subjects of Narnia as are nine- or ten-year-olds. Adult readers may also be interested to know some of the history behind the creation of the series. Together with other friends, Lewis and J. R. R. Tolkien met regularly at an Oxford pub to read aloud from works in progress, and to give and receive criticism. One result was the *Chronicles;* the other was Tolkien's *The Hobbit,* and its sequel, *The Lord of the Rings.* The other titles in the Narnia *Chronicles* are *Prince Caspian, The Voyage of the "Dawn Treader," The Silver Chair, The Horse and His Boy, The Magician's Nephew,* and *The Last Battle.*

Cracker Jackson. Betsy Byars. Viking Kestrel, 1985. 147 pp. Macmillan, 1988, 124 pp.

"Cracker" Jackson Hunter grows up a lot when his beloved

babysitter, Alma, is threatened by an abusive husband. Jackson's inept—and hilarious—attempts to overcome grown-up inertia and help his babysitter are the focus of this story: his mother and father merely tell him to stay away from a potentially dangerous situation, and even the babysitter refuses at first to take the escape he offers her. Byars illustrates the difference between breaking a rule for kicks and breaking a rule in an emergency (Jackson "borrows" his mother's car without permission when Alma is in physical danger; later Jackson resists his buddy's urging to take a drive for a lark). The story, although it involves wife and child abuse, is not too distressing for young readers, because the actual abuse occurs "offstage"—that is, Jackson (and the reader) learns of it only after Alma has already reached safety. As always, Byars's style is very funny but also quite moving. Jackson shows love and loyalty for Alma; and he learns that, undemonstrative as she is, his mother cares deeply about him and about those he loves.

Dear Mr. Henshaw. Beverly Cleary. Illus. by Paul O. Zelinsky. Morrow, 1963. 133 pp. Macmillan, 1987. 134 pp.

Through a young boy's letters to his favorite author (the Mr. Henshaw of the title), and later through the boy's diary, we learn of young Leigh's efforts to foil a school lunchbag thief, and of his desire to become a writer. We also discover Leigh's hurt and anger over his parents' divorce. Gradually Leigh matures and comes to understand and even forgive his parents' faults, and to recognize and appreciate the good in them. The appealing aspect of this book is the dual enlightenment that the reader experiences: the reader gradually learns about Leigh, the narrator, and also observes as Leigh learns about himself, his parents, and his peers.

A Dog on Barkham Street. Mary Stolz. Illus. by Leonard Shortall. Harper, 1960, 1985. 184 pp. **The Bully of Barkham Street.** Mary Stolz. Illus. by Leonard Shortall. Harper, 1963, 1985. 194 pp.

These companion novels tell the same story from two different points of view, and what a difference that makes! In *A Dog on Barkham Street*, Edward Frost wants a dog desperately, but his mom says he is too young and irresponsible. When his footloose uncle visits, bringing along the perfect dog, Argess, a true boy-dog bond forms between Edward and Argess. But will Uncle Josh, in his careless way, take Argess away with him again? Before a happy resolution is reached, Edward gets in plenty of trouble and learns a lot about responsibility, dependability, and commitment. His initial infatuation with his uncle's wandering lifestyle fades, and he realizes that his dad's reliable, steady ways have a great deal to recommend them. The companion volume retells the story of *A Dog on Barkham Street* from the point of view of Edward's next-door neighbor, Martin, the "bully of Barkham Street." Edward is terrified of Martin; Martin views Edward as a pest who constantly infuriates him by taunting him as "Fatso." Martin's painful struggle to leave behind his bullying ways is told with sympathy, honesty—and humor. The reader feels compassion for the inept Martin, and learns a lesson in perspective taking.

The story of Martin (the relatively reformed bully) is continued in another good book, *The Explorer of Barkham Street* (Illus. by Emily A. McCully. Harper, 1985, 1987. 192 pp.). Martin is not exactly a *good* example, but he is an appealing, trying-to-be-good example.

A Dog So Small. Philippa Pearce. Lippincott, 1962. 142 pp. Puffin, 1982. 155 pp.

The London apartment where Ben Blewitt's family lives is too cramped for young Ben to have the dog he longs for, so he begins to imagine the perfect dog, a dog that would fit—"a dog so small you can only see it with your eyes shut." Ben becomes so deeply involved with his imaginary companion that he becomes dangerously detached from reality. His imaginary dog leads him into real disaster, first physically, when a terrible accident occurs, and later mentally: when Ben finally gets the chance to own a real dog, he refuses to accept a reality that falls short of his imaginary dog's tiny perfection, and he almost allows his only chance at a real bond with a real dog to slip away from him. The author vividly depicts the human longing for perfection and the disappointment in flawed reality. There is an unstated parallel here with the use of illegal drugs to avoid disappointing or painful reality. The book has a happy ending, but it comes so late that the reader is left breathless: Ben comes very close to not waking up in time. This sense of averted disaster makes the reader sigh with relief—and brings home the point that an imaginary ideal must not be a substitute for a living reality.

The 18th Emergency. Betsy Byars. Illus. by Robert Grossman. Viking, 1973, 1988. 126 pp.

When Benjie, a slight sixth-grade boy whom everyone calls "Mouse," insults Marv Hammerman, the class tough guy, Benjie's first reaction is to flee. Benjie continues to run from his problem (and Marv's vengeance) until he finally realizes that, painful as it will be, the only honorable thing to do is face the consequences of his actions and confront Marv—even if it means getting beat up. In doing so, Benjie matures emotionally, demonstrated figuratively when his friend stops using his hated nickname. In this book, Byars has made the notion of honor comprehensible to young readers, while maintaining her lively, outrageously funny style.

Five Children and It. Edith Nesbit Bland (pen name: E. Nesbit). Illus. by H. R. Millar. Benn, 1902. 301 pp. Scholastic, 1988. 197 pp.

In this whimsical and very funny story, five siblings discover a "psammead"—a sand-fairy—while on an otherwise ordinary holiday. Naturally, the children think they are in for good times when they learn that each day the sand-fairy must grant them a single wish; but the literal-minded sand-fairy usually manages to land the children in unexpected difficulties, which are quite amusing, at least to the reader. The children's adventures are told in a lighthearted manner, but the lesson is just beneath the surface: Watch what you say! Words are powerful!

Gaffer Samson's Luck. Jill Paton Walsh. Illus. by Brock Cole. Puffin, 1984. 112 pp. Farrar, Straus, 1990. 118 pp.

This moving and life-affirming story takes place in England's fen country, richly described through the eyes of James, a boy new to the wide-open, flat countryside. The story involves two parallel plots: the young boy's attempts to gain a place among the village children, and the boy's involvement with his elderly neighbor, old Gaffer Samson. In befriending—and helping—his elderly neighbor, and in finding the courage to confront the village children, James comes face-to-face with his fears and overcomes them. Similarly, the old Gaffer faces and overcomes his own fear of death. The boy learns that death, represented by the old man's death, is a natural and proper part of life, a sad but necessary process of letting go. His deeper understanding of life and death does not diminish but only gives a clearer edge to his happiness at his eventual acceptance by the village children.

A Girl Called Al. Constance C. Greene. Illus. by Byron Barton. Viking, 1969. 127 pp. Viking Penguin, 1991.

In this pert, sassy, and honest story of friendship across generations, our narrator (who never gives her name) makes friends with a new girl in her apartment building, a girl who calls herself "Al" rather than "Alexandra," who is too fat, and who literally refuses to let her hair down. Together the two girls befriend old Mr. Richards, the colorful, tattoo-bearing maintenance man who tends their building. This unlikely friendship between the girls and the kind, gentle, delightfully eccentric old fellow becomes especially important to Al, who masks her distress over her absentee father's neglect by gaining weight. The children's sorrow at Mr. Richards's death is touching, and yet entirely in keeping with the lively, clear-sighted, and unsentimental insights of the narrator. This story presents a blueprint of hope for children who might otherwise believe that the lack of an involved, loving father in their lives is an insurmountable handicap; it is also a perceptive tale of loneliness alleviated by loving friendship between old and young.

Good Morning, Miss Dove. Frances Gray Patton. Illus. by Garrett Price. Dodd, Mead, 1946. 218 pp. Pocket Books, 1956. 218 pp.

"Good Morning, Miss Dove," recite her students at the start of each day to their no-nonsense geography teacher, the feared and respected Miss Dove. The story of this dedicated teacher and her students is revealed in a series of flashbacks when Miss Dove is ill in the hospital. She is shown to be a woman of rare strength, courage, and stalwartness of soul. She is a rare heroine in another way, too: an older single woman, satisfied with her life and interesting not for husband or family but for herself. Miss Dove is a Teacher, first and foremost, and though she recognizes that mothers are necessary (without them she would have no students), nonetheless, she regards mothers as slightly weak and silly—in need of assistance from Teachers such as herself. This is a well-told story of moral character, of doing one's duty, and of the joy of duty well done. In addition to meeting Miss Dove, the reader is allowed to share the story of Miss Dove's students, present and past, as Miss Dove sees them, with her clear, unsentimental vision. Miss Dove knows right from wrong. Readers of the book might find that as they make Miss Dove's acquaintance, they begin to see right from wrong more clearly as well.

Harriet Tubman: Conductor on the Underground Railroad. Ann Petry. Harper, 1955. 227 pp. Grey Castle Press, 1991. 175 pp.

In 1849 Harriet Tubman (1821?–1913), an illiterate slave, escaped from a Maryland plantation to freedom in the North—and then she fearlessly returned to the South again and again, in order to lead other slaves out of bondage. Eventually more than 300 slaves were guided to freedom by Harriet Tubman, who became known as "Moses." This moving biography brings Harriet to life, and shows the terrible hardships faced by slaves who worked on the plantations and by those who fled; it also describes the workings of the Underground Railroad, and the selfless goodness of those who assisted the runaways. Harriet Tubman's courage, determination, and strength were nourished by her faith in God and her deep love of liberty. The story of her remarkable and eventful life deserves to be widely known; this absorbing account is a fine introduction.

Heather and Broom: Tales of the Scottish Highlands. LeClaire G. Alger (pen name: Sorche Nic Leodhas). Holt, 1960, 1965. 128 pp. ***Thistle and Thyme: Tales and Legends from Scotland.*** LeClaire G. Alger. Holt, 1962. 143 pp.

Here are two collections of wonderful Scottish stories, from high tales of bravery and valor, to sweet tales of romance, to funny household stories. In *Heather and Broom,* for example, we find a lighthearted fairy tale, "The Woman Who Flummoxed the Fairies." The mischievous fairies kidnap a woman to bake for them, but she makes them let her go by using her wits; then she shows her kind heart by baking for them of her own free will. In "The Daughter of the King Ron," also found in *Heather and Broom,* we learn of a great lord who loses the bride of his heart when he speaks to her in anger. He is transformed by his grief from an arrogant ruler to one who is just and kind, and in the end, he is reunited with his love. The morals of the stories are unstated but clear, and the stories are delightful and well told, with a Scottish flavor you can eat with a spoon.

Heidi. Johanna Spyri. Originally published in 1880. Dell, 1990. 294 pp. Heinemann, 1991. 188 pp.

In the beautiful mountains of the Alps, a little girl's love for her grandfather transforms the old man from a bitter and lonely misanthrope into a person once again capable of returning love and devotion. But then comes a terrible separation as Heidi is taken to a distant city, where she suffers agonies of homesickness. How Heidi finds her way back to her grandfather—and how her grandfather endures the separation—makes a lovely story. The reader enters a mountain world of nostalgic delight, and meets characters who make memorable the ideals of kindness, loyalty, and love of family.

The House of Sixty Fathers. Meindert DeJong. Illus. by Maurice Sendak. Harper, 1956, 1987. 189 pp.

Tien Pao, a little Chinese boy, and his small family escape the Japanese invaders of their country during World War II and achieve temporary safety by fleeing upriver to the city of Hengyang in an abandoned sampan; but then the river floods and Tien Pao is separated from his family and carried downriver—into Japanese-occupied territory. The story of Tien Pao's bravery and heroism—he makes his painful way back upriver, saves a downed American airman, falls in with Chinese guerrillas who are fighting the Japanese, escapes the destruction of the city of Hengyang, and searches relentlessly for his family, all the while protecting the family's small pig—is told with such realism that the reader feels a part of Tien Pao's exhaustion, hunger, fear—and loneliness. The "sixty fathers" are the American soldiers who finally take Tien Pao in when the search for his family appears hopeless. Tien Pao, however, never gives up, and neither does his American airman. This story of courage, selflessness, and kindness in the midst of war and upheaval is both touching and inspiring.

The Hundred Dresses. Eleanor Estes. Illus. by Louis Slobodkin. Harcourt, 1944, 1974. 80 pp.

Even though she knows it is wrong, Maddie goes along with her friends' daily teasing of Wanda, the daughter of Polish immigrants. The outcast girl's unexpected move to another city leaves Maddie resolved to stand up for others in the future, but it also leaves her smitten with the realization that it is too late to make amends to Wanda herself. As Michelle Landsberg points out, this complex, subtle story stands in refreshing contrast to Judy Blume's amoral treatment of the same theme in *Blubber*.

Ida Early Comes Over the Mountain. Robert Burch. Viking, 1980. 145 pp. Puffin, 1990.

Ida Early looks a mess, but when she decides to stay with the Sutton family for a while, she brings happiness back to a household still grieving for its dead mother. Although the children enjoy and appreciate Ida, they fail to acknowledge her worth to their friends and instead stand silently by while their friends make fun of her. After this betrayal, Ida leaves, and the children realize, too late, how much they need her—and how much they love her. The children feel impelled to take steps to let Ida know that they are her true friends. This story introduces lively characters and a satisfying plot while teaching valuable lessons about loyalty and friendship.

The Indian in the Cupboard. Lynne Reid Banks. Illus. by Brock Cole. Doubleday, 1980. 181 pp. ABC-Clio, 1988. 213 pp.

Widely regarded as among the very best of recent children's fiction, *The Indian in the Cupboard* gives a whole new meaning to that somewhat shopworn phrase "the dignity of human life." Omri, an English boy, is disappointed at receiving a small plastic Indian and an old medicine cabinet for his birthday. But disappointment turns to excitement when he discovers that by locking the Indian in the cabinet, it magically comes to life. After the initial thrill wears off, Omri is confronted with the sobering responsibility of taking care of his fiercely independent new friend, and of hiding Little Bear from his parents. The story becomes more complicated when Omri's best friend, Patrick, is let in on the secret, and Patrick thinks nothing of adding a cowboy, an old chief, and horses to the tiny cast of characters. Realizing the irresponsibility of the act, Omri scolds Patrick: "They're people, you can't use people." Omri quickly comes to understand that relative size and power provide no justification for playing with the lives of others. Exciting, absorbing, and thought-provoking, this story, like the Indian in the title, is alive with magic.

Island of the Blue Dolphins. Scott O'Dell. Houghton Mifflin, 1960, 1990. 181 pp.

A poignant and powerful story of a twelve-year-old Indian girl who is accidentally abandoned on a remote island. After sacrificing her safe passage to the mainland in an unsuccessful attempt to save her brother's life, Karana spends the next eighteen years in solitude. Relying on skill and inner strength, she manages not only to survive but to grow in serenity and charity (exemplified by her rescue of a wild dog that had previously attacked her). This *Robinson Crusoe*–like story is a tribute to human resilience. O'-Dell is a skillful writer whose popularity with young readers is well deserved.

Johnny Tremain. Esther Forbes. Illus. by Lynd Ward. Houghton Mifflin, 1943. 305 pp. Puffin, 1979. 251 pp.

Awarded the Newbery Medal in 1944, this novel of the American Revolution has lost none of its appeal. With careful attention to factual accuracy, Esther Forbes skillfully weaves Johnny's story into the story of the fight for freedom. A talented and cocky silversmith's apprentice in Boston, Johnny has high hopes for his future. When a crippling accident puts an end to his dreams, he at first retreats into bitterness, but, helped by a friend, he discovers a new role for himself as a messenger for the Sons of Liberty. Johnny's struggle with his handicap and with his equally crippling pride makes for a moving and engrossing story.

Ladder of Angels. Madeleine L'Engle. Illus. by Children of the World. Penguin, 1980. 128 pp.

The renowned children's author tries her hand at retelling the stories of the Old Testament—and succeeds brilliantly. Her stories are accompanied by thought-provoking meditations and reflections.

Lassie Come-Home. Eric Knight. Holt, 1938, 1978. 248 pp.

Lassie is a purebred collie, beloved of Joe Carraclough, her young Yorkshire master, and the pride of their small family. Hard times and lack of work, however, force Joe's father to sell Lassie to the wealthy duke of Rudling, who has long coveted this fine animal for his own kennels, far away in northern Scotland. But Lassie, dog fashion, cannot understand the human sales contract; she escapes and makes her painful, slow, hazardous way across the hundreds of miles to the boy who is her true master. Along the way, Lassie encounters cruelty, kindness, and indifference from those she meets, but her determination to get home never wavers. Here is a story that is touching without sentimentality, with sharply depicted characters, a strong sense of place, and an exciting plot. Although it has some of the conventions of other dog stories, *Lassie* is in a class by itself.

A Little Princess. Frances Hodgson Burnett. Warne, 1905. 256 pp. Dell, 1990. 240 pp.

The heroine of this story, Sara Crewe, is one of the noblest and most appealing heroines in all children's fiction. When the story begins, Sara is the cosseted daughter of a wealthy Englishman, who has brought her to London from India to attend boarding school. Her situation worsens dramatically when her father's sudden death and financial ruin put Sara into the clutches of the mercenary headmistress of the school. Wealth and indulgence did not spoil the clear-sighted Sara, however, and neither do poverty and ill-usage. Throughout, Sara tries to act as she imagines a princess might: with kindness and consideration for those less fortunate than she, even when she herself is cold and hungry and exhausted from overwork and cruel treatment. With a heroine worthy of emulation, a gripping and satisfying plot, and richly depicted characters, this elegantly written book is well worth reading and rereading.

Pagan the Black. Dorothy Potter Benedict. Pantheon, 1960. 188 pp.

In this story of the American West, a twelve-year-old boy, Sandy, is challenged by the sudden arrival of a forlorn foster sister. Sandy wants to make her feel that she belongs with his family on their ranch—even if it means he has to give her his beloved horse, Pagan. The integration of this hostile, emotionally deprived waif into the family, and the threats to her well-being that develop later, make for a page-turning plot. This is a rewarding story which strongly affirms family values.

Plain Girl. Virginia Sorenson. Harcourt, 1955, 1988. 151 pp.

Every day, Esther, an Amish girl, prays that her brother Dan will come back home. Dan has left home and family, but even more distressing, he has abandoned the Amish ways—the ways of the "Plain People," the pattern of work and worship that has been handed down among the Amish for generations. When Esther must attend a regular public school under the state's compulsory attendance law, she is exposed for the first time to non-Amish ways, and she begins to understand her brother's departure. Eventually both Esther and her brother come to a renewed respect for their own tradition. The respect for elders and for old ways, the value placed on kindness and honesty, and the love Esther feels for her people all combine to make rewarding reading in this straightforward story.

Pollyanna. Eleanor H. Porter. Grosset, 1912. 305 pp. Scholastic, 1987. 231 pp.

Forget the saccharine reputation; forget the lousy Disney movie: the *real* Pollyanna, found only in the book, is well worth knowing. Young Pollyanna, recently orphaned, moves in with her tight-lipped Aunt Polly, whose grim sense of duty casts a gray pall upon everyone around her—everyone, that is, except Pollyanna. Pollyanna has an attitude to die for: she always looks for the best in everything around her; she looks for something to be "glad" about. Pollyanna shows the people of her town—and the reader—that it is easy to see the dismal in a situation, but it takes a special effort, and earns a special reward, to see the good. The reward is simple: Pollyanna carries her happiness inside her; it is not subject to the whims of others. Petty put-downs can't touch her. But more than all that glad philosophy, here is a tale of a winsome child whose friendliness and bright outlook make her lovable. Her story is immensely worthwhile.

The Potlatch Family. Evelyn Sibley Lampman. Atheneum, 1976. 135 pp.

Teenaged Plum Longor does not like herself. Why should she? She's an Indian, after all, and if that weren't bad enough, her dad's a drunk. Her white schoolmates exclude her, and Plum can't blame them: she believes herself, her family, and her Chinook Indian heritage to be without value. So her older brother has an uphill battle, when he returns from the war and the hospital, to convince her, her family, and other Indian families to get together and hold "potlatches"—traditional Indian communal feasts—for the tourists. The goal is to make money; but before the first dime is earned, the Indians benefit from working together toward a common goal, learning about their own heritage (which many have forgotten or dismissed as worthless), and discovering that some white folks are friends who can be counted on. The self-respect engendered by the potlatch project is reflected in Plum's new self-esteem and in her own ability to make hard choices. The devastating effect on the Indians of prejudice, loss of place, and loss of culture is well presented in this story, while the hopeful resolution prevents these aspects from overwhelming young readers.

The Rabbi's Girls. Johanna Hurwitz. Illus. by Pamela Johnson. Morrow, 1982. 158 pp. Puffin, 1989. 158 pp.

Carrie Levin is proud to be one of "the rabbi's girls." Her father is rabbi to the small Jewish community in Lorain, Ohio; he is also father to six daughters. In an understated though intensely moving account, Carrie tells of her father's strength, love, and devotion, and of their life as observant Jews, during the year 1923. When the youngest daughter, a tiny baby, develops pneumonia, a terrible tornado devastates the town, and her father's health fails, Carrie learns that life is both bitter and good, that without the bitter, one would be unable to appreciate the good. Her father's death, shortly after the tornado, brings to Carrie the realization of all he has given her, especially the knowledge that "the year is a circle, and that life goes on." The love and devotion of this father survives even death.

The Railway Children. Edith Nesbit Bland (pen name: E. Nesbit). Macmillan, 1906. 309 pp. Derrydale, 1992. 182 pp.

Two sisters and a brother are uprooted from their suburban home and moved to the country near a railway line, which they come to know well in the absence of other amusements. Their brave mother is supporting the family after the sudden disappearance of their father. How the children find out what has become of their father, and how their games with the train passengers end up helping their father in unexpected ways, form an engrossing and moving story. Nesbit's children are very real: they can be cross, sometimes they misbehave, and occasionally they fail at their endeavors; but they are basically decent and long to do right. In this story, love and justice and family prevail, and loyalty and courage find their reward.

Roll of Thunder, Hear My Cry. Mildred Taylor. Dial, 1976. 276 pp. Puffin, 1991. 276 pp.

This powerful story of a black family's resistance to injustice and poverty is set during the Depression years in Mississippi, and is observed through the eyes of Cassie, a spirited nine-year-old. Cassie and her family have a strong sense of right and wrong, plus an abundant supply of courage and determination. They need every bit of it. The novel, drawn from stories the author heard as a child, attests to the importance of storytelling as a vehicle for transmitting family virtues.

The Sign of the Beaver. Elizabeth Speare. Houghton Mifflin, 1983. 135 pp. ABC-Clio, 1988. 146 pp.

This story, set in 1768, tells of a young boy's experience of self-discovery when he is left alone on the Maine frontier while his father travels back to Massachusetts to fetch his mother and sister. Young Matt has been left behind to tend the family's new homestead, and though he makes a diligent effort, he is not learned in forest ways, and minor carelessness and impulsiveness on his part result in major disaster. Matt's life is saved only by the intervention of Indians who live nearby. Gradually the boy is forced to acknowledge that the Indians are not brute savages but highly skilled, complex, worthy people from whom he has much to learn. Eventually Matt is able to earn the respect of his Indian friends, though in a totally unexpected way. Here is a well-written frontier survival story which provides much food for thought. A Newbery Honor winner.

Snow Treasure. Marie McSwigan. Dutton, 1942. 197 pp. Scholastic, 1986. 104 pp.

In 1940 the Nazis invaded Norway. This story, which has a basis in fact, tells how Norwegian schoolchildren smuggled $9 million of gold bullion past German sentries and onto a hidden ship bound for America. How did they do it? By sledding right under the noses of the unwitting Nazi guards. A suspenseful plot and a series of close calls make this a real page-turner.

Sounder. William H. Armstrong. Illus. by James Barkley. Harper, 1969. 116 pp. Perennial Library, 1989.

A poor black sharecropper's family struggles to survive after the father is imprisoned for stealing a ham. Sounder is the family coon dog, and his courage and dedication are matched by those of his young master, who is thrust abruptly into the world of adult responsibilities. A heart-wrenching tale of family love, determination, and perseverance. A Newbery Medal winner.

The Taizé Picture Bible. Illus. by Brother Eric de Saussure. Darton Longman & Todd Ltd., 1968. 277 pp. Fortress Press, 1978. 277 pp.

These Bible stories are adapted from the text of the Jerusalem Bible and are accompanied every few pages by illustrations that arc brilliant in both senses of the word. Although it is published as a picture Bible, this edition is really more appropriate for middle readers than for younger readers.

Thank You, Jackie Robinson. Barbara Cohen. Illus. by Richard Cuffari. Lothrop, 1974. 125 pp. Cornerstone, 1990. 125 pp.

It is 1947, the year Jackie Robinson joined the Brooklyn Dodgers as the first black baseball player in the major leagues. Sam Green is a fatherless Jewish boy and a devout baseball fan, who lives with his three sisters at a New Jersey inn run by his widowed mother. When Sam meets Davy, an older black man who is the new cook at the inn, the two immediately discover that they share a passion for baseball, especially the Brooklyn Dodgers, and even more especially Jackie Robinson. The young white boy comes to understand Davy's pride in Jackie Robinson's accomplishments, and the old man becomes like a father to Sam. When Davy suffers a heart attack, Sam goes to great lengths to get Davy a baseball autographed by Jackie Robinson himself—the magic he hopes will make Davy well again. But the autographed ball does not work a miracle, and Sam must face and accept the loss of his friend. This book is a natural for baseball fans of all ages, but even those who are not fans can share its themes of friendship and loss.

Tuck Everlasting. Natalie Babbitt. Farrar, Straus, 1975, 1991. 139 pp.

This profound tale of adventure leads Winnie Foster, an over-protected ten-year-old, into the forest where she encounters the Tuck family, who have received eternal life by drinking from a certain spring. A moral dilemma develops for the young girl as she is forced to choose between mortality and everlasting life. Just as Winnie is caught up in the rapture of the possibility of eternal life, she is sobered by the words of Pa Tuck, who knows the burden it carries: "Us Tucks are stuck. We ain't part of the wheel no more. Dropped off, Winnie. Left behind." A thought-provoking explanation of the meaning of life—and death—this book, like the Tucks, seems destined to last for a good long time.

Understood Betsy. Dorothy Canfield. Grosset, 1916. 271 pp. Grosset, 1970. 212 pp.

Little Elizabeth Ann is, at age nine, the most impossibly sheltered little girl there ever was, sheltered by her doting Aunt Frances, who cares for her completely in the kindest and most understanding way; so kind and understanding is Aunt Frances that little Elizabeth Ann has never had even a thought of her own. But Aunt Frances is suddenly called away to care for her sick mother, and Elizabeth Ann must go to live in Vermont, with cousins who call her "Betsy" and treat her without question as a capable person—even though she is not, at least not at first. Initially, Betsy is terrified, and the joy of the story lies in sharing Betsy's astonished delight over each new accomplishment. This book tells the story of every person's passage—remembered or not—from incapable baby to competent adult. Betsy earns her self-esteem through her own efforts, and the praise of her Vermont relatives is even richer for being so rarely granted. The farmhouse in turn-of-the-century Vermont, and the Vermonters themselves, are depicted with heart-stirring clarity; the setting is so real that, just as with Heidi's mountainside, every reader longs to go there for a visit.

Walking the Road to Freedom: A Story About Sojourner Truth. Jeri Ferris. Illus. by Peter E. Hanson. Carolrhoda, 1988. 64 pp.

Sojourner Truth once admonished a complacent group of white men in her audience in the following words: "With all your opportunities for reading and writing, you don't take a hold and do anything. I wonder what you are in the world for!" There can be little doubt why Sojourner Truth was in the world. Born a slave in New York in 1799, she spent her adult life traveling through twenty states speaking out against slavery and campaigning for women's rights. "Speaking and singing" would be more accurate. Upon arriving in a new town, Sojourner (a name she gave herself) would stand in the street and begin to sing, and her deep, powerful voice would quickly draw a crowd. In one instance she sang down a mob of young men who were trying to break up a camp meeting. Written in tightly packed prose, this compelling narrative is both moving and memorable. A stirring account of a woman who refused to accept any master except Truth.

See also Jeri Ferris's *Go Free or Die: A Story About Harriet Tubman* (Illus. by Karen Ritz. Carolrhoda, 1988. 63 pp.).

The Wheel on the School. Meindert DeJong. Illus. by Maurice Sendak. Penguin, 1954. 204 pp. Puffin, 1983. 203 pp.

When the children of Shora, a tiny Dutch fishing village, ask their teacher why no storks come to nest there, little do they realize what adventures will result. The children learn that the storks disappeared many years before, when the village lost all its trees to a storm, and in the children's hearts is born the desire to bring the storks back to Shora. Since there are no trees in Shora, the children become determined to find a wagon wheel to put on the school roof for the storks to nest on. Their efforts eventually involve the entire village; in particular, Janus, an old man embittered since he lost his legs many years before, is drawn out of his seclusion, and by taking part in this effort, he finds the heart to rejoin his community. The storks come to symbolize new life for the village; no one remains outside the glad circle. The story dramatically illustrates how a worthwhile common goal can unite and uplift those who pursue it.

The Witch of Blackbird Pond. Elizabeth Speare. Houghton Mifflin, 1958. 249 pp. Cornerstone, 1989. 249 pp.

A thoroughly entertaining account of a young girl's entrance into womanhood. Kit Tyler leaves the sheltered and carefree world of Barbados, and lands in the provincial town of seventeenth-century Wethersfield, Connecticut, where she is shocked to learn that she must perform menial tasks such as baking bread and dipping candles if she is to earn her keep in her aunt's overcrowded house. Kit's initiation into the hardships of New England is turbulent both for Kit and for her adoptive family. However, after her encounter with the town outcast (the witch), she comes to realize that there is more to life than the silk gowns and lace handkerchiefs she had once prized so highly. Kit learns to commit herself to her new family and friends, and begins to appreciate the importance of hard work and sharing. The beauty of the changing New England seasons is skillfully rendered, as is the not-so-beautiful paranoia that occasionally gripped New England towns during the days when suspicion of witchcraft was a serious matter.

OLDER READERS

Abraham Lincoln: From Log Cabin to White House. Sterling North. Random House, 1956, 1987. 184 pp.

This excellent introductory biography of our sixteenth president, by a well-known children's author, focuses on Lincoln's career prior to his presidency, and especially on his younger days on the frontier. North writes clearly and concisely, and does full justice to both the nobility and the complexity of Lincoln's character. He does not sentimentalize his subject, and his history is reliable. A memorable story of a man who was truly "self-made," and who overcame both poverty and ignorance.

The Adventures of Huckleberry Finn. Mark Twain. Courage Books, 1884, 1990. 238 pp.

Twain's greatest book, sometimes considered the finest novel in American literature. Despite this intimidating reputation, the book is simple and unpretentious, an adult story that any child can read and understand. Twain's hero is a young outcast, the son of a drunken and abusive father, who acts and thinks for himself and often shows more kindness and understanding than the respectable southern citizens among whom he finds himself. Through the character of Huck, Twain arraigns and denounces all the evils he most hated: self-righteousness, ignorance, violence, mob law, and racism. In the story of Huck's relationship with Jim, the runaway slave, Twain showed a racial tolerance a hundred years ahead of its time. The book is never messagy, is full of action and intrigue, and is very funny.

April Morning. Howard Fast. Bantam, 1961, 1987. 202 pp.

Set in Lexington, Massachusetts, during the American Revolution, Fast's novel tells of a boy's rapid transformation from self-absorption to responsible manhood. While the nation wins its independence, Adam Cooper wins the approval and trust of his elders. Fast paints a detailed and dramatic portrait of the Revolution, and of the men and women who made it happen.

Building Blocks. Cynthia Voigt. Atheneum, 1984, 1985. 128 pp.

A heartwarming time-travel story in which a twelve-year-old boy is mysteriously transported from the present day back to the time of the Great Depression. While playing with his blocks and listening to his parents argue, Brann falls asleep and awakens to find himself in the bedroom of a ten-year-old boy, who he discovers is his own father. The scenes of Brann playing with his father are very touching and revealing. Brann, who has always seen his father as passive and weak, develops a new understanding of his parent's strengths and weaknesses. A book that opens up a new perspective on parenthood for middle readers and young adults.

Call of the Wild. Jack London. Illus. by Philip R. Goodwin and Charles Livingston Bull. Macmillan, 1903. 231 pp. Children's Classics, 1991. 254 pp.

A gripping story of a courageous sled dog's devotion to his master. Set amidst the Klondike gold rush, the story pits dog and man against the weather and the wilderness. London's portrayals of love and loyalty are all the more compelling for being set against the background of his generally unsentimental view of man and nature. A classic.

Captains Courageous. Rudyard Kipling. Doubleday, 1896. 224 pp. Scholastic, 1990. 197 pp.

Captains Courageous is the story of a bored and spoiled young rich boy, Harvey Cheyne. Harvey falls overboard from the ocean liner on which he is traveling and is rescued by the men of the Gloucester fishing schooner *We're Here.* Aboard the schooner, Harvey is shocked to discover that his money counts for nothing: for the first time in his life he will have to work. The rest of the book is a chronicle of the schooner's cruise, and all the dangers and hard work of the fisherman's life. Under the stern tutelage of Captain Disko Troop, Harvey slowly learns to do his share and accept responsibility. For all its hardships, he comes to love life at sea. As Harvey matures, he gradually learns to appreciate and understand his own father, a hardworking industrialist and railroad tycoon. Full of fascinating details of sea life, *Captains Courageous* is exciting and well written, though it may take time for some readers to adjust to Kipling's use of dialect.

Cheaper by the Dozen. Frank Gilbreth, Jr., and Ernestine Gilbreth Carey. Crowell, 1948. 237 pp. Bantam, 1988. 180 pp.

In one of the funniest books ever written, two of the Gilbreth children recall the adventures and high jinks of growing up in a family of twelve boisterous children, governed by a truly memorable father and an equally engaging mother. The family's best-developed trait is their sense of humor (who can forget the car horn incident?—and that's only the beginning). Underlying the fun and high spirits, however, is the father's dedication to the training and education of his children, in order that they may grow into competent, responsible, and fun-loving adults. This book is a happy memorial to an unforgettable father.

The mother, Lilian Gilbreth, is the focus of the sequel, *Belles on Their Toes* (Crowell, 1950. 237 pp.), also a lively and hilarious story, which tells of the family's struggles, joys, and sorrows after the death of the father.

A Child's History of England. Charles Dickens. Arlington, 1840. 344 pp. Dent, 1978. 396 pp.

The only complete book-length work of nonfiction that Dickens ever wrote, *A Child's History* tells the story of England from Roman times to the end of the seventeenth century. Dickens's history is a personalized one, told mainly through the actions of a large cast of heroes (Alfred the Great, Stephen Langton, Simon de Montfort) and villains (Henry VIII, John, Charles I and II). Dickens simplifies the character of these historical figures and gives little space to such standard historical fixations as economics and institutions. His representation of the Catholic Church and of the Puritans is purely Anglican, but these are minor flaws. On the whole, Dickens's history is sound, and this book is an excellent introduction to its subject. The style is lively, and Dickens's wit is often evident.

The Chosen. Chaim Potok. Simon & Schuster, 1967. 284 pp. Knopf, 1992. 284 pp.

The Chosen is a book of a special kind: one of the few modern novels to concern itself with the life of the mind and the joy of intellectual discovery as well as the spiritual aspect of human nature. In form the novel is very simple. It tells of two Jewish boys growing up in Brooklyn, their friendship, their relationships with their fathers, and the choices they face for the future. One boy, Reuven Malter, is Americanized, the son of a prominent Zionist professor. His friend, Danny Saunders, a brilliant young scholar, is the son of the leader of a strict Hasidic sect. As these unlikely friends grow up, they slowly learn to appreciate each other's worlds. *The Chosen* is more than a standard coming-of-age story; it is a story of spiritual and intellectual maturation, of the deepening of two young souls. A specifically Jewish story, its theme and implications are universal.

The Count of Monte Cristo. Alexandre Dumas. Dodd, Mead, 1889. 472 pp. New American Library, 1988. 509 pp.

The classic adventure story of Edmond Dantes, the prisoner of the Château d'If, who escapes, assumes a new identity, and remorselessly tracks down and exposes the men who had him imprisoned. The plot moves at lightning speed, with the full Victorian array of improbable coincidences, intricate conspiracies, long-lost wills, and plenty of action along the way. The villains are eminently hatable, and Dumas creates a convincing picture of a truly good man in the figure of Abbé Faria, the fellow prisoner and benefactor of Dantes. In the full, original version, Dumas's story deals subtly and intelligently with the themes of vengeance and mercy. In the end the villains are justly punished but Dantes learns that only forgiveness can really heal injustice.

David Copperfield. Charles Dickens. Originally published in 1849–50. Bantam, 1988. 817 pp.

Once again, Dickens deals with his favorite themes: childhood (especially the unhappy kind), simplicity versus snobbery, and good against evil. This is the most nearly autobiographical of Dickens's works, and contains some of his most deeply felt scenes of childhood misery. Young David is abused by his greedy and merciless stepfather, whipped, sent to heavy labor in a factory, and confined in a ghastly boarding school. Yet along the way he finds some unexpected friends: the comical Mr. Micawber, the amiably mad Mr. Dick, Aunt Betsy Trotwood, and the kind and hospitable Peggotty family. If the book contains some of Dickens's best good people, it also contains some of his best bad ones, such as Uriah Heep, the loathsome law clerk, and the corrupt aristocrats, the Steerforth family.

Diary of a Young Girl. Anne Frank. Originally published in 1947. Pocket Books, 1990. 258 pp.

This extraordinary book is the daily record of one young Jewish girl, Anne Frank, written during the two years she and her family spent hiding from the Nazis in Amsterdam. A sad and moving story of hardship and persecution, it is also an absolutely honest account of Anne's coming of age. With disarming simplicity, she writes of her adolescent longings and confusion and of the beginnings of her first real romance. Despite her dire situation, Anne remains full of hope and dreams for the future, and she refuses to neglect her mind or her education. Anne does not sentimentalize herself or her fellow Jews; the petty quarrels and misunderstandings in the family are honestly reported. The reader comes away from this book with a powerful impression of Anne's own personality, of her brilliant mind, decency, and sensitivity to others.

Drums Along the Mohawk. Walter D. Edmonds. Little, Brown, 1936. 592 pp. Bantam, 1988. 466 pp.

An outstanding historical novel of the Mohawk Valley during the American Revolution, remarkable both for its historical accuracy and for its psychological verisimilitude. Edmonds follows the fortunes of a young pioneer couple through their long struggle against the British and their Indian and Tory allies. The author paints a vivid picture of the danger and privation of frontier life and the courage, patience, and determination of the pioneers. Edmonds is realistic and unsentimental in his characterizations. His people are real human beings: the heroes make mistakes and commit injustices, while the Indian and Tory villains also have qualities of bravery and determination. Highly recommended for more mature readers.

The Endless Steppe: A Girl in Exile. Esther Hautzig. Scholastic, 1968, 1970. 240 pp.

In June 1941, ten-year-old Esther's sheltered life in Vilna, Poland, was abruptly shattered when Russian soldiers arrested and deported her, her family, and other Polish Jews to work at forced labor in Siberia. The carefree life of Poland, the terror of arrest by the Russians, the grim journey by cattle car to unknown destinations far from home, and the struggle to keep body and soul together in an unfamiliar, hostile land are all vividly depicted in this true-life account. After the war's end, the family learned of the irony of their five years' exile: by removing the Polish Jews from the reach of the Germans, the Russians had unintentionally saved their lives. Those of Esther's large extended family who were not deported had been murdered by the Nazis. Esther's courage, resilience, and strength in the face of these hardships is an inspiring example, made all the more telling by the author's honest depiction of her own immaturities and moments of self-pity. The reader soon finds himself giving thanks for things taken for granted—peace, freedom, family.

Great Expectations. Charles Dickens. Chapman and Hall, 1860. 509 pp. Knopf, 1992. 460 pp.

The story of Pip, an orphan who comes mysteriously into a great fortune, and his efforts to rise in the world and discover his benefactor. The book is long, full of incident, and complexly plotted, like all Dickens's works. The crux of the novel is Pip's relationship with the two men who play the part of father to him: Joe Gargery, his foster father, a kind, simple country blacksmith, and the sinister Abel Magwitch, the escaped convict whom Pip befriends. In the end Pip turns away from snobbery and social ambition and learns the value of true affection. The early scenes, when Pip is a boy, are among the truest renderings in literature of a child's vision of the world.

The Great Gilly Hopkins. Katherine Paterson. Crowell, 1978. 148 pp. Harper, 1987. 148 pp.

In this heart-wrenching story of the emotional cost of serial foster care, the protagonist is Gilly Hopkins, an eleven-year-old foster child and a smart-mouthed veteran of a string of foster homes. Now she is off to yet another foster home, but she has become so hardened to rejection that she refuses to notice that this time she has landed in a safe place. The story's universal appeal lies in the opportunities Gilly misses because of her well-founded fear of forming loving attachments: Gilly idolizes her mother, who abandoned her; she throws away a treasure (her new foster home), realizing its value only as it slips away (Gilly manages to get herself removed to yet another unfamiliar place); and she finally learns, in a devastating revelation, that the false god she has so loved—her mother—has never been worthy of her affection. The ending is ambiguous, but hopeful: Gilly seems able to face the future, strengthened by the short time she has spent with one loving family. Gilly is never the same, and neither is the reader.

Gulliver's Travels. Jonathan Swift. Motte, 1726. Oxford University Press, 1987. 432 pp.

Like his contemporary Daniel Defoe, Jonathan Swift was one of the first practitioners of the English novel; like Defoe's, his best-known work is a story of fantasy and adventure. Swift sends Gulliver, his hero, on a voyage to undiscovered islands in the South Seas. There Gulliver visits the land of Lilliput, where human beings are only a few inches high; the kingdom of Brobdingnag, inhabited by giants; and many others. By constantly changing the perspective of his protagonist, Swift highlights all the pretensions and idiocies of mankind. (Two kingdoms fight each other over the critical issue of how to crack an egg properly.) Swift was one of the most brilliant and bitter satirists who ever lived, and his jokes are pointed enough to make everyone feel uncomfortable, even as they laugh. Some of his humor is concerned with the politics of his own day, and may be lost to the average reader, and as with Defoe, his old-fashioned style may take some getting used to. That said, *Gulliver's Travels* still remains one of the most important books in English. It can be read with enjoyment either as satire or as fantastic adventure.

Hard Times. Charles Dickens. Originally published in 1854. Oxford University Press, 1989. 464 pp.

One of Dickens's best novels, *Hard Times* is distinguished by a relatively simple plot and less of the sentimentality to be found elsewhere in Dickens. The novel tells the story of Charles Gradgrind, a successful businessman whose theory of materialistic and utilitarian education ruins the lives of his children and nearly destroys all love within his family. Dickens is at his most scathing (and his funniest) in his bitter denunciations of the Gradgrind system. Dickens's Coketown is a horrifying picture of the industrial towns of Victorian England, a place where imagination has been outlawed and nature defiled.

The Hero and the Crown. Robin McKinley. Greenwillow, 1984. 246 pp. ABC-Clio, 1988. *The Blue Sword.* Robin McKinley. Greenwillow, 1982. 272 pp. Ace, 1987. 248 pp.

Fantasy lovers of all ages will appreciate these tales of romantic adventure. Both novels have richly detailed and masterfully crafted plots in which the struggle for adolescent identity is woven together with the battle between good and evil. In *The Hero and the Crown,* the unlikely heroine is Aerin, a Damarian princess. Totally lacking in courtly graces, she is nevertheless strong and independent, and proves her worth by freeing Damar from fire-breathing dragons and an evil wizard. This gracefully written fantasy offers a refreshing twist as the heroine performs the daring deeds. The action of *The Blue Sword* takes place 500 years later and concerns the exploits of another heroine, Harry Crew. Kidnapped by the magic-working Corlath, king of the Old Damarians, Harry soon discovers that she, too, possesses mysterious powers. Like the legendary Aerin who preceded her, Harry finds herself battling the evil forces that threaten the Damarians. McKinley has given us two utterly engrossing stories about heroines who display uncommon courage, ingenuity, and wit.

Hobberdy Dick. Katherine M. Briggs. Canongate, 1955, 1988. 207 pp.

This wonderful, warm story is told through the eyes of a "hob" (a brownie or helpful sprite), who is attached to an old country house during the interregnum of seventeenth-century England. New owners, coldhearted followers of Cromwell, move into the house, and Hobberdy Dick undertakes to educate them in proper English country ways. Christians, especially fundamentalist Christians, are too often the bad guys in books for children, but this story presents a balanced view: on the one hand, there is the father, a hard-eyed, self-righteous—but ultimately honest—Calvinist; and on the other, his mother-in-law, a sweet, warmhearted soul, whose love and forgiveness can comfort and put to rest even a wicked ghost who has terrified a young servant girl. Hobberdy Dick sees all this with his elfin eyes. This book re-creates and brings to life old English customs and beliefs; and even though these beliefs include a firm belief in the supernatural, the story is never "occult" in an evil sense; on the contrary, it resembles the Narnia stories in its sense of respect for the whole of creation.

The Hobbit. J. R. R. Tolkien. Houghton Mifflin, 1957, 1988. 315 pp.

The famous story of Bilbo Baggins, the peaceful hobbit of Middle Earth, who is virtually kidnapped by a wizard, joins a treasure-hunting expedition of dwarfs, helps to slay a dragon, and finds a mysterious magic ring. Bilbo has plenty of help, but his own courage, resourcefulness, and common sense emerge in the course of his action-filled journey. The book is full of monsters, perils, and mysterious creatures (including the memorably evil Gollum), all the products of the author's fertile imagination. It can be read either on its own or as a prologue to the epic fantasy *The Lord of the Rings.*

Kidnapped. Robert Louis Stevenson. Originally published in 1886. Gollancz Paperbacks, 1991. 304 pp. ***David Balfour.*** Scribner, 1893. 356 pp. Gilberton, 1968.

These two books together form one of the most exciting and convincing historical romances ever written. Stevenson tells the story of David Balfour, a young Scot of the eighteenth century, who is abducted by agents of his evil uncle. Imprisoned on shipboard, Balfour escapes with the aid of Alan Breck Stewart, a Highlander and Jacobite rebel. Despite their vast difference in outlook and political principles, Alan and David become loyal friends as they make their way through a maze of perils and political intrigue. David comes to admire Alan for his bravery in the service of his cause; in the end Alan, out of friendship for David, accepts the punishment for his crimes. The story moves rapidly, with plenty of shipwrecks, sword fights, and battles along the way. Stevenson gives a detailed and sympathetic description of the culture of the Scottish Highlands in its last days of existence.

Knight's Fee. Rosemary Sutcliff. Walck, 1960. 237 pp. Oxford University Press, 1974. 241 pp.

The rich and detailed prose of this historical novel re-creates for the reader life in England in the late eleventh century, the decades following the death of William the Conqueror. In this story, a pitiful, defiant kennel boy is transformed by the love of his foster father and foster brother from a bitter, abused, terrified child into an honest, courageous knight capable of serving the king. Loyalty, courage, and devotion all play a part in this well-told, gripping story.

Little Women. Louisa May Alcott. Originally published in 1868. Puffin, 1988. 303 pp.

In this well-beloved story of four lively sisters and their devoted mother, set during the Civil War, each of the four girls is challenged in a different way by the genteel poverty of the family, and each is nurtured by her mother, who treasures and strives to protect her girls' purity and high ideals. The Victorian style of writing and the author's strongly stated moral judgments may require the reader's patience at first, but such patience will be richly rewarded. On becoming better acquainted with the March girls, the reader soon comes to appreciate the refreshing and appealing quality of their hopes and ideals. Like the best in children's literature, *Little Women* can be enjoyed by audiences of all ages.

Moby-Dick. Herman Melville. Originally published in 1852. Vintage, 1991. 660 pp.

One of the greatest of American novels, *Moby-Dick* can be read on several levels. In an abridged edition, it is a fine adventure story and a superb re-creation of the vanished days of whaling under sail. In the full, adult version, *Moby-Dick* is a profound and complex story of good and evil. In Captain Ahab, Melville creates one of the classic figures of literature, a good man destroyed by pride, arrogance, and vengefulness. Tragically, Ahab corrupts the good and half-good men around him and takes them with him to destruction. A difficult book, but rewarding to those young readers who enjoy a challenge.

Narrative of the Life of Frederick Douglass. Frederick Douglass. Boston Anti-Slavery Office, 1845. 126 pp. Belknap, Harvard University Press, 1960. 163 pp.

The early life of one of the great heroes of the antislavery movement in America, as written by himself. Born a slave in Maryland before the Civil War, Douglass educated himself, escaped from bondage after several attempts, and went on to become the most powerful black politician in America. A moving record of one man's triumph over prejudice, ignorance, and oppression.

1984. George Orwell. Signet, 1948. New American Library, 1984. 268 pp.

The classic novel of an antiutopia, set in a socialist England of the (then) distant future. Orwell follows the misfortunes of a single unhappy bureaucrat, Winston Smith, in a state where art, nature, and love have nearly disappeared. War has become perpetual, truth has ceased to exist even as a concept, and the spies and listening devices of "Big Brother" are everywhere. The novel is grim and there is no happy ending; but as a cautionary tale, an example of the kind of hell that human beings can create on earth, *1984* remains unequaled. Young readers should also learn that the type of society Orwell depicted was no fantasy but actually existed in his own time—and still exists in ours.

The Old Man and the Sea. Ernest Hemingway. Scribner, 1952, 1988. 127 pp.

A Pulitzer Prize winner, this finely crafted novella tells of an aging Cuban fisherman who battles a giant marlin. Sharks take most of the marlin, but they cannot deprive the old man of his inner victory. The story is notable for its depiction of the old man's relationship with a young boy. Along with lessons in fishing, the boy learns valuable lessons about persistence and self-discipline.

Old Yeller. Fred Gipson. Harper, 1956, 1990. 184 pp.

The story of a young boy on the Texas frontier and the big yellow dog who becomes his friend and helper. Written in a clear, unsentimental style, it offers a detailed picture of the constant dangers and difficulties of frontier life and the courage and unity with which frontier families confronted those hazards. Reminds us that boys and girls on the frontier had awesome responsibilities thrust on them at a very early age—responsibilities that they met.

Oliver Twist. Charles Dickens. Bon Marchbe, 1837. 112 pp. Knopf, 1992. 380 pp.

One of Dickens's best-known works, this novel recounts the perilous adventures of an orphan condemned at birth to one of the frightful workhouses of Victorian England. Oliver escapes his prison only to fall into the clutches of the most hatable villains in English literature; Fagin, the corrupter of children and trainer of pickpockets; Toby Cratchit, the ace burglar; and the hideous murderer Bill Sikes. The book is full of dramatic scenes and vivid characters, and Dickens paints a comprehensive portrait of the England of his day. One of the most scathing attacks on social and legal injustices ever written.

Paul Harvey's "The Rest of the Story." Paul Aurandt. Doubleday, 1977. 234 pp. Bantam, 1978. 180 pp.

A collection of eighty-one of Paul Harvey's stories of little-known incidents in the lives of famous people, past and present. The trademark of Harvey's suspenseful stories is the surprise ending. We aren't told, and often can't guess, the person's identity until it is revealed at the story's end. These brief anecdotes usually focus on incidents that manifest admirable character traits in those involved.

The Phantom Tollbooth. Norton Juster. Illus. by Jules Feiffer. Knopf, 1961, 1989. 256 pp.

This is the story of a bored young boy named Milo, who drives through a magic tollbooth to discover an amazing world where words, numbers, and ideas can take the form of individuals, and where nothing is quite what it seems. Milo journeys from Dictionopolis (the city of letters) to Digitopolis (the city of numbers) and finally into the Mountains of Ignorance, in his quest to rescue the Princesses Rhyme and Reason. Milo finds allies in Tock (the ticking dog) and the pompous Humbug, and encounters such villains as the Everpresent Wordsnatcher, the Gelatinous Giant, and the Lethargians. The book is very funny, full of wordplay and puns, and has excellent drawings by Jules Feiffer. A celebration of knowledge and learning, which all readers can enjoy.

The Red Badge of Courage. Stephen Crane. The Modern Library, 1894. 267 pp. Vintage, 1990. 143 pp.

Acclaimed as one of the greatest fictional depictions of war, Crane's short, straightforward novel is easily accessible to advanced young readers. Crane's hero, a young Civil War soldier, experiences all the horrors of war in his first battle. Despite this, he slowly learns to conquer his fear and to do his duty. Crane talked to many veterans of the war before he wrote his story, and his historical and psychological realism is unmatched.

Rifles for Watie. Harold Keith. Crowell, 1957. 332 pp. Harper, 1987. 332 pp.

Rifles for Watie is the story of a young Kansas boy, Jeff Bussey, who runs away to fight with the Union army on the western frontier during the Civil War. A convincing chronicle of one boy's growing to manhood, the story is well written and based on very solid historical research. Keith, a native of the region he writes about, knows his period and brings it to life. The book is valuable for the light it sheds on a little-known aspect of the Civil War: the involvement (on both sides) of American Indians in that conflict. Young Jeff comes to know, and respect, men and women on both sides of the lines. An excellent historical novel for younger readers.

Robinson Crusoe. Daniel Defoe. Originally published in 1719. Knopf, 1991. 256 pp.

This book, one of the first novels in the English language, is a classic of adventure. Crusoe, Defoe's first-person narrator, runs away to sea as a young man, and experiences every kind of peril and misfortune, including slavery. He is at length cast away upon a deserted island, where he slowly learns to survive by his wits. Defoe's narrative is full of all the accurate minor details that make a story convincing—so convincing, indeed, that when the book first appeared, many took it to be fact. The reader comes to admire the inventiveness, pluck, and hard work of Crusoe, as Crusoe learns to trust in the goodness of a power greater than himself.

The Scarlet Pimpernel. Baroness Emmuska Orczy. Putnam, 1905. 341 pp. Bantam, 1992. 264 pp.

This historical romance, set during the French Revolution, is the story of a small band of selfless Englishmen and their mysterious leader who work to rescue French aristocrats from the horrible death of the guillotine. Fast-paced and exciting, it also features some remarkable characters: Chauvelin, the sinister French diplomat and secret policeman; Sir Percy Blakeney, the empty-headed young man of fashion; and the mysterious Scarlet Pimpernel himself, who has a flair for disguise to rival Sherlock Holmes's. The intricately plotted story moves from cliff-hanger to cliff-hanger, to a conclusion guaranteed to take the reader by surprise.

Something Wicked This Way Comes. Ray Bradbury. Simon & Schuster, 1962. 215 pp. Bantam, 1990. 215 pp.

An allegorical fable by one of America's best-known science fiction and fantasy writers. Two young boys in the American Midwest, Jim and Will, are, like all boys, looking for excitement, preferably with a spice of danger. They get far more than they bargain for when a mysterious carnival comes to town: Cooger and Dark's Pandemonium Shadow Show, run by the sinister Mr. Dark, the Illustrated Man. Strange and deadly things begin to happen as the show's temptations draw people into Mr. Dark's clutches. Before they know it, the boys are fighting for their own souls against all the powers of darkness. An exciting story with profound implications, *Something Wicked This Way Comes* is written in an innovative style that may prove difficult for some readers, but the reward is more than worth the effort.

The Space Trilogy: Out of the Silent Planet, Perelandra, That Hideous Strength. C. S. Lewis. Macmillan, 1944–46, 1990.

A sophisticated science fiction fantasy by one of the leading Christian writers of our era. The trilogy follows the fortunes of Ransom, an innocent academic who is kidnapped by mad scientists and transported to Mars by spaceship. Together with the angelic spirits of the solar system and a small band of humans, Ransom battles and defeats the mad scientists and secret police of the evil N.I.C.E. on Mars, Venus, and finally Earth. The trilogy is at the same time a futuristic adventure story, a religious allegory, and a philosophical drama of the struggle between good and evil. Well-written, exciting, and profound.

Stories for Children. Isaac Bashevis Singer. Farrar, Straus, 1984, 1985. 337 pp.

A superb collection of children's stories by the well-known American Yiddish writer. The stories are mostly set in the typical milieu of Singer's work, the Jewish communities of Poland in the years and centuries before the Holocaust. They tell of demons and angels, miracles and visions, and have the flavor of the ancient and the magical that is typical of Singer. The background, characters, and spiritual context are Jewish, but the themes are universal: the struggle between good and evil, the saving power of love and hope, and man's quest for God. On this level these stories (like all the best children's literature) can be read with equal enjoyment by adults and children. Despite the depth and subtlety of their content, Singer's stories are written with beautiful simplicity and clarity. The book also contains a fine essay by Singer on children's literature.

A Study in Scarlet. Sir Arthur Conan Doyle. Ward Lock, 1888. 169 pp. Watermill Press, 1987. 151 pp. *The Sign of the Four.* Sir Arthur Conan Doyle. Spencer Blackett, 1890. 283 pp. Watermill Press, 1987. 142 pp. *The Hound of the Baskervilles.* Sir Arthur Conan Doyle. Caldwell, 1902. 248 pp. Oxford University Press, 1989. 91 pp.

These are the novel-length adventures of fiction's most famous detective, Sherlock Holmes, and his loyal companion, Dr. Watson. It is almost impossible to imagine a reader of any age who is impervious to the appeal of Holmes, and young readers will enjoy his wit and supernatural intelligence. Doyle knows how to keep the action and the riddles coming, and his stories seldom drag. Holmes is relentless in his pursuit of criminals, but he dispenses his own brand of justice, often showing a great deal of compassion for those unwittingly involved in crime.

A Tale of Two Cities. Charles Dickens. All the Year Round, 1859. HarperCollins, 1992. 240 pp.

Dickens's novel of the French Revolution, as seen through the eyes of a large cast of characters in London and Paris. The book contains some of Dickens's best writing, and is more tightly and coherently plotted than some of his other works. The themes of vengeance, justice, and mercy are developed throughout the novel, as each character finds himself drawn into the events of the Revolution by the power of fate. The book features many memorable characters: Dr. Manette, a kind and wise man who suffers injustice and inflicts it on others in spite of himself; the corrupt and merciless noblemen, the Evremonde brothers; Jerry Cruncher, the comical grave robber; and Dickens's greatest villainess, the bloodthirsty and implacable Madame Defarge. Last but not least is Sydney Carton, a decent man ruined by his misfortunes, who rises to a supreme act of self-sacrifice. Dickens's history is not always accurate, but few have excelled him in re-creating the true atmosphere of revolution.

This Hallowed Ground: The Story of the Union Side of the Civil War. Bruce Catton. Doubleday, 1956. 437 pp. Pocket Books, 1975. 559 pp.

A single-volume history of the American Civil War, accessible to mature young readers and written by one of our foremost Civil War historians. The book is mainly a military and political history, but Catton also devotes considerable attention to the life of the common soldier on both sides. The outstanding characters of the war—Lincoln, Grant, Sherman, Davis, Lee, Jackson—are powerfully and convincingly portrayed. The hardcover edition contains many excellent illustrations.

Typhoon. Joseph Conrad. Putnam, 1902. 205 pp. Knopf, 1991.

An outstanding adventure story by the Pole who became one of England's greatest authors. The story is short and simple in outline: a fierce tropical storm, as experienced by the crew of a single beleaguered freighter. Conrad's description of the storm's power is frighteningly vivid, but the focus of the story is on the vessel's crew and their reactions to the crisis. As always in Conrad, the characters are faced with stark choices between duty and cowardice. Conrad's unlikely hero, Captain MacWhirr, shows a bravery and moral responsibility of which many more intelligent men are incapable. An excellent introduction to a major writer.

Warrior Scarlet. Rosemary Sutcliff. Oxford University Press, 1958, 1979. 207 pp.

Among the tribes of Bronze Age Britain, to be different was often the same as being outcast. The boy Drem knows this well. Drem struggles fiercely to overcome the handicap of his withered right arm, and to pass his tribe's test of manhood in order to wear the warrior's red robe, the "warrior scarlet." Because Drem tries so desperately to succeed, his failure is all the more unbearable. The heart of the story is found in Drem's positive response to this failure: sick at heart, he nonetheless faces the loss of all his hopes without becoming resigned or bitter. The deep sorrow he experiences works an inward change in Drem, giving him more compassion toward others who also suffer because they are different. The swift, stirring plot culminates in a satisfying conclusion.

Watership Down. Richard Adams. Rex Collings, 1972. 413 pp. Penguin, 1983. 431 pp.

Courage, resourcefulness, loyalty, bravery in battle—who would expect to find these themes in a story about rabbits? Richard Adams's wonderful story of Hazel, the Chief Rabbit who rules by wisdom, and his loyal followers, who flee their doomed warren and encounter numerous adventures, is fascinating and believable. Adams has created an entire rabbit world, complete with its own language and mythology (such as the stories of Al-ahrairah, the Prince with a Thousand Enemies). Part of the appeal comes from the carefully drawn character of each rabbit, and the close attention given to every detail of the rabbit environment; but another part of the appeal comes from the glimpses of a second level, an allegorical one. One strange warren the rabbits chance across resembles a welfare state; another warren, even scarier, resembles a fascist dictatorship. The allegorical aspects of the book, however, never overwhelm the action-filled plot. Written for adults, the book can also be enjoyed by advanced younger readers.

NOTES

CHAPTER ONE. THE CRISIS IN MORAL EDUCATION

PAGE

13 *In 1955, Rudolf Flesch wrote:* Rudolf Flesch, *Why Johnny Can't Read* (New York: Harper & Row, 1955); *Why Johnny Still Can't Read* (New York: Harper Colophon Books, 1981). Flesch points out that "look-say" was originally designed for deaf children. In current terminology, "look-say" is called the "sight method" or the "whole word" approach.

13 *In 1986, the U.S. Department of Education endorsed: What Works: Research About Teaching and Learning* (Washington, D.C.: U.S. Department of Education, 1986), 21. The Department of Education endorsement also includes a qualifier: "phonics should be taught early but not over-used. If phonics instruction extends for too many years, it can defeat the spirit and excitement of learning to read." It should be kept in mind that, aside from the question of what reading method should be used in schools, the best *preparation* for reading is a home where songs and rhymes are sung, books are valued, and stories are read aloud.

14 *An estimated 525,000 attacks:* Ronald D. Stephens, *Safe Schools and*

PAGE

Quality Schooling: The Public Responds (Malibu, Calif.: National School Safety Center, 1988), 5.

14 *Each year nearly three million crimes:* Ronald D. Stephens, *National Crime Survey* (National School Safety Center, 1990), cited in *Newsweek* (March 9, 1992), 26.

14 *135,000 students carry guns: Caught in the Crossfire: A Report on Gun Violence in Our Nation's Schools* (Washington, D.C.: Center to Prevent Handgun Violence, 1990), 7. The figure of one student in five is provided by the Centers for Disease Control and is cited in *Newsweek* (March 9, 1992), 25.

14 *students avoid using the rest rooms:* Karl Zinsmeister, "Juvenile Crime: An Overview," *The World & I* (April 1990), 475.

14 *Surveys of school children:* Stephens, *Safe Schools and Quality Schooling,* 5–6.

14 *one third of public school teachers:* "Public School Teacher Perspectives on School Discipline," Office of Educational Research and Improvement Bulletin (Washington, D.C.: Center for Education Statistics, Department of Education, October 1987), 1.

14 *Suicides among young people:* Based on 1987 data from the National Center for Health Statistics. Cited in Thomas Lickona, *Educating for Character: How Our Schools Can Teach Respect and Responsibility* (New York: Bantam Books, 1991), 19. The figure of one teen in seven is based on a 1988 survey by the U.S. Department of Health and Human Services cited in Lickona.

14 *Forty percent of today's fourteen-year-old girls:* William J. Bennett, *Our Children and Our Country* (New York: A Touchstone Book, 1989), 92.

16 *the merits of wife swapping:* For "wife swapping" and "cannibalism" see M. Blatt, A. Colby, and B. Speicher, *Hypothetical Dilemmas for Use in Moral Discussions,* No. 23 on the list *Kohlberg Reprints Available from the Center for Moral Education* (Cambridge, Mass.: Moral Education and Research Foundation, Harvard University, 1974). For the merits of teaching children to masturbate see Sidney B. Simon, Leland W. Howe, and Howard Kirschenbaum, *Values Clarification* (New York: Hart Publishing Company, 1972), 52. For a discussion of nonjudgmental drug education see Chapter Two.

17 *the collapse of a large Catholic school system:* The Immaculate Heart of Mary Parochial School System in Los Angeles. See Chapter Two for details.

18 *a questionnaire used in several Massachusetts schools:* My thanks to June Kevorkian for this example.

18 *From the* Values Clarification *handbook:* Simon et al., 143, 180–81, 186–88.

PAGE

19   *the chief architect:* I refer to Carl R. Rogers. See Chapter Two for details.

19   • *"Each group takes a minute":* Skills for Adolescence (Granville, Ohio: Quest International, 1985), Unit Six Energizers, 115.

19   • *"Ask the children to lie down":* Don Dinkmeyer, Ph.D., and Don Dinkmeyer, Jr., Ph.D., DUSO 1 (Circle Pines, Minn., 1982), Guided Fantasy Card 13.

19   *in an elementary school in St. Louis:* Jacqueline R. Kasun, "Sex Education: The Hidden Agenda," *The World & I* (September 1989), 489. The second example is cited in Dr. James Dobson and Gary L. Bauer, *Children at Risk* (Dallas: Word Publishing, 1990), 48.

20   • *On Valentine's Day in Missoula:* Beverly LaHaye, "Education in the Year 2020," in Beverly LaHaye, ed., *Who Will Save Our Children?* (Brentwood, Tenn.: Wolgemuth & Hyatt Publishers, 1990), 82.

20   • *"In a southern high school classroom:* This incident is described at length in George Grant, *Grand Illusions* (Brentwood, Tenn.: Wolgemuth & Hyatt Publishers, 1988), 105-8, 321 (n 1).

20   • Changing Bodies, Changing Lives: Ruth Bell (and other coauthors of *Our Bodies, Ourselves*), *Changing Bodies, Changing Lives* (New York: Vintage Books, 1988), 114, 99, 4, 91, 76.

20   • *A man's wife is dying:* A condensed version of the "Heinz dilemma" developed by Lawrence Kohlberg. See Blatt et al., *Hypothetical Dilemmas.*

20   • *A girl and boy are in love:* A condensed version of a dilemma in the *Values Clarification* handbook. See Simon et al., *Values Clarification,* 290–94.

21   • *A band of settlers is hiding:* A condensation of a dilemma used in the Vancouver, Canada, public schools. Cited in Kathleen M. Gow, *Yes, Virginia, There Is Right and Wrong* (Wheaton, Ill.: Tyndale House, 1985), 189. A similar dilemma was developed by Lawrence Kohlberg.

21   *when drug education programs:* See Chapters Two and Three for the research on the effectiveness of such programs.

22   *Moral values cannot be taught:* From a collection of student letters sent to *The Toronto Star* and cited in a March 18, 1978, article, A8. Quoted in Gow, *Yes, Virginia,* 86.

22   *"You call it 'life skills':* Gow, *Yes, Virginia,* 191.

23   *"always bootlegged the values stuff":* Quoted in Gow, *Yes, Virginia,* 192.

CHAPTER TWO. DRUG EDUCATION

PAGE

32 *In 1976 at Stanford:* Richard H. Blum with Eva Blum and Emily Garfield, *Drug Education: Results and Recommendations* (Lexington, Mass.: Lexington Books, 1976).

32 *similar study of Decide in 1978:* Richard H. Blum, Emily F. Garfield, Judy L. Johnstone, and John G. Magistad, "Drug Education: Further Results and Recommendations," *Journal of Drug Issues* (Fall 1978), 379–426.

32 *evaluated by other researchers:* W. B. Hansen, C. A. Johnson, B. R. Flay, J. W. Graham, and J. Sobel, "Affective and Social Influences Approaches to the Prevention of Multiple Substance Abuse Among Seventh Grade Students: Results from Project Smart," *Preventive Medicine* 17 (1988), 135–54; see also R. A. Hopkins, A. L. Mauss, K. A. Kearney, and A. Weisheit, "Comprehensive Evaluation of a Model Alcohol Education Curriculum," *Journal of Studies on Alcohol* 49:1 (1988), 38–50; W. R. Coulson, "Quest: Internal Memorandum Reveals More Drug Use After Skills for Adolescence," from the *La Jolla Program Newsletter* (August 1990), Publication of the Research Council on Ethnopsychology, San Diego.

32 *one of Coulson's colleagues:* This story is told by Coulson in "Affective Education" speech given at Livonia, Mich. (September 5, 1990). Available on videotape from the Paradigm Company, Box 45161, Boise, Idaho 83711.

32 *Once she arrived:* William R. Coulson, "Principled Morality vs. Consequentialism" in *Questianity: Why the War on Drugs Drags* (San Diego: Research Council on Ethnopsychology, 1990), 32. The essentials of the story are confirmed in Rasa Gustaitis's book, *Turning On* (New York: Macmillan, 1969). According to Gustaitis, however, the LSD trip came at the end of the first week.

33 *Who should teach whom?* Richard J. Lowry, ed., *The Journals of A. H. Maslow* (Monterey, Calif.: Brooks/Cole Publishing Company, 1979) May 5, 1968, 919.

33 *Maslow was concerned:* Quoted in Coulson, "Principled Morality," 21.

33 *"made the psychology of the time":* Lowry, ed., *Journals of A. H. Maslow,* February 1, 1969, 1109.

33 *In Chapter 11:* Abraham H. Maslow, *Motivation and Personality,* 2d ed. (New York: Harper & Row, 1970), XX.

33 *Educational Innovation Project:* The project is described at length in W. R. Coulson, *Groups, Gimmicks, and Instant Gurus* (New York: Harper & Row, 1972); and in W. R. Coulson, "Tearing Down the

PAGE

Temple: Confessions of a Catholic School Dismantler," *Fidelity* (December 1983), 18–22.

34   *When I got back:* Carl R. Rogers, *Freedom to Learn* (Columbus Ohio: Charles E. Merrill Publishing Company, 1969), 332–33.

34   *Some of you might be frightened:* Ibid., 332.

34   *"When we started":* Coulson, *Groups, Gimmicks, and Instant Gurus,* 99.

35   *"Why did I ever write":* Quoted in W. R. Coulson, "Too Much Psychology," *Bulletin of the Research Council on Ethnopsychology,* San Diego (October 1, 1990), 1.

35   *"a pattern of failure":* Coulson, "Principled Morality," 20.

35   *Rogers's therapeutic approach:* For a thorough exposition of these ideas see Carl R. Rogers, *On Becoming a Person* (Boston: Houghton Mifflin, 1961).

36   *The intensive group:* Rogers, *Freedom to Learn,* 304–5.

36   *"When I write up my theories":* Coulson, "Principled Morality," 41.

36   *He had two other misgivings.* William R. Coulson, *A Sense of Community* (Columbus, Ohio: Charles E. Merrill Publishing Company, 1973), 31–32.

36   *Dr. Coulson, who knew:* W. R. Coulson, "The Californication of Carl Rogers," *Fidelity* (November 1987), 25.

36   *"wild psychologizing":* Coulson, "Too Much Psychology," 1.

37   *"non-profit educational organization":* Cited in *Questianity: Why the War on Drugs Drags,* 1.

37   *"more than 2000 school systems":* *Skills for Adolescence: Workshop Guidebook* (Granville, Ohio: Quest International, 1989), 12A.

37   *Howard Kirschenbaum:* Howard Kirschenbaum, *On Becoming Carl Rogers* (New York: Delacorte Press, 1979).

37   • *Paraphrase:* Excerpts from *Skills for Adolescence Workshop Guidebook,* 43, 93.

38   *the cardinal rule of the clinic:* Coulson "Principled Morality," 6–7.

38   *Children need "authoritative guidance":* Ibid., 8.

38   *Students, says Coulson, will gain the impression:* Ibid., 7.

38   *"Try not to lecture":* Instruction booklet for teachers to accompany Ortho Straight Talk program. Cited in Pearl Evans, *Hidden Danger in the Classroom* (Petaluma, Calif.: Small Helm Press, 1990), 43. Other quote is from *Skills for Adolescence: Workshop Guidebook,* 49.

38   *"a really good time":* From a tape recording of a Project Charlie Recruitment meeting. Cited in Coulson, "Principled Morality," 26.

39   *"We were to be the first generation":* Coulson, "Affective Education" speech.

39   *"Remember that these techniques":* *Helping Youth Decide* (Alexandria, Va.: National Association of State Boards of Education, 1984),

PAGE

13. NASBE no longer publishes this booklet. It has been re-released by the Tobacco Institute.

39   *"The Family,"* says one Quest worksheet: *Skills for Adolescence: Student Workbook* (Granville, Ohio: Quest International, 1985) Unit 5, Worksheet 4, V23.

39   *"It seemed as if the parents":* Cited in *Questianity: Why the War on Drugs Drags,* 5.

39   *"You must decide for yourself":* V. Ryder, *Contemporary Living* (South Holland, Ill.: Goodheart-Wilcox, 1979), 16; H. McGinley, *Caring, Deciding and Growing* (Lexington, Mass.: Ginn, 1983), 20; J. Kelly and E. Eubanks, *Today's Teen* (Peoria, Ill.: Bennett, 1981), 27.

40   *"choosing for himself":* Coulson, "Affective Education" speech.

40   *"This evocation of feeling":* Coulson, *Questianity,* 32.

40   *exercise titled "Emotion Clock":* **Skills for Adolescence: Student Workbook,** Unit 3, Worksheet 3; Unit 1, Worksheet 2.

40   *drawing a "Rainbow of Feelings":* **Skills for Adolescence** (Granville, Ohio: Quest International, 1988), III–8 to III–11.

40   *"The most wonderful thing":* Coulson, *Questianity,* 31–32.

40   *"There was no talk of drugs":* Ibid., 27.

40   *Out of a total of seven units:* **Skills for Adolescence** (Granville, Ohio: Quest International, 1985, 1988).

40   *"The subject is not":* Coulson, *Questianity,* 27.

41   *"the lack of self-esteem":* Final report, "Task Force to Promote Self-Esteem and Personal and Social Responsibility," cited in Chester E. Finn, Jr., "Narcissus Goes to School," *Commentary* (June 1990), 40.

41   *Other states followed suit:* Finn, ibid., 41.

41   *Rita Kramer concluded that:* Ibid.

41   *Chester Finn, who served:* Ibid., 40.

41   *"inoculates us against the lures":* Ibid.

42   *"If I'm really quite wonderful":* W. R. Coulson, "Always Ready for a Good Time," *La Jolla Program Newsletter* (March 1991), 1.

42   *At a drug education fair:* Coulson, *Questianity,* 13.

42   *psychologist Joseph Adelson writes:* Joseph Adelson, "Drugs and Youth," *Commentary* (May 1989), 27.

43   *"By risktaking we mean":* Donald Read, Sidney Simon, Joel Goodman, *Health Education: The Search for Values* (Englewood Cliffs, N.J.: Prentice-Hall, 1977), 152.

43   *"There is no assurance":* Taken from a letter written to Janice Rinks by Dr. Harold Voth on September 12, 1986, after reviewing Quest's *Skills for Adolescence.*

43   *"knew or should have known":* "Parents of Two Teenagers in Smart Case to Sue School," *The Manchester Union Leader* (Manchester, N.H.: May 22, 1991). The program is Project Self-Esteem.

44 *the profile of the teen-age girl smoker:* Yankelovich, Skelly, and White, Inc., *"A Study of Cigarette Smoking Among Teen-age Girls and Young Women,"* unpublished research report submitted to the American Cancer Society, February, 1976, 17–18. See also the summary of this research published in 1977 by the National Cancer Institute, "Cigarette Smoking Among Teen-agers and Young Women" (DHEW Pub. No. [NIH] 77-1203).

44 *to "demonstrate tolerance": Skills for Adolescence: Workshop Guidebook* (1989), 33.

45 *Under this induction:* Coulson, *Questianity,* 29.

45 *In 1978 and 1985 Professor Stephen Jurs:* "Errors in 'Quest Facts' corrected by professor," letter to the editor of *The Norman (Oklahoma) Transcript* from Stephen Jurs (November 11, 1990).

45 *The study compared Quest students:* From a six-page memorandum on *Skills for Adolescence,* "Phase II Findings," dated June 26/July 11, 1989. Sent by Quest to Dr. Stephen M. Conway, School of Dental Medicine, Southern Illinois University, at his request.

45 *We have a program:* From Howard Kirschenbaum, "Humanistic Education: What Have We Learned in 20 Years?" Tape available from Association for Supervision and Curriculum Development (ASCD). Cited in Coulson, "Principled Morality," 23.

46 *". . . humanistic education, holistic education":* Ibid.

46 • *Nearly six out of ten high school seniors.* These statistics are cited in Thomas Lickona, *Educating for Character* (New York: Bantam Books, 1991), 376.

46 • *The percentage of children:* Ibid., 377.

46 • *One in fifteen high school senior boys:* Ibid.

46 • *One in twelve high school students:* Ibid.

46 • *More than half of high school seniors:* Ibid., 388.

46 • *The average age of first alcohol use:* Ibid.

46 • *A 1985 study showed:* Cited in Coulson, *Questianity,* 24.

46 *In 1988 the U.S. Department of Education published a guide: Drug Prevention Curricula: A Guide to Selection and Implementation* (Washington, D.C.: Office of Educational Research and Improvement, U.S. Department of Education, 1988), 10–13.

47 *"it is important that these choices":* Ibid., 19.

47 *child-centered approach: Quest International Resource Catalog, 1991–1992* (Granville, Ohio: Quest International), 12.

47 *even the parent meetings: Supporting Young Adolescents: A Guide to Leading Parent Meetings* (Granville, Ohio: Quest International, 1987), 72, 33-35, 74.

48 *"his soft fur and warm smile": Quest International Resource Catalog, 1991–1992,* 37.

PAGE

48 *"guided fantasy activities"*: Don Dinkmeyer, Ph.D., and Don Dink-meyer, Jr., Ph.D., *DUSO-1: Teacher's Guide* (Circle Pines, Minn.: American Guidance Service, 1982), 19.

48 *"a loveable young dragon"*: "Join Pumsy in a Self-Esteem Adventure of Positive Thinking Skills." Curriculum catalog (Eugene, Ore.: Timberline Press, 1991).

48 *"may trivialize the message"*: *Drug Prevention Curricula: A Guide to Selection and Implementation,* 16.

48 *The children loved these police officers:* Thomas P. Masty, Testimony before the Michigan State Senate Subcommittee on the Michigan Model (November 18, 1991), 13.

49 *Research on the effectiveness of DARE:* Ted Rohrlich, "DARE's Results Prove Difficult to Measure," *The Los Angeles Times* (Jan. 19, 1992). DARE has also been criticized because of incidents in which children have turned in their drug-using parents to police. See "The Informants," *The Wall Street Journal* (April 20, 1992), 1, A7.

49 *"A strong school policy"*: *Drug Prevention Curricula: A Guide to Selection and Implementation,* 7.

49 *"that's very difficult to do"*: From *Building Drug-Free Schools,* a videotape provided by the American Council for Drug Education, 2021 Monroe Street, Rockville, Md., 20852.

50 *no known incidents of Gompers students: Schools Without Drugs* (Washington, D.C.: U.S. Department of Education, 1987), 28.

CHAPTER THREE. SEX EDUCATION

53 *It's Friday afternoon:* James Patterson and Peter Kim, *The Day America Told the Truth* (New York: Prentice Hall Books, 1991), 102–3.

53 *"If you feel your parents are overprotective"*: Ruth Bell et al., *Changing Bodies, Changing Lives,* 90.

53 *"Many Catholics, Protestants"*: Ibid., 91.

54 *both of which failed to show:* Deborah A. Dawson, "The Effects of Sex Education on Adolescent Behavior," *Family Planning Perspectives* (July/August 1986), 162–70. William Marsiglio and Frank L. Mott, "The Impact of Sex Education on Sexual Activity, Contraceptive Use and Premarital Pregnancy Among American Teenagers," *Family Planning Perspectives* (July/August 1986), 151–62.

54 *(1986) a Lou Harris poll:* Lou Harris and Associates, "American Teens Speak: Sex, Myths, TV, and Birth Control: The Planned Parenthood Poll," 1986.

54 *The best that is claimed:* See, for example, Beth Frederick, "Columnist Twists Statistics to Blame Sex Education," *Washington Times,* June 5, 1992, F2.

PAGE

54 *"We find basically that"*: Douglas Kirby, speaking at the Sixteenth Annual Meeting of the National Family Planning and Reproductive Health Association, March 2, 1988, Washington, D.C. Cited in Jacqueline R. Kasun, "Sex Education: The Hidden Agenda," *The World & I* (September 1989), 497.

54 *Study by the Guttmacher Institute.* F. Sonenstein et al., "Sexual Activity, Condom Use and AIDS Awareness Among Adolescent Males," *Family Planning Perspectives* (July–August 1989), 152–58.

54 *In Virginia, for example:* Josh McDowell, *The Myths of Sex Education* (San Bernardino, Calif.: Here's Life Publishers, 1990), 126, 227–237.

54 *Dr. Jacqueline Kasun:* Ibid., 128.

55 • *In 1950 genital herpes: New England Journal of Medicine* (July 6, 1989). See also Marsha F. Goldsmith, " 'Silent Epidemic' of 'Social Disease' Makes STD Experts Raise Their Voices," *Journal of the American Medical Association* (June 23/30, 1989).

55 • Chlamydia trachomatis: "Safer Sex," *Newsweek* (December 9, 1991), 58; "The Dangers of Doing It," *Newsweek* (Special Edition, Summer/Fall, 1990), 56.

55 *1 million new cases of genital warts: Newsweek* (December 9, 1991), 59; *Newsweek* (Special Edition, Summer/Fall 1990), 56–57.

55 • *The risk of cervical cancer:* Kermit E. Krantz, Javier Magrina, C. V. Capen, "Sexual Risk Factors for Developing Cervical Cancer," *Medical Aspects of Human Sexuality* (November 1984); "Cervical Neoplasia Caused by Condyloma Virus," *Medical Aspects of Human Sexuality* (October 1985). Quote is from "Cervical Cancer Epidemic With Current Lifestyles," *Family Practice News* (August 1–14, 1984), 3.

55 • *The incidence of gonorrhea: Newsweek* (Special Edition, Summer/Fall 1990), 57.

55 • *The rate of syphillis infection:* Ellen Flax, "Explosive Data Confirm Prediction: AIDS Is Spreading Among Teenagers," *Education Week* (October 25, 1989), 1, 12.

55 • *Each year more babies:* Jean Seligmann, "A Nasty New Epidemic," *Newsweek* (February 4, 1985), 73. For a thorough survey of STD rates among teens see McDowell, *Myths of Sex Education,* 158–76.

56 *"The permissiveness of American society"*: Linus Wright, "Sex Education: How to Respond," *The World & I* (September 1989), 506.

56 *a demonstration video: AIDS and Adolescents: A Frank Discussion with Shoshona Rosenfeld, R.N.,* a videotape produced by the Massachusetts Department of Public Health, © Boston University, 1989.

59 *Lou Harris/Planned Parenthood Poll of late 1986:* Lou Harris and Associates, "American Teens Speak."

60 *a national survey by Zelnick and Kantner:* McDowell, *Myths of Sex Education,* 31.

PAGE

60   *"it is not unusual for normal teenagers"*: Douglas H. Powell, *Teenagers* (New York: Doubleday, 1987), 95.

60   *the rate of condom failure:* William Grady, Mark D. Hayward, and Junichi Yagi, "Contraceptive Failure in the United States: Estimates from the 1982 National Survey of Family Growth," *Family Planning Perspectives* (September/October 1986), 204–7. See also Melvin Zelnik, Michael A. Koenig, and Kim J. Young, "Sources of Prescription Contraceptives and Subsequent Pregnancy Among Young Women," *Family Planning Perspectives* (January/February 1984), 6–13.

60   *Extrapolated over time:* These figures were worked out for me by members of the Boston College Department of Research Methods. A higher figure of an 87 percent chance of pregnancy before finishing college is given by Robert Ruff, *Aborting Planned Parenthood* (Houston: New Vision Books, 1988).

60   *a Department of Education position paper:* Cited in McDowell, *Myths of Sex Education,* 61.

60   *A 1987 study of seventeen homosexual couples:* Ibid., 63.

60   *A 1985 study published in the British medical journal* Lancet: *The Lancet* (December 21–28, 1985), cited in Richard Bishirjian, "AIDS Education and the Tale of Two Cities," *The World & I* (September 1989), 560. In another study "About 30 percent of men reporting condom use in anal sex had experienced at least one instance of breakage in the previous six months": F. Pollner, "Experts Hedge on Condom Value," *Medical World News* (August 28, 1988), 60.

61   "To say that the use of condoms": Theresa Crenshaw, M.D., "Condom Advertising." Testimony before the House Subcommittee on Health and the Environment, February 10, 1987. Cited in McDowell, *Myths of Sex Education,* 63.

61   *"Many adolescents report"*: Wanda Franz, "Sex and the American Teenager," *The World & I* (September 1989), 475.

61   *"I was sitting at a table"*: Quoted in McDowell, *Myths of Sex Education,* 68.

61   *A study of gay men in 1987:* Ronald Valdiserri, O. D. Lyter, C. Callahan, L. Kingsley, and C. Rinaldo, "Condom Use in a Cohort of Gay and Bisexual Men." Third International Conference on AIDS, Washington, D.C., June 1–5, 1987. *Abstracts volume.*

62   *One of the latest "concepts"*: Debra Haffner, "Safe Sex and Teens," *SIECUS Report* (September/October 1988).

62   *"teaching teens about oral sex"*: Ibid., 9.

62   *a video about AIDS prevention: AIDS: Can I Get It?* Videotape produced by Michael Shane and Light Videotelevision, Inc., 1987.

63   *"How safe is sex"*: McDowell, *Myths of Sex Education,* 91.

PAGE

63 *a survey of over 400 college men and women:* Susan Cochran and
    Vickie Mays, "Correspondence," *New England Journal of Medicine*
    (March 15, 1990), 774. See also McDowell, *Myths of Sex Education,*
    91–93.

63 *"One can probably assume":* Quoted in Daniel Q. Haney, "Lies and
    Sex Make Dishonest Bedfellows," *San Diego Union* (March 15,
    1990), C4.

64 *"Our main aim in this section":* Ruth Bell et al., *Changing Bodies,
    Changing Lives,* 75.

64 *"if you are involved with someone else":* Ibid., 76.

64 *According to FBI statistics:* McDowell, *Myths of Sex Education,* 100.

64 *surveys of male college students:* Ibid., 102.

64 *A national study of 1,700 sixth- to ninth-grade students:* Reported
    by Jacqueline Jackson Kikuchi, staff member of the Rhode Island
    Rape Crisis Center, at the 1988 National Symposium on Child Victim-
    ization, Anaheim, California.

64 *"leaves young people with unclear boundaries":* McDowell, *Myths of
    Sex Education,* 100, 101.

65 *According to psychologist Mary Koss's:* "Date Rape," *Ms.* magazine
    (October 1985).

65 *A fairly standard practice in fifth and sixth-grade classrooms:*
    Masty, Testimony before the Michigan State Senate Subcommittee, 6.
    See also Kasun, "Sex Education: The Hidden Agenda," 489. See also
    Franz, "Sex and the American Teenager," 484.

65 *Other curriculums require:* Kasun, ibid. Example taken from Fern-
    dale Elementary School District and Ferndale Union High School
    District, *Family Life/Sex Education Curriculum Guide: Kindergar-
    ten–Twelfth Grade* (Ferndale, Calif.: July 1978), 285–86, 303.

66 *diaphragm as a puppet:* Franz, "Sex and the American Teenager,"
    484.

66 *In one eighth-grade class:* Testimony of Janet Brossard, concerning
    Bellevue, Washington, schools, given before the U.S. Department of
    Education, March 13, 1984, Seattle, Washington. In Phyllis Schlafly,
    ed., *Child Abuse in the Classroom: Excerpts from Official Transcript
    of Proceedings Before the U.S. Department of Education in the Mat-
    ter of Section 439 of the GEPA.* (Alton, Ill.: Père Marquette Press,
    1984), 44.

66 *"See, feel, smell":* Masty, Testimony before the Michigan State Sub-
    committee, 7.

66 • *At a suburban high school in Massachusetts:* This was personally
    related to me by the parents of a boy who was given the assignment.

66 *"safer-sex dance party":* "Safety Dance" developed by Planned Par-
    enthood of Tompkins County, Ithaca, N.Y., suggested as "home-

PAGE

work" by Vermont Department of Health, brochure, 1989. Richard P. Barth, *Enhancing Skills to Prevent Pregnancy* (Santa Cruz: ETR Associates, draft, 1988). In the same vein, *The Chattanooga News* (September 21, 1991), A7, carries a story about school officials defending a health care worker's suggestion to seventh graders to practice putting a condom on a banana.

66   • *Wardell Pomeroy's* Boys and Sex: Wardell Pomeroy, *Boys and Sex* (New York: Dell Publishing, 1981), 171–72.

66   *Pomeroy's book* Girls and Sex: Wardell Pomeroy, *Girls and Sex* (New York: Dell Publishing, 1981).

66   Changing Bodies, Changing Lives: Ruth Bell et al., 115, 126.

67   • *At a high school assembly in Cincinnati:* Mike Arata, "The Dangerous Trends in Sex Education," *The Blumenfeld Education Letter* (February 1988), 8.

67   *a filmstrip accompanying a multimedia program:* Deryck Calderwood, *About Your Sexuality,* a multimedia program produced by the Unitarian Universalist Association. Described in William E. Dannemeyer, "The New Sex Education: Homosexuality," *The World & I* (September 1989), 524–28.

67   *"it may take some time":* Quoted in Dannemeyer, ibid., 526.

67   *A brochure in use at the eighth-grade level:* Ibid., 536. A description of "an AIDS brochure circulated in Buffalo, New York, among eighth graders" and published by the Western New York AIDS Program. The 1972 Gay Rights Platform adopted by the National Coalition of Gay Organizations contains a plank calling for "Federal encouragement and support for sex education courses, prepared and taught by gay women and men, presenting homosexuality as a valid healthy preference and lifestyle as a viable alternative to heterosexuality."

67   *"Sex," as one Planned Parenthood pamphlet puts it:* Sheri Tepper, *The Perils of Puberty* (Denver: Rocky Mountain Planned Parenthood, 1974). Tepper is also the author of a pamphlet with the interesting title, *The Great Orgasm Robbery* (Denver: Rocky Mountain Planned Parenthood, 1977).

67   *"What's so special about sex?" Sex: A Topic for Conversation with Dr. Sol Gordon.* A videotape (Dallas: Mondell Productions, Inc., 1987).

69   *"dreaming of systems so perfect":* T. S. Eliot, *The Rock* (London: Faber & Faber, Ltd., 1934), 42.

69   *There is abundant evidence:* For example, see Harris and Associates, "American Teens Speak," 16.

69   *Harvard sociologist David Riesman says:* Quoted in John Sedgwick, "The Wrenching of America," *Boston* (December 1991), 105.

70   *a 1987 "Survey of High Achievers":* Cited in McDowell, *Myths of Sex Education,* 31.

PAGE

70 *In Japan:* Ibid., 30.

70 *"If an unfriendly foreign power":* Quoted in Chester E. Finn, Jr., "A Nation Still at Risk," *Commentary* (May 1989), 17.

70 *Adolescent Family Life Act:* Title XX of the Public Health Service Act, Section 2001 (a) (1) (A).

70 *To do something helpful:* Quoted in Nabers Cabaniss, "A Look at the Adolescent Family Life Act," *The World & I* (September 1989), 606.

71 *"If they want to have a future":* L. Douglas Wilder, "To Save the Black Family, the Young Must Abstain," *The Wall Street Journal* (March 28, 1991).

71 *Among the more successful are:* For descriptions and addresses of abstinence-based programs see Margaret Whitehead and Onalee McGraw, *Foundations for Family Life Education: A Guidebook for Professionals and Parents* (Arlington, Va.: Educational Guidance Institute, 1991), Appendix A. Contact Onalee McGraw, Director, Educational Guidance Institute, 927 South Walter Reed Drive, Suite 4, Arlington, Va. 22204; Tel. (703) 486-8313. See also Dinah Richard, "Exemplary Abstinence-Based Sex Education Programs," *The World & I,* (September 1989).

72 *In the shelter of a good marriage:* Coleen Kelly Mast, *Sex Respect: The Option of True Sexual Freedom* (Bradley, Ill.: Project Respect, 1986), 31.

72 *the San Marcos school district north of San Diego:* Richard, "Exemplary Abstinence-Based Sex Education Programs," 569–89. See also McDowell, *Myths of Sex Education,* 212. Another highly successful program is Postponing Sexual Involvement developed by Emory/Grady Teen Services Program, Atlanta, Georgia. See M. Howard and J. McCabe, "Helping Teenagers Postpone Sexual Involvement," *Family Planning Perspectives* 22:1 (1990), 21–26.

73 *A five year pilot study: Project Respect Performance Summary,* Final Report, Office of Adolescent Pregnancy Programs, #000816, Title XX, 1985–1990.

73 *"teens will be totally turned off":* Cited in Susan Newcomer, "Is It O.K. for PPFA to Say 'No Way'?" (Distributed by Planned Parenthood Federation of America, 810 7th Avenue, New York, N.Y. 10019), 4.

73 *The American Civil Liberties Union:* Cabaniss, "Adolescent Family Life Act," 610.

73 *The sharpest rise: Newsweek* (Special Edition, Summer/Fall 1990), 56.

74 *"to graft an abstinence message":* Nancy Pearcey, "Recovering Sanity: New Trends in Sex Education," *The Family in America* (July 1991), 7.

74 *"Although we adults feel":* Cited in ibid., 8.

75 *a group of parents in Wisconsin: National Review* (July 8, 1991), 12.

PAGE

76 *"I have never had a parent tell me":* Bennett, *Our Children and Our Country,* 96–97.

77 *rote learning, repetition, memorization:* These examples are drawn from the collection of articles on sex education in *The World & I* (September 1989), 466–612.

CHAPTER FOUR. HOW NOT TO TEACH MORALITY

78 *"It ought to be the oldest things":* G. K. Chesterton, *What's Wrong with the World?* (New York: Dodd Mead, 1910), 213.

80 Values and Teaching: L. Raths, M. Harmin, and S. Simon, *Values and Teaching* (Columbus, Ohio: Charles E. Merrill Publishing Company, 1966).

80 *"fostering the immorality":* Quoted in Barbara Morris, *Change Agents in the Schools* (Upland, Calif.: Barbara M. Morris Report, 1979), 144.

80 *"aware of* their own *feelings:* Simon et al., *Values Clarification.*

81 *"it is entirely possible":* Raths et al., *Values and Teaching,* 48.

81 *"Twenty Things You Love to Do"* Simon et al., *Values Clarification,* 30.

81 *"sex, drugs, drinking":* Lickona, *Educating for Character,* 237.

81 *"Everyone drinks":* Ibid.

81 *"Values Voting":* Simon et al., *Values Clarification,* 38–57.

82 *the research, which shows Values Clarification to be ineffectual:* See, for example, Alan Lockwood, "The Effect of Value-Clarification and Moral Development Curricula on School-Age Subjects: A Critical Review of Recent Research," *Review of Educational Research* 48 (1978), 325–64.

82 *Kohlberg was a serious scholar:* See Lawrence Kohlberg, *Essays on Moral Development,* vol. 1: *The Philosophy of Moral Development* (San Francisco: Harper & Row, 1978).

83 *Kohlberg felt that the Socratic dialogue:* Ibid.

83 *Kohlberg and his colleagues:* Blatt et al., *Hypothetical Dilemmas.*

83 *Sharon and Jill were best friends:* A condensation of a dilemma created by Dr. Frank Alessi, a member of the staff of the Carnegie-Mellon/Harvard Values Education Project. Cited in Barry K. Beyer, "Conducting Moral Discussions in the Classroom" in Peter Scharf, ed., *Readings in Moral Education* (Minneapolis, Minn.: Winston Press, 1978), 62–63.

84 *Suppose a ten-year-old boy:* A condensation of a dilemma in Blatt et al., *Hypothetical Dilemmas.*

85 *The Donner Party dilemma:* Ibid.

85 *a mother must choose:* Ibid.

PAGE

85 *a government bureaucrat who must decide:* Simon et al., *Values Clarification,* 281–86.

85 *"that almost everything in ethics":* Richard A. Baer, Jr., "Character Education and Public Schools: The Question of Context," *Content, Character and Choice in Schooling,* proceedings of a symposium sponsored by the National Council on Educational Research, Washington, D.C. (April 24, 1986), 81.

85 *"I often discuss cheating":* An example cited in Christina Hoff Sommers, "Ethics Without Virtue: Moral Education in America," *The American Scholar* (Summer 1984), 383.

86 *He [Kohlberg] expressed perplexity:* Edwin J. Delattre, "Ethics and Education in America," *Network News & Views* (February 1991), 19.

87 *"no one can really have a dilemma":* Ibid.

87 *"Not all of what constitutes":* Craig R. Dykstra, *Vision and Character* (New York: Paulist Press, 1981), 21.

87 *the "swapping" dilemma:* Blatt et al., *Hypothetical Dilemmas.*

87 *"This approach":* Delattre, "Ethics and Education," 19–20.

88 *"We should not":* Bennett, *Our Children and Our Country,* 84.

89 *Plato maintained that:* Plato, *The Republic,* trans. Allan Bloom (New York: Basic Books, 1968), Book VII, 216–17, 218.

90 *"when tolerance is the sole virtue":* Sommers, "Ethics Without Virtue," 386.

91 *Consequently, drawing an audience:* Camille Paglia and Neil Postman, "She Wants Her TV! He Wants His Book!" *Harper's* (March 1991), 55. See also, Neil Postman, *Amusing Ourselves to Death* (New York: Penguin Books, 1985).

91 *these student-citizens:* Sommers, "Ethics Without Virtue," 384.

92 *Some years of active involvement:* Lawrence Kohlberg, "Moral Education Reappraised," *The Humanist* (November/December 1978), 14–15.

92 *West Indians snub:* "A Just Corner of the Bronx," *Newsweek* (July 1, 1991), 59.

CHAPTER FIVE. A HISTORY LESSON

97 *"its underlying philosophy":* Personal communication from Professor Wynne.

97 *An example is John Dean:* D. Goldman, "Exclusive Interview with John Dean," *Comment,* Boston University School of Law (February 1979), 7.

98 *"Plato, Aristotle, and the whole throng":* Seneca, *Ad Lucilium Epistulae Morales,* vol. 1, trans. Richard M. Gummere (Cambridge, Mass.: Harvard University Press, 1934), 29 (emphasis not in original).

99 *The study of the humanities:* For a scholarly treatment of this thesis see Robert E. Proctor, *Education's Great Amnesia: Reconsidering the Humanities from Petrarch to Freud* (Bloomington: Indiana University Press, 1988).

100 *FBI statistics show startling increases:* For a thorough discussion of rising crime rates see Marvin Wolfgang and Paul E. Tracy, "The 1945 and 1958 Birth Cohorts: A Comparison of the Prevalence, Incidence, and Severity of Delinquent Behavior," paper presented to the Conference on Public Danger, Dangerous Offenders, and the Criminal Justice System, Kennedy School of Government, Harvard University, 1982; Dane Archer and Rosemary Gartner, *Violence and Crime in Cross-National Perspective* (New Haven: Yale University Press, 1984); James Q. Wilson and Richard J. Herrnstein, *Crime and Human Nature* (New York: Simon and Schuster, 1985); *Age-Specific Arrest Rates and Race-Specific Arrest Rates for Selected Offenses, 1965–1988* (Washington, D.C.: FBI, 1990).

100 *Compare what classroom teachers identified:* Source: Fullerton, California, Police Department. Based on interview data compiled for 1988 Conference of Educators and Law Enforcement Officers, San Francisco, Calif., sponsored by the California State Department of Education.

101 *"My God," he proclaims:* Gustave Flaubert, *Madame Bovary,* trans. Alan Russell (New York: Greenwich House, 1982), 90.

102 *Following Kant's lead, Kohlberg argued:* See Kohlberg, *Essays on Moral Development,* vol. 1.

103 *"a math problem with humans":* Carol Gilligan, *In a Different Voice,* (Cambridge, Mass.: Harvard University Press, 1982). The quotes are from page 28.

104 *Benjamin Franklin, for example, sported a beaver cap:* See Simon Schama, *Citizens* (New York: Alfred A. Knopf, 1989), 43.

104 *the voyages of Cook and de Bougainville:* John Chodes, "Mutiny in Paradise," *Chronicles* (February 1988), 11.

104 *"What could your miseries":* These statements of Rousseau are collected in J. H. Huizinga, *The Making of a Saint: The Tragi-Comedy of Jean-Jacques Rousseau* (London: Hamish Hamilton Publishers, 1976).

105 *"I am made unlike anyone":* Jean-Jacques Rousseau, *The Confessions,* Book One, trans. J. M. Cohen (Harmondsworth: Penguin Books, 1953), 17.

105 *"The basic nature of the human being":* Rogers, *Freedom to Learn,* 290.

107 *Previously in much of children's literature:* David Elkind, *The Hurried Child* (Reading, Mass.: Addison-Wesley Publishing Company, 1981), 85.

PAGE

108 *"When I was young":* Quoted in Michelle Landsberg, *Reading for the Love of It* (New York: Prentice Hall Press, 1987), 205.

108 *no "enlargements of the self":* Ibid, 207.

108 *"Saint Rousseau":* Quoted in Paul Johnson, *Intellectuals* (New York: Harper & Row, 1988), 27.

109 *Betsy was thirteen:* Quoted in Marie Winn, *Children Without Childhood* (New York: Pantheon, 1983), 30.

109 *There we were, put in the role:* Ibid., 32–33.

109 *Finally we all went:* Ibid., 33

CHAPTER SIX. MORAL ILLITERACY

113 *The trouble with character education:* See Lawrence Kohlberg and Rochelle Mayer, "Development as the Aim of Education," *Harvard Educational Review* 42 (1972), 449–96; see also Kohlberg, "Moral Education in the Schools: A Developmental View," *The School Review* (Chicago. The University of Chicago Press, 1966).

113 *an extensive study of individuals who rescued Jews:* Samuel P. Oliner and Pearl M. Oliner, *The Altruistic Personality: Rescuers of Jews in Nazi Europe* (New York: The Free Press, 1988), 221.

113 *not "moral heroes, arriving at their own conclusions":* Ibid., 257.

113 *"what most distinguished them":* Ibid., 259.

114 *I cannot give:* Ibid., 216.

114 *They taught me:* Ibid., 220.

114 *When you see a need:* Ibid., 169.

114 *The basic morality:* Ibid., 204.

114 *My father taught me:* Ibid., 166.

114 *At my grandfather's place:* Ibid., 208.

114 *"Asked how long it took":* Ibid., 169.

115 *he was steeped in Bible stories:* See Lewis V. Baldwin, *There Is a Balm in Gilead: The Cultural Roots of Martin Luther King, Jr.* (Minneapolis, Minn.: Fortress Press, 1991); see also Bennett, "Martin Luther King and the Liberal Arts" in *Our Children and Our Country,* 117–25.

115 *"Morally autonomous people":* Constance Kamii and Mieko Kamii, "Why Achievement Testing Should Stop," in Constance Kamii, ed., *Achievement Testing in the Early Grades: The Games Grownups Play* (Washington, D.C.: National Association for Education of Young Children, 1990), 22.

115 *"There is no such thing":* Mortimer J. Adler, "Why 'Critical Thinking' Programs Won't Work" in James Wm. Noll, ed., *Taking Sides* (Guilford, Conn.: The Dushkin Publishing Group, Inc., 1989), 216.

116 *a 1989 survey of* college seniors: A Survey of College Seniors:

Knowledge of History and Literature conducted by the Gallup Organization for the National Endowment for the Humanities, Washington, D.C., 1989, 33–56; see also Diane Ravitch and Chester E. Finn, Jr., *What Do Our Seventeen-Year-Olds Know?* (New York: Harper & Row, 1987); see also Benjamin J. Stein," The Cheerful Ignorance of the Young in L.A.," *Washington Post,* (October 3, 1983). The case of the students who couldn't find the United States on the world map is cited in Solveig Eggerz, "Permanence and the History Curriculum" in Joseph Baldacchino, ed., *Educating for Virtue* (Washington, D.C.: National Humanities Institute, 1988), 94.

117 *Communities and cultures depend:* E. D. Hirsch, Jr., *Cultural Literacy* (New York: Vintage Books, 1988).

119 *"prizing and cherishing":* Simon et al., *Values Clarification,* 19.

120 *two university students:* Charles J. Sykes, *The Hollow Men* (Washington, D.C.: Regnery Gateway, 1990), 14.

120 *In 1985 Professor Paul Vitz:* Paul C. Vitz, *Censorship: Evidence of Bias in Our Children's Textbooks* (Ann Arbor: Servant Books, 1986).

120 *"there are no stories that":* Ibid., 72.

120 *None of the social studies books:* Ibid., 2.

120 *story by Isaac Bashevis Singer:* Ibid., 3–4.

121 *"college students rarely confess":* Lickona, *Educating for Character,* 393.

121 *About ten years ago:* Ibid., 34.

122 *Robert Coles shows:* Robert Coles, *The Moral Life of Children* (Boston: The Atlantic Monthly Press, 1986).

123 *For one group of multiculturalists:* For a thorough discussion of the two approaches to multiculturalism see Diane Ravitch, "Multiculturalism," *The American Scholar* (Summer 1990), 337–54.

123 *Stanford University in 1988:* See Sykes, *Hollow Men,* 60–67, for a discussion of the Stanford University affair.

124 *"if separatist tendencies go unchecked":* Arthur M. Schlesinger, Jr., "The Cult of Ethnicity, Good and Bad," *Time* (July 8, 1991), 21.

124 *D'Souza makes a convincing case:* Dinesh D'Souza, *Illiberal Education* (New York: The Free Press, 1991).

124 *fall of the Berlin Wall:* Ravitch, "Multiculturalism," 349.

124 *A substitute teacher in a Virginia suburb:* Cited in Dobson and Bauer, *Children at Risk,* 180.

125 *"are consistently portrayed as plausible":* Dr. Donald Oppewal, "Religion in American Textbooks: A Review of the Literature." Part of Final Report: NIE-G-84-0012; Project No. 2-0099. Included in Vitz, *Censorship,* Appendix A, 120.

125 *A task force on minority education:* Cited in Don Feder, "History

PAGE

Failing to Repeat Itself," *Boston Sunday Herald* (March 18, 1990), 31.

125   *exponents of "Afrocentric" education:* "The Afrocentric Idea," *Social Studies Review: A Bulletin of the American Textbook Council* (Winter, 1991), 3–6; see also Midge Decter, "E Pluribus Nihil: Multiculturalism and Black Children," *Commentary* (September 1991), 25–29.

125   *According to Professor Peggy Means McIntosh:* Robert Costrell, "The Mother of All Curriculums," *Brookline (Mass.) Citizen* (March 15, 1991), 7.

126   *according to another educator:* Derald Wing Sue, "The Challenge of Multiculturalism," *American Counselor* (Winter 1992), 6–14.

126   *"the support of explorations":* Cited in Robert C. Serow, *Schooling for Social Diversity* (New York: Teachers College Press, 1983), 95.

126   *"skills for values clarification":* Cited in *The Blumenfeld Education Letter* (October 1991), 1.

126   *"it is wrong to assume":* Alba A. Rosenman, "The Value of Multicultural Curricula" in Noll, ed., *Taking Sides,* 40, 42.

126   *"tolerance for diversity":* Serow, *Schooling for Social Diversity.*

126   *"holistic processes," "many realities":* These two phrases are contained in *African American Baseline Essays* cited in *Social Studies Review* (Winter 1991), 5.

126   *"multiple perspectives":* This phrase appears in "A Curriculum of Inclusion," a task force report to the New York State Commissioner of Education, 1989. Cited in Decter, "E Pluribus Nihil," 28.

126   *the danger of "imposing values":* Sue, "Challenge of Multiculturalism," 11.

126   *"We are the creative cause":* Quoted in Andrew Sullivan, "Racism 101," *The New Republic* (November 26, 1990), 20.

127   *This Atlanta-based conference:* Ibid., 20–21.

127   *"radically changing the curriculums":* Robert Hughes, "The Fraying of America," *Time* (February 3, 1992), 48.

127   *The reporter who covered it:* Sullivan, "Racism 101," 20, 21.

128   *"The crimes of the West":* Arthur M. Schlesinger, Jr., *The Disuniting of America* (Knoxville, Tenn.: Whittle Books, 1991), 76.

128   *"Paradoxical though it may seem":* Ravitch, "Multiculturalism," 339.

CHAPTER SEVEN. VISION AND VIRTUE

PAGE

129 *Do we want our children to know:* Bennett, *Our Children and Our Country,* 82, 83–84.

130 *"Bennett's aversion to conscious moral decision making":* William Damon, *The Moral Child* (New York: The Free Press, 1988), 145.

130 *Socrates sometimes talked as if:* Derek C. Bok, "The Death and Rebirth of Morality," Terry Sanford Lectures, Duke University, April 1988. Published in Derek Bok, *Universities and the Future of America* (Durham: Duke University Press, 1990), 76–77.

132 *Who really cares about Heinz:* This is the dilemma mentioned in the first chapter; it concerns a man who steals a cancer-treatment drug for his wife.

132 *"A story is a way to say something":* Flannery O'Connor, *Mystery and Manners* (New York: Farrar, Straus, Giroux, 1981), 96.

133 *"That is to say, inasmuch as you":* Quoted in Harry V. Jaffa, "Of Men, Hogs, and Law," *National Review* (February 3, 1992), 40.

135 *most notably, Alasdair MacIntyre:* Alasdair MacIntyre, *After Virtue* (Notre Dame, Ind.: University of Notre Dame Press, 1981), Chapter Fifteen.

136 *Bruno Bettelheim argued that fairy tales:* Bruno Bettelheim, *The Uses of Enchantment* (New York: Vintage Books, 1977).

136 *the indispensable role of stories:* Robert Coles, *Moral Life of Children; The Spiritual Life of Children* (Boston: Houghton Mifflin, 1990); *The Call of Stories* (Boston: Houghton Mifflin, 1989).

136 *this narrative thought:* Jerome Bruner, *Actual Minds, Possible Worlds* (Cambridge, Mass.: Harvard University Press, 1986).

136 *A number of other psychologists:* For an excellent summary of the literature in this area see Paul Vitz, "The Uses of Stories in Moral Development: New Psychological Reasons for an Old Education Method," *American Psychologist* (June 1990), 709–20.

136 *"Indeed," writes Vitz:* Ibid., 711.

136 *"the children he came to know":* Coles, *Moral Life of Children.*

136 *the foundation of all education:* Kieran Egan, *Teaching as Storytelling* (Chicago: University of Chicago Press, 1986), 2.

137 *"Most of the world's cultures":* Kieran Egan, *Primary Understanding* (New York: Routledge, 1988), 66.

137 *"The Lifeboat Exercise":* Maury Smith, *A Practical Guide to Values Clarification* (San Diego, Calif.: University Associates, 1977), 120–121.

138 "A Night to Remember": *A Night to Remember* (London: The Rank Organization Film Productions, Ltd., 1958).

PAGE

140 *"If all the [white] people"*: Coles, *Moral Life of Children*, 65.
140 *"All my seven Narnian books"*: C. S. Lewis, *Of Other Worlds: Essays and Stories*, ed. Walter Hooper (New York: A Harvest/HBJ Book, 1975), 42.
141 *"tangibly right"*: Bettelheim, *Uses of Enchantment*, 5.
142 *"At the core of every moral code"*: Walter Lippmann, *Public Opinion* (New York: The Free Press, 1965), 80.
142 *"a single image breaks"*: William Barrett, *The Truants* (New York: Anchor Press/Doubleday, 1982), 174.
142 *"My dear children"*: Fyodor Dostoevsky, *The Brothers Karamazov*, trans. Constance Garnett (New York: The Heritage Press, 1961), 602.

CHAPTER EIGHT. MORALITY MAKES STRANGE BEDFELLOWS

145 *"to bring a new order"*: Carol Gilligan, "Joining the Resistance: Psychology, Politics, Girls and Women," *Michigan Quarterly Review* (Fall 1990), 533.
145 *Professor Gilligan built her theory*: See Gilligan, *In a Different Voice*.
146 *"that repository of experience"*: Gilligan, "Joining the Resistance," 523.
146 *"may also discover"*: Ibid., 531. The slightly different wording that I quote appears in a condensed version of the article in *Harvard Graduate School of Education Alumni Bulletin* (Fall 1991), 4.
146 *"the temptation to model perfection"*: Gilligan, "Joining the Resistance," 531.
146 *"The mesmerizing presence"*: Ibid., 522.
146 *"disconnecting themselves"*: Ibid., 523.
146 *"desire or passion"*: Ibid., 524.
146 *"know what they know"*: Ibid., 529. See also Gilligan, *Alumni Bulletin*, 4.
147 *"intersection between political resistance"*: Gilligan, "Joining the Resistance," 529.
147 *the word "resistance"*: Gilligan, *Alumni Bulletin*, 3–4.
147 *A recent book*: Mary M. Brabeck, ed., *Who Cares? Theory, Research, and Educational Implications of the Ethic of Care* (New York: Praeger, 1989).
148 *a place for raising consciousness*: For examples of feminist consciousness-raising on the campus see Sykes, *Hollow Men*, 36–45. See also D'Souza, *Illiberal Education*, 194–228.

148 *After spending two years:* Rita Kramer, *Ed School Follies* (New York: The Free Press, 1991).

148 *a widely publicized report: How Schools Shortchange Girls: A Study of Major Findings on Girls and Education* (Washington, D.C.: A joint publication of the American Association of University Women Educational Foundation and National Education Association, 1992), 66, 82.

148 *The report calls for stricter reinforcement:* Ibid., 84–85.

148 *"full of "musts":* Ibid., 85, 86, 88.

149 *"the assumption of heterosexuality":* Ibid., 40, 80.

149 *"Western culture":* Ibid., 38.

150 *"where girls and boys":* Ibid., 80.

150 *"conventional conceptions of":* Carol Gilligan, Janie Victoria Ward, and Jill McLean Taylor, eds., *Mapping the Moral Domain* (Cambridge, Mass.: Center for the Study of Gender, Education and Human Development, Harvard University Graduate School of Education, 1988), from the preface by Gilligan, iv.

151 *"Put it down in capital letters":* Gilligan, *In a Different Voice,* 129.

151 The Rise of Selfishness: James Lincoln Collier, *The Rise of Selfishness in America* (New York: Oxford University Press, 1991).

151 *"It was only in the nineteenth century":* Nona Lyons, "Two Perspectives: On Self, Relationships, and Morality" in Gilligan et al., *Mapping the Moral Domain,* 44, n. 5.

151 *Gilligan suggests that a proper orientation:* Gilligan et al., *Mapping the Moral Domain,* iii.

151 *"the persistent error":* Carol Gilligan and Grant Wiggins, "The Origins of Morality in Early Childhood Relationships" in ibid., 134.

152 *"If I cannot act":* Gilligan, *In a Different Voice,* 131.

152 *"care can be 'principled' ":* Gilligan and Wiggins, "Origins of Morality," 129.

153 *explaining Gilligan's concept of "voices":* Bell et al., *Changing Bodies, Changing Lives,* 90–93.

153 *the idea is "generally fatal":* Christina Hoff Sommers, "Philosophers Against the Family" in Hugh LaFollette and George Graham, eds., *Person to Person* (Philadelphia: Temple University Press, 1989), 96.

153 *According to Sommers:* Ibid., 82–105.

153 *"Relativism is a good thing":* Kramer, *Ed School Follies,* 29.

155 *"Much of Nietzsche's writing":* Terry Eagleton, *The Ideology of the Aesthetic* (Oxford: Basil Blackwell, 1990), 244.

155 *"What is good?"* Friedrich Nietzsche, *The Antichrist,* Book II, trans. R. J. Hollingdale (Penguin Classics, 1968).

155 *"I fear I am the one":* A letter to Franz Overbeck quoted in Thomas

Molnar, *God and the Knowledge of Reality* (New York: Basic Books, 1973), 181.

156 *Sartre was once asked:* Cited in Will Herberg, "What Is the Moral Crisis of Our Time?" *The Intercollegiate Review* (Fall 1986), 12.

156 *"No woman should be authorized":* "Sex, Society and the Female Dilemma: A Dialogue Between Simone de Beauvoir and Betty Friedan," *Saturday Review* (June 14, 1975), 18.

157 *Hitler's ideas about life and politics:* For an informative discussion of this topic see Modris Eksteins, *Rites of Spring: The Great War and the Birth of the Modern Age* (New York: Anchor Books, 1990), 300–31.

157 *Others go further:* Bill Puka, "The Liberation of Caring: A Different Voice for Gilligan's 'Different Voice,' " in Brabeck, ed., *Who Cares?*, 26.

158 *"Standards and role obligations":* Lyn Mikel Brown, "When Is a Moral Problem Not a Moral Problem?" in Carol Gilligan, Nona P. Lyons, and Trudy J. Hanmer, eds., *Making Connections: The Relational Worlds of Adolescent Girls at Emma Willard School* (Troy, N.Y.: Emma Willard School, 1989), 107.

160 *"In the early 1800s":* Norman H. Clark quoted in Collier, *Rise of Selfishness,* 5.

160 *Average alcohol consumption:* For a more detailed description of the social climate of this era see Collier, ibid., 3–7. See also James Q. Wilson, "Incivility and Crime," *The World & I* (March 1992), 541, 547.

160 *In the 1830s and 1840s a reaction set in:* Collier, ibid., 8–18; Wilson, ibid., 547–49.

161 *Victorianism was a revolution:* Collier, ibid., 9–10.

161 *organizations that were dedicated to improving:* For an informative discussion of this topic see Joel Schwartz, "The Moral Environment of the Poor," *The Public Interest* (Spring 1991), 21–37.

162 *Rather than banish the Chinaman:* Quoted in Schwartz, ibid., 25.

163 *"The classroom is":* Neil Postman, *Teaching as a Conserving Activity* (New York: Delacorte Press, 1979), 202, 204, 209.

163 *"a recovery of anger":* Gilligan, "Joining the Resistance," 527.

CHAPTER NINE. BEAUTY AND THE BEASTS

165 *"It is only as an* aesthetic phenomenon": Friedrich Nietzsche, *The Birth of Tragedy* in Walter Kaufmann, trans. and ed., *Basic Writings of Nietzsche* (New York: The Modern Library, 1968), 52.

166 *"The enthusiasm was kindled":* Eksteins, *Rites of Spring,* 323, 313.

166   Triumph of the Will: After the war the film was banned in this country and in Europe for a period of twenty years.

166   *Hitler's deranged attempt:* The connection between the genocidal policies of the Nazis and Hitler's aesthetics is detailed in a recent German documentary film, *The Architecture of Doom,* produced, directed and written by Peter Cohen.

167   *Yves Montand:* Richard Grenier, *Capturing the Culture; Film, Art, and Politics* (Washington, D.C.: Ethics and Public Policy Center, 1991), 196.

167   *"The question for a child":* Bettelheim, *The Uses of Enchantment,* 10.

167   *A good education, says Ryn:* Claes G. Ryn, "The Humanities and Moral Reality" in Baldacchino, ed., *Educating for Virtue,* p. 27, 28, 29, 30. See also Claes G. Ryn, *Will, Imagination and Reason* (Chicago: Regnery Books, 1986).

168   *"When we read":* John Gardner, *The Art of Fiction* (New York: Vintage Books, 1985), 63.

169   *When fiction works for us:* Wayne Booth, *The Company We Keep* (Berkeley: University of California Press, 1988), 202, 204, 223.

169   *An informative book:* Jack Katz, *Seductions of Crime; Moral and Sensual Attractions in Doing Evil* (New York: Basic Books, 1988).

169   *"Esthetic leadership appears to be":* Ibid., 151.

CHAPTER TEN. MUSIC AND MORALITY

173   *"Education in such cultures":* Kieran Egan, "The Origins of Imagination and the Curriculum" in Kieran Egan and Dan Nadaner, eds., *Imagination and Education* (New York: Teachers College Press, 1988), 98.

173   *music should be at the center:* Allan Bloom, *The Closing of the American Mind* (New York: Simon and Schuster, 1987), 68–81.

173   *"since it's considered to be":* Plato, *Republic* IV, 424d.

174   *"illiberality," "insolence":* Republic III, 400b.

174   *"orderly and courageous life":* Republic III, 400a.

174   *"he would have the sharpest sense":* Republic III, 401e.

174   *children ought to be brought up:* Republic III, 401e, 402a.

174   *"erotic attachment" to virtue:* Plato, *Laws,* trans. A. E. Taylor in *Collected Dialogues of Plato,* Edith Hamilton and Huntington Cairns, eds. (Princeton, N.J.: Princeton University Press, 1961), 1243.

174   *statues that graced the cities of Greece:* Bloom, *Closing of the American Mind,* 80.

PAGE

175 *"a common highway":* Allan Bloom, "Too Much Tolerance" in Robert L. Stone, ed., *Essays on* The Closing of the American Mind (Chicago: Chicago Review Press, 1989), 240.

175 *"rock has the beat":* Bloom, *Closing of the American Mind,* 73.

175 *"nasty, reactionary attack":* William Greider, "Bloom and Doom" in Stone, ed., *Essays,* 245.

175 *"is, in fact, much closer":* Steven Crockett, "Blam! Bam! Bloom! Boom !" in Stone, ed., *Essays,* 255.

175 *"That kind of critique":* Bloom, "Too Much Tolerance" in Stone, ed., *Essays,* 239.

176 *"avoid noticing what the words say":* Bloom, *Closing of the American Mind,* 76.

176 *"The issue here":* Ibid., 79.

176 *"It is only through the spirit of music":* Nietzsche, *Birth of Tragedy* in Kaufmann, trans. and ed., *Basic Writings of Nietzsche,* 104.

177 *"indestructibly powerful":* Ibid., 59.

177 The Triumph of Vulgarity: Robert Pattison, *The Triumph of Vulgarity: Rock Music in the Mirror of Romanticism* (New York: Oxford University Press, 1987).

177 *"the rocker feels":* Stuart Goldman, "That Old Devil Music," *National Review* (February 24, 1989), 30.

178 *"The Live Aid concert":* John Leland, "Welcome to the Jungle," *Newsweek* (September 23, 1991), 53.

179 *"So what about":* NWA, "Straight Outta Compton," Priority Records, 1988.

179 *"unabashed espousal of violence":* Quoted in *Boston Herald* (November 19, 1991), 13.

179 *"laugh at honor":* C. S. Lewis, *The Abolition of Man* (New York: Macmillan, 1955), 35.

180 the *"best discs" of 1991:* "Music Writers Choose Best Discs of the Year," *The Heights* (Independent Student Weekly of Boston College, December 9, 1991), 24–25.

180 *"The anger is what helps you relate":* Quoted in Tipper Gore, *Raising PG Kids in an X-Rated Society* (Nashville: Abingdon Press, 1987), 53.

180 *"music to kill":* Quote ascribed to radio consultant Lee Abrams in Gore, *Raising PG Kids,* 57.

180 *"It's all attitude":* Ron Powers, "The Cool Dark Telegenius of Robert Pittman," *The Beast, the Eunuch and the Glass-Eyed Child* (San Diego: Harcourt Brace Jovanovich, 1990), 24.

181 *"I'll either break her face":* Mötley Crüe, "Live Wire," *Too Fast for Love,* Elektra/Asylum EI-G0174. Written by N. Sixx. Published by Warner-Tamerlane Publishing Corp./Mötley Crüe Publishing.

PAGE

181   *"Gonna drive my love":* Great White, "On Your Knees," *Great White,* EMI America ST 17111. Written by Kendall, Russell, Holland, Black, Dokken. Lyrics copyright © 1984 Great White.

181   *the cover of the W.A.S.P. single:* Gore, *Raising PG Kids,* 52.

181   *a report of the American Medical Association:* Cited in Dobson and Bauer, *Children at Risk,* 213.

181   *more definitive studies:* Edward Donnerstein, "The Effects of Exposure to Violent Pornographic Mass Media Images," *Engage/Social Action* (July/August 1985), 16–19.

181   *two recent studies conducted in the Northeast:* M. A. J. McKenna, "One-third of Teen Girlfriends May Be Abused," *Boston Sunday Herald* (September 8, 1991), 1, 8–9.

182   *"Some dreamers have hoped":* Pattison, *Triumph of Vulgarity,* 137.

183   *"has all the moral dignity of drug trafficking":* Bloom, *Closing of the American Mind,* 76.

183   *"It may well be":* Ibid., 75.

183   *"You know what I say?":* Quoted in Gore, *Raising PG Kids,* 86.

185   *Such harmony is in immortal souls:* William Shakespeare, *The Merchant of Venice,* Act V, sc. 1.

185   *. . . disproportion'd sin:* John Milton, "At a Solemn Musick," *The Poetical Works of John Milton,* vol II, Helen Darbishire, ed. (Oxford: Clarendon Press, 1955), 133.

185   *"some philosophers say":* Aristotle, *Politica,* trans. Benjamin Jowett in *The Works of Aristotle,* vol. x, W. D. Ross, ed. (Oxford: Clarendon Press, 1952), 1340b, 19–20.

186   *"the melodies* sounded important": Thomas Day, *Why Catholics Can't Sing* (New York: Crossroad, 1990), 86.

186   *The rocker lives his music:* Pattison, *Triumph of Vulgarity,* 183–84.

187   *"You can't be a teenager forever":* From an NBC television interview.

187   *"I said, 'There is no beginning' ":* Quoted in Powers, "Cool Dark Telegenius," 24.

187   *"This is a non-narrative generation":* Ibid., 25.

188   *"the most honest form":* Pattison, *Triumph of Vulgarity,* 182.

188   *"musical training is":* Plato, *Republic* III, 401b.

CHAPTER ELEVEN. LIFE IS A STORY

190   *"Whether I shall":* Charles Dickens, *David Copperfield* (Garden City, N.Y.: The Literary Guild, 1948), 1.

191   *"Does this have a plot?":* Fernando Savater, *Childhood Regained: The Art of the Storyteller* (New York: Columbia University Press, 1982), 3.

PAGE

192   *Our greatest need, says Frankl:* Viktor E. Frankl, *Psychotherapy and Existentialism* (New York: Washington Square Press, 1967).

192   *"to restore meaning":* Bettelheim, *Uses of Enchantment,* 4.

192   *"a struggle against severe difficulties":* Ibid., 8.

193   *"To find deeper meaning:* Ibid., 3–4.

193   *"My first and last philosophy":* G. K. Chesterton, *Orthodoxy* (New York: Image Books, 1990), 49.

193   *"I had always felt life":* Ibid., 61.

193   *Like many another adult:* Landsberg, *Reading for the Love of It,* 22–23.

194   *"endless numbers of characters":* Paul Zweig, *The Adventurer* (Princeton: Princeton University Press, 1981), 84.

195   *"She told me":* Lance Morrow, "The Best Refuge for Insomniacs," *Time* (April 29, 1991), 82.

196   *"If stories weren't told":* Isaac Bashevis Singer, *Stories for Children* (New York: Farrar, Straus, Giroux, 1990), 173 (from "Naftali the Storyteller and His Horse, Sus").

196   *But what about the other kind:* Lynne Cheney, "The Importance of Stories," *Academic Questions* (Spring 1991), 8–9.

199   *a distinction between hero and adventurer:* For a scholarly discussion of the distinction between "hero" and "adventurer" see Zweig, *Adventurer,* 34–47.

199   *half the adventure consists in telling:* Zweig also provides a good treatment of the relation between adventure and storytelling. Ibid., 81–96.

204   *"the best part of an adventure tale":* Fernando Savater, *Childhood Regained,* 8.

205   *"roles into which we have been drafted":* MacIntyre, *After Virtue,* 201. MacIntyre provides an excellent scholarly treatment of the relationship between morality and narrative. See especially pages 190–209.

CHAPTER TWELVE. MYTH WARS

206   *A number of books:* Jean Shinoda Bolen, *Goddesses in Everywoman* (New York: Harper Colophon Books, 1984); Stanley Krippner and David Feinstein, *Personal Mythology* (Los Angeles: J. P. Tarcher, Inc., 1988).

207   *in some elementary schools:* Joy Hakim, "Classics Are for Kids," *American Educator* (Spring 1990), 35–40.

208   *The first term is discussed:* Irving Babbitt, *Rousseau and Romanticism* (Boston: Houghton Mifflin, 1919).

PAGE

208   *the second term originates with:* Edmund Burke, *Reflections on the Revolution in France* in Russell Kirk, ed., *The Portable Conservative Reader* (New York: Penguin Books, 1982), 22.

208   *When the idyllic imagination:* See Babbitt, *Rousseau and Romanticism,* 114–86.

208   *I love to dream:* Ibid., 75.

209   *to describe the frame of mind:* Russell Kirk, *Eliot and His Age* (LaSalle Ill.: Sherwood Sugden & Company, 1984).

209   *"Christian romantics":* Kathryn Lindskoog, *The Lion of Judah in Never-Never Land* (Grand Rapids, Mich.: William B. Eerdmans Publishing Company, 1973), 21.

210   *"Apollo cannot always be bending":* Babbitt, *Rousseau and Romanticism,* 209.

210   *"There is no such thing":* Ibid., 217.

210   *"terminates in disillusion":* Russell Kirk, "The Perversity of Recent Fiction: Reflections on the Moral Imagination" in *Reclaiming a Patrimony: A Collection of Lectures by Russell Kirk* (Washington, D.C.: The Heritage Foundation, 1982), 47.

210   *"began by asserting the goodness":* Babbitt, *Rousseau and Romanticism,* 307.

210   *suggest that the idyllic imagination:* Kirk, "Perversity of Recent Fiction," 47–48.

210   *"the Satanic School":* Quoted in Babbitt, *Rousseau and Romanticism,* 319.

211   *"If you're going to San Francisco":* Scott McKenzie, "San Francisco," *The Voice of Scott McKenzie,* ODE Z12 4401. Written by John Phillips.

211   *"Imagine there's no countries":* John Lennon, "Imagine," *Shaved Fish* (New York: Apple Records, Inc., 1975) copyright 1971 Maclen Music, Inc./EMI.

212   *"out of date":* Quoted in Andrew Ferguson, "The Power of Myth," *The New Republic* (August 19 & 26, 1991), 24.

212   *"follow your bliss":* Joseph Campbell, *The Power of Myth* (New York: Doubleday, 1988), 117–21.

213   *drew his inspiration for Luke Skywalker:* Owen Jones, "Joseph Campbell and *The Power of Myth,"* *The Intercollegiate Review* (Fall 1989), 21.

213   *Paul Vitz's content analysis:* Vitz, *Censorship,* 65–70, 75.

214   *"of the Aquarian Conspirators surveyed":* Marilyn Ferguson, *The Aquarian Conspiracy* (Los Angeles: J. P. Tarcher, Inc., 1980), 280.

214   *"its members have broken":* Ibid., 23.

214   *"extraordinary reaches of conscious experience":* Ibid., 31.

PAGE

214   *"revolt against imposed patterns"*: Ibid., 55.

214   *"awesome capacities"*: Ibid., 41.

214   *"the mystical experience"*: Ibid., 380.

214   *"self-transcendence"*: Ibid., 62.

214   *"God-within"*: Ibid., 382.

214   *"Together," says Ferguson*: Ibid., 406.

215   *"new paradigm"*: Ibid., 289.

215   *Canfield and co-author Paula Klimek recommend*: Jack Canfield and Paula Klimek, "Education in the New Age," *New Age* (February 1978), 27–39.

215   *When you get to the top*: Jack Canfield, "The Inner Classroom: Teaching with Guided Imagery" in Anastas Harris, ed., *Holistic Education: Education for Living* (Del Mar, Calif.: The Holistic Education Network, 1981), 38–39.

216   *Canfield describes one girl*: Ibid., 39.

216   *"To me," writes Canfield*: Ibid., 38.

216   *"Experience the good"*: Ibid.

217   *"These children of the New Age"*: Canfield and Klimek, "Education in the New Age," 39.

217   *"his now famous children's story"*: Ibid., 33.

217   *the four most frequently mentioned*: Ferguson, *Aquarian Conspiracy*, 420.

217   *"a bridge between"*: Carl R. Rogers, *A Way of Being* (Boston: Houghton Mifflin, 1980), 41.

217   *Canfield now seems to serve*: Richard Beswick, "Education in the New Age" copyright © 1991 by Richard Beswick, Ph.D., 6.

217   *"I now consider it possible"*: Rogers, *Way of Being*, 92.

218   *it is essentially at an opposite pole*: Babbitt, *Rousseau and Romanticism*, 149–50.

218   *New Age themes are beginning to show up in reading series*: For example, Harcourt Brace Jovanovich markets a kindergarten through sixth-grade reading series entitled Impressions in thirty-four states and in Canada. Impressions mixes children's classics with occult and New Age stories. The accompanying curriculum calls upon children to sit in circles and chant and to create and cast spells. Several of the stories in Impressions are examples of what T. S. Eliot refers to as the "diabolic imagination."

219   *This, according to Canfield*: Canfield and Klimek, "Education in the New Age," 33.

220   *"I continue to be amazed"*: William J. Bennett, "Drugs and the Face of Evil," *First Things* (December 1990), 5–6.

221   *"If one doesn't believe"*: Ibid., 6.

222   *"If the school"*: Postman, *Teaching as a Conserving Activity*, 115.

222 *"unlike the problems of earlier generations":* Bennett, "Drugs and the Face of Evil," 6.

223 *The approach of the commission:* Ibid.

CHAPTER THIRTEEN. WHAT SCHOOLS CAN DO

227 *since the mid-fifties school budgets:* James Q. Wilson, "Reforming the Schools," *Commentary* (December 1991), 60: "In real (that is, inflation-adjusted) dollars, per-pupil spending on public education has tripled since the mid-1950s and doubled since the mid-1960s. It rose by nearly 30 percent in the 1980s alone . . . At the same time the number of pupils in the classroom has gone down. Between 1961 and 1986, median classroom size fell in the elementary schools from 30 to 24 and in secondary schools from 27 to 22."

227 *"a spirit of devotion":* The American Heritage Dictionary of the English Language (Boston: Houghton Mifflin, 1979).

227 *universities are far more segregated:* D'Souza, *Illiberal Education.*

229 *study conducted by sociologist James Coleman:* James S. Coleman, Thomas Hoffer, and Sally Kilgore, *High School Achievement* (New York: Basic Books, 1982).

229 Reclaiming Our Schools: Edward Wynne and Kevin Ryan, *Reclaiming Our Schools: A Handbook on Teaching Character, Academics and Discipline* (Columbus Ohio: Merrill Books, in press).

232 *successful drug rehabilitation programs:* Straight, a drug rehabilitation program with a high rate of success, employs group singing.

234 *boys* are *inherently—biologically:* One of the most comprehensive discussions of the biological differences is Steven Goldberg's *The Inevitability of Patriarchy* (New York: William Morrow, 1973).

234 *Initiation rites:* See Mircea Eliade, *Rites and Symbols of Initiation* (New York: Harper Torchbooks, 1958); see also Colin Turnbull, *The Human Cycle* (New York: Simon and Schuster, 1983); and Margaret Mead, *Male and Female: A Study of the Sexes in a Changing World* (New York: Dell, 1968).

235 *"The worry that boys":* Mead, ibid., 123.

236 *The importance of transformative institutions:* For an excellent discussion of the male need for transformative rituals and institutions see George Gilder, *Men and Marriage* (Gretna, La.: Pelican Publishing Company, 1987).

236 *Why can't some schools:* Leon J. Podles, "Susan B. Anthony and the Bad Dudes," *Fidelity* (December 1989), 17.

237 *in Detroit, a federal judge:* "Judge Halts Plan for Male Schools," *The New York Times* (August 16, 1991), A6.

PAGE

237 *Virginia Military Institute:* Chester E. Finn, Jr., "Quotas and the Bush Administration," *Commentary* (November 1991), 20.

239 *Patience is a calm endurance:* Character Education Program (North Clackamas School District, Instructional Development Department: September 1988), 7.

240 *Still heroism is more:* Edwin J. Delattre, "No Empty Heads, No Hollow Chests," *American Educator* (Summer 1981).

241 *"What is a good life?":* The Jefferson Institute on the Foundations of Ethics in Western Society, descriptive paper (December 4, 1989), 1.

241 *During the summer institute:* Thanks for this information to Carolyn E. Gecan and Bernadette M. Glaze and other faculty at Thomas Jefferson High School for Science and Technology.

241 *"I learned there was no such thing":* Christina Hoff Sommers, "Teaching the Virtues," *Imprimis* (November 1991), 2.

241 *Students find a great deal:* Ibid., 3.

CHAPTER FOURTEEN. WHAT PARENTS CAN DO

246 *response to an Ann Landers column:* Cited in Jeane Westin, *The Coming Parent Revolution* (Chicago: Rand McNally & Company, 1981), 25.

246 *American parents spend less than fifteen minutes a week:* The *Wall Street Journal* (April 6, 1990), B1.

247 *"One of the biggest reasons":* Mary Pride, *The Way Home* (Westchester, Ill.: Crossway Books, 1985), 106.

249 *a study of child-rearing articles:* C. B. Stendler, "Sixty Years of Child Training Practices," *Journal of Pediatrics* 36 (1950), 122–34; and Martha Wolfenstein, "Fun Morality: An Analysis of Recent American Child-training Literature" in Margaret Mead and Martha Wolfenstein, eds., *Childhood in Contemporary Cultures* (Chicago: University of Chicago Press, 1955).

249 *The problem is divorce:* Armand M. Nicholi, Jr., "The Impact of Parental Absence on Childhood Development: An Overview of the Literature," *The Journal of Family and Culture* (Autumn 1985), 25.

250 *children from single-parent homes:* Ibid., 19–28; see also Nicholas Davidson, "Life Without Father," *Policy Review* (Winter 1990), 40–44.

250 *"Children felt that":* Judith S. Wallerstein and Joan Berlin Kelly, *Surviving the Breakup: How Children and Parents Cope with Divorce* (New York: Basic Books, 1980), 76.

250 *"the shaky family structure":* Ibid., 83.

PAGE

250   *Some psychologists have even concluded:* From research conducted by Michael Rutter of the University of London. Cited in James Q. Wilson *On Character* (Washington, D.C.: The AEI Press, 1991), 72.

251   *"We refuse to accept":* Nicholi, Jr., "Impact of Parental Absence," 22.

251   *"I don't think a female running a house":* Toni Morrison, interview in *Time* magazine (May 22, 1989), 122.

251   *"Fathers must be there":* Dobson and Bauer, *Children at Risk,* 169–70.

251   *A Canadian study:* Martin Day and Margo Wilson, "Child Abuse and Other Risks of Not Living with Both Parents," *Journal of Ethology and Sociobiology* 6 (1985), 197–206.

252   *"culture of character":* Louis W. Sullivan, "We Must Revive Character," *The Dallas Morning News* (December 21, 1990).

252   *John Dewey:* See Bryce J. Christensen, *Utopia Against the Family* (San Francisco: Ignatius Press, 1990), 88.

252   *"traditional family values":* Paul C. Vitz "Censors at Work: (Anti) Family Values in Public School Textbooks," *The Family in America* (November 1991), 1.

252   *"a decided animus":* Quoted in Christensen, *Utopia Against the Family,* 93.

252   *"education of the junior generation":* Quoted in ibid., 87.

254   *a survey of schools:* Philip C. Clarke "Teaching Morality in Our Schools," *Behind the Headlines—Philip C. Clarke Commentary,* Program C-223 (January 30, 1991). Produced by America's Future, 514 Main St., New Rochelle, N.Y. 10801.

254   *"the nation's faith in its public schools"* "The Flight from Public Schools," *U.S. News & World Report* (December 9, 1991), 66.

255   *"If a school says":* Ibid., 71.

256   *"A family is a group":* Vitz, "Censors at Work," 2.

256   *"A family is a little church":* William Gouge, "Of Domesticall Duties" (London, 1622); quoted by John Demos in *A Little Commonwealth: Family Life in Plymouth Colony* (New York: Oxford University Press, 1970), XIX.

257   *"increased discipline":* Westin, *Coming Parent Revolution,* 181–96.

257   *"Without struggling with the ambivalent emotions":* Christopher Lasch, *Haven in a Heartless World* (New York: Basic Books, 1979), 123.

257   *She found that:* Diana Baumrind, "Parenting Styles and Adolescent Development." In J. Brooks-Gunn, R. Lerner and A. C. Petersen, eds., *The Encyclopedia of Adolescence* (New York: Garland, 1989).

258   *they "are able to do":* William R. Coulson, "Don't Coddle the Piano Player," *San Diego Magazine* (June 1977).

PAGE

258   *"The child's respect for parental authority"*: Damon, *Moral Child*, 52.

258   *"Boys who worked in the home"*: Quoted in Edwin Kiester, Jr., and Sally Valente Kiester, "How to Raise a Happy Child," *Reader's Digest* (January 1986), 96.

259   *"The grass was too high"*: Beverly Beckham, "What Happened to Caring for Others?" *Boston Herald* (May 10, 1991).

260   *"harmonious" families*: Diana Baumrind, "Note: Harmonious Parents and Their Pre-school Children," *Developmental Psychology* 4 (1973), 99–102. See also D. Baumrind, "Rearing Competent Children" in William Damon, ed., *Child Development Today and Tomorrow* (San Francisco: Jossey-Bass, 1989).

260   *"In these families, the parent rarely needs"*: Damon, *Moral Child*, 60.

260   *"families don't really work if"*: Francis Fukuyama, *The End of History and the Last Man* (New York: The Free Press, 1992), 324.

262   *Religious rituals*: Edward Hoffman, "Thriving Families in Urban America: The Lubavitcher Hasidim," *The Family in America* (October 1990), 6, 7.

262   *"Lubavitchers partly attribute"*: Ibid., 6.

264   *"it is our culture"*: Kenneth A. Myers, *All God's Children and Blue Suede Shoes* (Wheaton, Ill · Crossway Books, 1989), 159, 160.

264   *almost never does a TV character go to church*: Benjamin Stein, "TV: A Religious Wasteland," *The Wall Street Journal* (January 19, 1985), 24.

265   *"It opens up the home"*: Hoffman, "Thriving Families in Urban America," 5, 6.

265   *"Instead of having to establish rules"*: Winn, *Children Without Childhood*, 45.

265   *"I do believe that addiction to television"*: Myers, *All God's Children*, 174.

266   *"Even the plot is a paradigm"*: Thomas J. Fleming, "Affection and Responsibility in the Family of Classical Greece," *The Journal of Family and Culture* (Autumn 1985), 46–47.

267   *I read because my father read to me*: Jim Trelease, *The New Read-Aloud Handbook* (New York: Penguin Books, 1989), xv.

INDEX